HOW TO SURVIVE A HOSTILE WORLD

HOW TO SURVIVE A HOSTILE WORLD

Power, Politics, and the Case for Realism

Patrick Porter

Stanford University Press
Stanford, California

Stanford University Press
Stanford, California

© 2025 by Patrick Porter. All rights reserved.

No part of this book may be reproduced or transmitted in any form or by any means, electronic or mechanical, including photocopying and recording, or in any information storage or retrieval system, without the prior written permission of Stanford University Press.

Library of Congress Cataloging-in-Publication Data
Names: Porter, Patrick, 1976– author
Title: How to survive a hostile world : power, politics, and the case for realism / Patrick Porter.
Description: Stanford, California : Stanford University Press, 2025. | Includes bibliographical references and index.
Identifiers: LCCN 2025017702 (print) | LCCN 2025017703 (ebook) |
    ISBN 9781503641839 cloth | ISBN 9781503644069 paperback | ISBN 9781503644076 ebook
Subjects: LCSH: Political realism | International relations | World politics—21st century
Classification: LCC JZ1307 .P67 2025 (print) | LCC JZ1307 (ebook) | DDC 327.101—dc23/eng/20250701
LC record available at https://lccn.loc.gov/2025017702
LC ebook record available at https://lccn.loc.gov/2025017703

Cover design: Michel Vrana
Cover art: iStock

The authorized representative in the EU for product safety and compliance is: Mare Nostrum Group B.V. | Mauritskade 21D | 1091 GC Amsterdam | The Netherlands | Email address: gpsr@mare-nostrum.co.uk | KVK chamber of commerce number: 96249943

For my father
Be light upon him, earth

Contents

	Acknowledgments	ix
	Introduction	1
One	**Realism Is Moral**	5
Two	**Realism Is Realistic**	56
Three	**Realism Is for Everyone**	101
	Epilogue	140
	Notes	145
	Bibliography	167
	Index	187

Acknowledgments

I am indebted to many people's inspiration, conversation, and argument for making this book possible. Thanks to David Blagden, Robert Saunders, Emma Ashford, Martin Skold, Robert Jervis, Justin Logan, Anders Wivel, Christian Bueger, Campbell Craig, Nina Tannenwald, Susan Martin, Yuan-Kang Wang, David Adesnik, Ronald Specter, Marco Viera, Haro Karkour, Errol Henderson, William Wohlforth, Jeanne Morefield, Sean Molloy, Marc Mulholland, Huw Bennett, Will Ruger, Stephen Wertheim, Elbridge Colby, Chris Brown, Dale Copeland, Stephen Walt, John Mearsheimer, Randall Schweller, Jonathan Kirshner, Joshua Shifrinson, Kelly Greenhill, Barry Posen, Joseph Parent, Arthur Eckstein, Michael Lind, Michael Desch, Pete Dombrowski, Nick Wheeler, Adam Quinn, Rita Floyd, Stefan Wolff, Will James, Ben Whitham, Sumantra Maitra, John Hulsman, Robert Ralston, Aurel Sari, Rob Johnson, Mark Webber, David Dunn, Dan LoPreto, Ryan Grauer, and Colin Dueck. Many thanks to the Koch Foundation, whose generous support for another book project helped inspire this one. Tipping my hat, too, to my students, whom it is a privilege to teach and learn from. To my family—Jane, Hugh, and Ella, as well as Muriel, Emily, Pat, Gus, and Molly, and Frances and John—thanks beyond telling. And to a certain British academic who advised undergraduates that realism is just a "throwback," I offer the reputed words of Gustav Mahler: "Tradition is not the worship of ashes, but the preservation of fire."

Introduction

LET US BEGIN IN the dark. For in that is where we existentially are in a time of war, atrocity, plague, economic dislocation and climate crisis, and political rancor. The darkness has several layers. It is partly the darkness of what we humans are capable of doing to one another. It is partly the darkness of facts we can't avoid—of impermanence and mortality. Everything ends. Life is fragile, and time is scarce. And there is the darkness of uncertainty. Our knowledge about life remains limited. In particular, we can't for certain know what others are thinking. Even if we could, we can't know whether, when, and how their minds will change. Understanding the political environment we live in matters. In order to build a richer and fuller existence, what President John F. Kennedy called "a more vital life," we must first see the world for what it is.[1] We must survive.

Morbid? A little. Granted, this author has a melancholy streak and is predisposed to look for the darkness. Still, thousands of years of history are pretty dark. There are moments when the darkness lifts. Moments. And even the peace of those interludes is uneasy and uneven. Nostalgists nowadays look back on the Cold War or the 1990s periods of stable "order." But the Cold War era turned continental Europe—the core of such nostalgia—into rival armed camps. And it featured brutal conflicts, coups, and purges through Indonesia, Korea, Tibet, Vietnam, Egypt, Hungary, Angola, Cuba, Chile, Cyprus, Greece, and beyond. And when, in the 1990s, the United States enjoyed a large and decisive power advantage and was unchecked by peer adversaries and expected its preponderance to last, the supposed holiday from history also featured the Second Congo War, Africa's Great War, and bloodletting in the Balkans. It is idle, therefore, to tell people studying International Relations (IR) that times have changed and to switch focus to other matters. To do so is to wish away the recent history of concentration camps and gulags, minefields and bomb craters, and the signs of their return.

That being so, the study of IR matters. Those who make foreign policy, after all, work from assumptions about how the world works—what we call "theory"—whether or not they admit it. Within IR, which is the best, or least bad, "first cut"? Which is the soundest starting point for understanding that part of politics that we call "international"? It is the tradition of realism despite the many and extensive attacks on it.

In a nutshell, realism is a pessimistic intellectual tradition about how the world of human politics is and how it is bound to be. It views international life as intrinsically dangerous given both our species' capacity for violence and the absence of a reliable protector to keep us safe. However remote it seems, the shadow of war conditions international life. All efforts at cooperation, prosperity, and peace are constrained by that reality—a reality that can't be changed. Likewise, human groups ought to make all foreign and defense policy with that shadow in mind. Most polities tend to act in self-serving ways and revert to competition under pressure. They do so not primarily because they are bad but because the imperatives of the international system shove them in that direction. Those that flout these imperatives court punishment. Realism takes as its analytical priority the external environment, its structure, or the "international system," and the pressures it generates. Realism need not be blind to other factors, like domestic politics or the type of regime or ruler, but these have lesser causal weight. Importantly, realists assume that international forces are the main source of domestic politics, rather than vice versa. It is hard to understand political strife from China to America, for instance, without factoring in global competition for muscle labor and how this drives up China's growth, drives down American wages, and moves industry offshore and creates a more discontent working class.

This book is a short defense of the realist worldview. It is written mainly for those who are new to the subject. It has in mind those who are curious and come at this with fresh minds. My goal isn't to convert you to realism. Or, at least, that's not the main goal. Rather, I want to show you that realism is a serious tradition worthy of consideration. It is not a typical academic book, as it isn't primarily a work of innovation. Rather, it is an attempt at rejuvenation. Realists spend much of their/our time arguing with each other about how best to formulate, refine, and apply the intellectual tradition. That's not a bad thing. A paradigm without internal dispute is a dead paradigm. But it has come at a price. By talking so much to one another and other scholars, not enough realists defend the church to a broader audience, though there are honorable exceptions, like the scholar Stephen Walt, and these deserve supporting fire.

This book makes three arguments. Against claims to the contrary, I argue realism has a moral basis. Against claims to the contrary, I argue realism is realistic, at least to the extent that it works like a decent map, simplifying enough to clarify without fundamentally distorting things. And against claims to the contrary, I argue realism is for everyone.

This is not the first bite-size defense of realism. I commend readers to two short articles by Robert Gilpin—one of the most penetrating realist minds—from 1984 and 1996, where he recapitulated and defended realism from new waves of criticism.[2] Gilpin's articles, though, appeared in the era of the late Cold War of 1984 and then at the climax of US global preeminence in 1996. Three decades later, advocacy on realism's behalf is again needed—this time, for a new context.

This book brings the discussion to a generation facing different circumstances: a more multipolar world where hierarchies and power balances are more unsettled and where Western youth are generally more skeptical about realism's core claims, more averse to the idea of militarized competition for security under anarchy, and more sensitive to the issue of whether any IR theory developed by Western minds can be truly universal. This discussion approaches realism through several problem areas that have taken on added salience in the present—namely, the climate crisis, the question of cultural difference and Eurocentrism, mounting crises in East Asia and the Middle East, and the largest war in Europe in generations. These issues are likely to intensify further in our time and beyond.

A few points of clarification are needed before we begin. First, in defending "realism," I am defending the common baseline of assumptions that realists share. Realists, like any "-ists," are not monolithic. Realism is more a paradigm or family of theories than a single one. Here, the focus is on the realist "minimum."

Throughout this book, I refer to "states." To be clear, I use this as shorthand not just for the kind of nation-states we have today but also for what Gilpin calls "conflict groups" more broadly, applicable from city-states to empires. At their core, they are organized and governed to rule a territory and population from a fixed abode. When I discuss nonstate actors, like insurgent movements or terrorist networks, I'll say so.

Last, skeptics will likely say that realists, like this author, don't have much to say about novel, cutting-edge, or resurgent problems away from realism's main focus, like artificial intelligence, robotics technology, food insecurity, social media disinformation, or preventable diseases. In truth, we don't. A general paradigm does not rise or fall on its capacity to pronounce on and incorporate every worthy topic or to be relevant across the board. The subjects above are important and deserve intensive study. They bear on realism, however, only to the extent that they challenge realism's fundamental claims about international politics. Aspects of today's existence may be more complex than earlier generations endured, though they often aren't more intense. We shouldn't be too impressed with how much more sophisticated we, or our circumstances, are than our forbears. Most people today would not swap their problems for what their ancestors endured. In those areas where things are more complex, other ideas and theories may help understand those issues that fall outside realism's main focus.[3] If you are after a Great Big Theory of Everything in IR, you've come to the wrong shop.

Studying international politics requires us to look carefully, to distinguish what is new from what only seems to be new. For sure, the internet is centrally important in our lives, but that doesn't mean online activity alters the offline balance between the weak and the strong. Other problems sometimes look more urgent, but that doesn't mean they will remain so. Terrorism and insurgency, for a time, persuaded some that realism, with its emphasis upon states and great power politics, was losing its salience. That dismissal, it turns out, presupposed the continuation of a stable international hierarchy, overseen by one superpower—conditions luxurious enough that strong states could focus so much on lesser threats. Those conditions ended. Indeed, the assumption that other things mattered more—in particular, the overinvestment in counterterrorism, nation building, and the extravagant global war on terror—diverted capital (intellectual and financial) from a more important development: the return of interstate competition. Realism's main focus is on conflict, power, and survival against the most intense and direct threats. Not a trendy topic, perhaps. But alas, once again, on trend.

1 Realism Is Moral

WHAT'S WRONG WITH REALISM, allegedly? Consider the indictment laid down by Ken Booth:

> Realism is not realistic (it does not provide an accurate picture of the world); it is a misnomer (it is an ideology masquerading as a theory of knowledge); it is a static theory (without a theory of change); it is reductive (it leaves out much of the picture); its methodology is unsophisticated (it sacrifices richness for efficiency of explanation); it fails the test of practice (it does not offer a reliable recipe book); its unspoken assumptions are regressive (it leaves no space for gender or class); its agenda is narrow (it over-concentrates on the military dimension to the exclusion of other threats); its ethics are hostile to the human interest (by placing the "cold monster" of the state at the centre); and it is intellectually rigid (its proponents have marginalized or silenced other approaches).

In short, realists are unrealistic, oblivious, immoral, rigid, overmilitarizing peddlers of simplism. Some of this is self-contradictory. If realism fails to grasp reality or an accurate picture of the world, it isn't clear how realism also "dominates the academies" nor how it supplies "a passport into the offices of power."[1] And some of Booth's charge is just plain wrong. Realism does not dominate the academies—certainly, not outside the United States. Few academics even in the United States would identify as fully-fledged realists. Realists do have theories of change. Critics of realism just dislike them. For realists, there can be change, but change is generally the product of shifts in the distribution of material capabilities. And realism offers insights beyond armed conflict. In an age of climate crisis, realism can help. Realists will advise those in the eye of environmental storms to be wary of others' benign assurances in the face of impersonal threats. Islanders who bank on major states curbing their emissions and lowering the tides may find themselves underwater.

Nonetheless, Booth's charges overall are serious and deserve weighing. In this chapter, I address the charge of moral bankruptcy and offer an account of realist morality.[2] The following chapters will address the two other main charges of intellectual poverty and cultural narrowness.

Let's focus on the charge that realists are inhumanely amoral (lacking principles that inform what is right and wrong) or downright immoral (knowingly violating those principles), promoting the hollow pursuit of power with little to no regard for right and wrong.[3] Critics draw this conclusion from something that is true: that realists up front are generally more accommodating of ruthless and brutal behavior.

These charges draw on a deeper objection to realism's complicity in oppression. That is, critics suggest that realism too readily takes for granted as inevitable what in fact is changeable. By doing so, by accepting as an inexorable fact of life the arbitrary, unjust way of things, realists place themselves in "secret complicity with an order of domination that reproduces the expectation of inequality as a motivating force and insecurity as an integrating principle."[4] Realists may think they are diagnosing the treacherousness of life as it is and the realities of self-serving behavior. But allegedly, they are naturalizing it. They are wrong to do so. Norms do not have to lose out to power. Violent self-seeking behavior does not have to be our future. Human affairs do not have to be anarchic.[5]

From this objection, critics suggest realists should do something more constructive. Instead of saying things are intrinsically anarchic and that international life necessarily revolves around material interests and competition for security, they argue realists should imagine a better, more humane global order and use their pulpit not to reinforce or provide alibis for destructive power politics but to challenge it. At a time of climate crisis, genocidal wars, and dangerous weapons' proliferation, we urgently need a sense of human solidarity that transcends national frontiers. It follows that we cannot afford realists' pessimism.

Are they right? Is realism inherently amoral/immoral? Or does it lay down meaningful constraints? Before considering how well realism accounts for the world, we should ask what realism is *for*.

Booth describes the state as "cold," and he's not wrong. States, even relatively benign ones, make decisions that fall heavily on people. They imprison them, deport them, or build freeways through their neighborhoods. And given policymaking is messy and full of trade-offs and resource constraints and will always harm someone's interests, to act is to harm. The sovereign's ultimate duty is to choose. This means there is a detachment inherent in holding office and arbitrating over the fate of millions and in the threat of force that necessarily underpins authority. Unchecked empathy with everyone would lead to paralysis. This is cold all right. But coldness is not the same thing as monstrousness. As an ancient tradition stretching back to classical antiquity in Greece, India, and China—societies that first codified realist thought—realism is both austere and morally concerned.

For thinkers in the realist tradition, those in power must work by an alternative moral standard—a morality that is more tolerant of (sometimes) doing terrible things and that presumes against relying on things apart from hard power. Realists stress rulers' duty to safeguard their citizens and husband power carefully, to strike ruthlessly when necessary but to avoid unnecessary harm to others, as a matter not only of expedience but of righteousness. We live in a fallen universe predisposed to conflict. In that condition, rulers are not entitled to make moral judgements as mere conscientious individuals but as leaders responsible to the ruled, with an eye to consequences. Realists, or at least insightful ones, don't say the state should work simply as a pitiless "monster," like the predator in *Alien* that embodies only pure egoistic hostility. Rather, realist morality advises the pursuit of survival and interests of one's own people on the basis of accepting what is inexorably "real"—hence the name "realism"—and this is a morally serious business. There can be defensible altruistic action, yet any attempt to serve universal morality must always be related back to the national interest, defined as self-preservation via the competitive pursuit of power. This is not an easy dialogue between the empirical (how things "are") and the normative (how they "ought" to be). Even realists like E. H. Carr, who at times defined "realism" as the belief that there is no place for ethics in International Relations, ended up regarding political life as an "uneasy compromise between power and morality."[6]

In what follows, I lay out the basis for a realist account of morality, known as "reason of state." This is a vast topic, so I'll just sketch the outlines. First, I define "realism." I then contrast realism with a family of alternatives—namely, moralism, idealism, and cosmopolitanism. I then show what realist morality looks like via three issues that restage the problems in our time: nuclear weapons, the climate crisis, and dictators. I conclude with a concession to realists' critics. While they are wrong to suggest realism is inherently amoral/immoral, they are right that realism can fall prey to immoral excess. Realism has a corrupt cousin: amoral machtpolitik—a form of self-destructive barbarism that not merely respects power but craves it as an end in itself and for the perverse benefit only of the powerful, not the wider polity.

WHAT IS REALISM?

Before we turn to morality, let's define "realism." Realists assume that the world is inherently dangerous. This is so because of two interacting things that are constant: humans and the system they inhabit. Our world is made up of people who can be violent and whose intentions are always uncertain. As history reveals, we are capable of barbarism without limit. And the international system is ultimately ungoverned. There is no higher benign earthly authority committed to superintending the globe or protecting us. Thus, the most important feature of the globe is not a thing but the absence of a thing. We call this condition "anarchy." It derives from a Greek word meaning absence of authority. Under anarchy, the organized human polity is the essential unit of world politics. While the choices and attitudes of polities vary, anarchy drives most polities, in the aggregate, toward similar behavior. Some scholars argue that the reality realists assume is really socially constructed and open to change. Realists, by contrast, see that different polities in similar conditions tend to construct their realities similarly, suggesting they are responding to objective conditions. Realists work from this shared basis. They have intramural disagreements too, and these are nontrivial, but we'll come to those later.

Realists are pessimists because they believe we cannot replace the state of anarchy with benign hierarchy, world government, or a permanent or deep peace based on some profound shift in human sensibility whether democratic, humanist, capitalist, or feminist. Anarchy leaves all groups in a state of ultimate solitude and self-help. Cooperation is possible but always impermanent and fragile. Peace is possible and at times prevalent. But it is always a product of power relations, and power relations shift. When power is in flux and interests diverge, securing peace is hard in such an international structure given its pressures drive polities who are at odds toward competition and perhaps coming to blows. Arguments about what "power" really is can take up many hours. Here, I simply mean the ability to get others to do what they otherwise might not do. In Robert Gilpin's words, realism asserts the "primacy in all political life of power and security in human motivation."[7] Realists mean this both descriptively—how things are—and prescriptively in terms of what they exhort us to do.

Real*ism* prescribes real*politik*—the recognition that to defend a desired political system at home, we must do what is necessary to shield it from the dangerous system of international politics. Since the world is unalterably and threateningly anarchic, defined by the possibility of war, realists both expect and advise the pursuit of security via the acquisition of power. Realists prize material and coercive power as the *ultima ratio* that protects vital interests when all else fails. Thus international politics is power politics—a form of self-seeking politics that privileges one's own group and is concerned with not only achieving objectives but also creating and sustaining power, including the ability to apply violence. As we will see, no paradigm can capture everything in its complexity. There are cases that puzzle realists. But realists expect patterns of power politics to dominate international life in the aggregate.

Our world is not one of constant war. But the prospect of armed conflict conditions it. Realists see the shadow of war as the defining, inexorable feature of international politics, as well as something worse: the prospect of annihilation without conflict. The danger of aggressors falling on one's own group in the dead of night and finding their targets unprepared haunts our species both as a proven possibility in history and as a trace memory. Others, without warning, can attack us, assault our interests, or annihilate us. And third parties may not turn up to rescue.

The fates of the cities Thebes, Carthage, Tenochtitlan, and Constantinople, besieged and overrun, show that people who assumed this could not happen to them or who counted on help from other parties or who thought their fortifications made them invulnerable can lose everything.[8] In our time, assailants turned Mosul, Mariupol, Darfur, and Gaza into brutal battlegrounds and sites of atrocity. In the latter case, the Gaza massacre followed a surprise cross-border attack and the largest slaughter of Jews since the Holocaust. For those of us lucky enough to live in more stable neighborhoods and behind moats, navies, and a nuclear deterrent, the storming and sacking of our cities by massed forces may be a remote prospect. But nuclear-missile strikes and mass-casualty terrorist attacks are not so remote. Neither are blockades at sea against the maritime chokepoints that are our windpipe. That food is on the table is no natural blessing but an achievement of power and deterrence. The country I live in, the United Kingdom, has depended on regular seaborne imports of food for centuries, hence the grace of the Royal Navy: "For what we are about to eat, we thank the Lord and the British fleet."

Does this make realists warmongers? It does not. A warmonger enthusiastically and incautiously encourages war and finds it attractive in itself. Realists, by contrast, advocate military preparedness but are also mindful that war can consume, not increase, power, destroy the state, and debase those who wage it. A continuing argument amongst realists is how best to balance defense and offense, competition and cooperation, to make wars rare and, if waged, short and victorious. Yet a common presumption against war unites them. If anything, today, it is less often realists and more often liberals of a certain muscular kind who are prone to advocating expansive military measures. The realist practitioners you will meet in this book are notable not for their promiscuity with the military instrument but their discipline and restraint.

Realists are skeptical of claims that these fundamental parameters can be changed. In particular, they regard anarchy as a constant. The lack of central authority is not something that can be supplanted by international institutions, no matter how well or benevolently designed. Institutions can never be disinterested, transcendent, and trusted governments, for they are made up of human groups with their own conflicting interests. The point was well made to the British member of Parliament Chris Mullin: "I once asked Vietnam's foreign minister Nguyen Co Thach why, after his country was attacked by the Khmer Rouge, it had not taken its case to the UN instead of invading Cambodia late in 1978. 'We do not have such a high regard for the UN as you do,' he replied. 'How so?' Because during the last forty years we have been invaded by four of the five permanent members of the Security Council."[9] History had taught Vietnam a hard lesson: not to defer the most important questions to international institutions, since behind their claim to authority always lies power politics.

It is useful to compare realism to alternatives. There are multiple nonrealist paradigms.[10] Two families are especially prominent in the debate: the liberal and the radical. Liberal internationalism is a family of optimistic visions, a continuously reinvented "fighting creed" more than a single theory.[11] Liberal internationalists from different backgrounds believe fundamental progress in a liberal direction is possible—that is, toward a human condition centered around a range of noble things. These include the integrity of the individual, freedom of commerce, the ascent of law, rules and transparency over the cynicism and darkness of traditional power politics, and a general cultural and social openness. For liberal internationalists, who walk in the tradition of Immanuel Kant, President Woodrow Wilson, and, today, G. John Ikenberry, enlightened states and especially the United States in its ascendancy can turn the world into an international community. They can do so by persuading states to forgo immediate, short-term gains and, in exchange for this self-denial, create enduring concord via the confidence-building power of institutions and under the benign watch of Washington. Analytically, they prioritize the domestic and the internal as the prime causes of international behavior, hence their preoccupation with the "type" of regime one is interacting with and hence their conviction that the spread of democratic capitalism would make the world significantly more peaceful.

The liberal tradition raises many internal disputes and predicaments:[12] What is the main cause of progress, economic interdependence, democracy, or the coming of supranational institutions? What should prevail when international institutions and liberal values come into collision? And how warlike should liberals be given their missionary outlook? Against determined adversaries, to bind oneself via institutions, rules, and norms is to risk impotence. Yet to relax those constraints and wield hard power to defend liberalism risks perpetuating illiberal behavior. Liberal internationalists have muscular and more bellicose cousins—"neoconservatives," or "Vulcans," with significant overlaps and strong differences—who assert the paramount importance of America as an agent of transformation, loosening its constraints and projecting power abroad. Like most histories of ideas, this is not a simple story. But you see the outline.

And then there are radical traditions.[13] Marxism, feminism, and postcolonialism are not all the same, to be clear, and on some fundamentals, they disagree. In common, they repudiate realism's assumption that state security, or the polity, is the primary and most important unit of analysis, that the world is bound to be anarchic and competitive, and that there are hard and oppressive constraints that bind us. Rather, they suggest, emancipation from oppression is both possible and imperative to pursue. Patriarchy, oppressive class systems, and/or colonial and racist projects of domination lie at the root of suffering in the international and domestic spheres and can be dismantled, just as the state, in its different forms, can be replaced by different organizations founded on human solidarity. As we will see, the predicament for radical traditions is how far to compromise with and accommodate the state. Historically, in crisis, radicals find that competitive power politics is hard to abolish. And despite radical convictions that state-based loyalties are a form of false consciousness, those loyalties also die hard. Economics often does not determine ideology, as shown by the elites who sacrificed themselves on the western front of World War One, in large numbers, for king and country. Also, radicals divide. The schisms that upended communist alliances or pan-Arab partnerships point to a further problem: that the search for alternative enduring international formations based on something else, whether class revolution or anticolonialism, have thus far proven elusive.

Like liberal and radical alternatives, realism also offers a morality. Yet realist morality is distinct because it is built on assumptions about a harsh predatory environment around us. It's not a nice paradigm. It's not a nice world.

REASON OF STATE

You can already sense why realist morality is contentious. Critics allege, and will say of this book, that all this talk of war is too central. They say we must decenter armed conflict and organized violence from our understanding of security and demilitarize our view of IR. From this perspective, this would better discourage war in the first place, enabling us to get on with tackling other urgent security matters from economic precarity to human trafficking, from criminal gangs to climate crisis.

These other issues obviously matter. But declaring the danger of predation or war passé in order to focus on other things will not reliably make that danger go away. To the contrary, it will create opportunities for predators to pounce. Indeed, it is simplistic to correlate military buildup with war: militarization and large defense budgets can be followed by conflict in some circumstances but not in others. If it were otherwise, Britain and France would have fought several wars in the late nineteenth and early twentieth century, the Cold War would have gotten directly hot, and North and South Korea would have gone to the mat more recently than 1953. Weapons don't make war; rulers make war as political choices, and the notion that excessive military technology itself drives actors into conflict is a suspect alibi for those responsible for decisions.[14] There is no certain formula for war avoidance. What increases insecurity in some circumstances generates deterrence in others. We can judge, more confidently, that the bleak history of defenseless or defeated peoples suggests repudiating arms is no way out. If neglecting one's defenses can also lead to conflict, groups then locked into crisis or war will have a hard time addressing other security problems, especially if they are wiped out.

It is no accident that literature urging that we marginalize conflict in security affairs spreads the most in countries enjoying more stable and tranquil times, after epochal conflicts end, as in the post–Cold War interregnum between 1991 and 2001. Some visionaries insist that we must never return to conflict and assume we can rise above it. Inured to peace, others cannot even imagine their nations being acted upon violently and mistake temporary lulls in strife with a permanent transformation of the world.[15] Luxury conditions encourage luxury ideas. And such conditions end. So realist morality begins from the premise that the possibility of war is hardwired into the human condition as we find it rather than being a demon that can be exorcised.

Were we always violent? Actually, perhaps not. It would be tempting and convenient at this point to say that we have always fought wars, that this proves the inherent force of anarchy, and that therefore our species is intrinsically war prone.[16] Some realist-friendly minds trace conflict far back in the animal kingdom and amongst primate societies, suggesting conflict is evolutionary and primordial.[17] Yet the notion that we are originally warlike may not be true.

In the study of prehistoric humans, the "state-of-the-art" judgement is that our hunter-gatherer nomadic ancestors of the Pleistocene era (from two million to ten thousand years ago), at least amongst the less organized and less clustered communities, may not have been very warlike compared to the societies that arose later.[18] We can't be too sure about this. We lack decisive evidence in either direction given the absence of written records in preliterate societies, the difficulty of distinguishing weapons from hunting implements, the rarity of burials amongst early humans, and the overreliance on observations of surviving indigenous societies with the problem of "contact" that potentially changes their behavior. Still, there isn't much positive evidence for frequent armed conflict in humanity's earliest chapters. Occasional massacre sites and the marks of weapon damage on skeletons and primitive fortifications indicate that war was not unknown. But the evidence we do have—for instance, from the patterns of cave painting, which took some time to feature actual armed conflict—suggests other things preoccupied the first people. The populations of small intimate tribes were too small and dispersed, the capabilities too limited, and the collisions of interests too isolated for frequent war making.

Warfare may have sprung up on an appreciable scale only later. And it may generally have been a biproduct of "complexification"—the coming of more settled agricultural and urban life with higher population density—that both created the capability to fight on a large scale and made possible the collision of groups. Given the rarity of war amongst the earliest nomads, some observers draw the optimistic conclusion that we can revert to that state, reimagine our future, and relegate the possibility of catastrophic violence to the margins.[19]

We can't resolve the debate about prehistoric war here. Importantly, though, even if conflict grew beyond isolated and sporadic levels only relatively late in our species' life, this does not disturb the core claims of realism. Realism's main insight is not dependent upon the original violence levels of apes or foragers.

Let me explain. Complexification and the coming of horticultural and agricultural societies came after the nomadic period but predated the formation of states. So it didn't take the creation of states to intensify conflict. In that intermediate era, the high percentages of skeletal injuries, palisades, and settlement nucleation suggest war was frequent enough. Whether in northern or middle America, the Amazon or Australia, there was variation but a notably high incidence of cranial injury, skewed toward the adult male populations. Contact with intrusive foreign empires may have intensified but did not introduce organized warfare, as precontact body armor and fortified settlements suggests. Some optimists try to reclassify cases of intergroup violence as mere feuds and "nonwar," straining to make facts fit a theory.[20] Despite valiant efforts to deny it, clearly, a capacity for organized conflict had formed.

So humans began fighting at a level beyond the sporadic as soon as they developed the capability, the resources, and the incentives. Even if war was not originally in our "nature" and if the plausible threat of war was not the original state of humanity and arrived later, those insights do not alter the pessimistic premise of realism. We won't be dismantling and reversing complexification, with its many benefits, and returning to a nomadic hunter-gathering low-population life. Any group that tries will find that others won't. They will become less, not more, secure. The only world we are likely to live in for the foreseeable future will share the fundamentals of the world we have inhabited for at least twelve thousand years—versions of the postnomadic and complexified life in which war began.

Our species, therefore, still comes out of this prehistory as pretty warlike under long-standing conditions that are likely to persist. Realist thinkers and advisors who wrote down their pessimistic thoughts came along well after these warlike patterns settled. They independently reached similar conclusions in separate parts of the world. So they did not sing such a hostile world into existence. The world they found was already bloody and volatile.

This point matters because the assumption that war is obsolete or outmoded, an artificial invention that we can uninvent, is fatal if it is unfounded. If we refuse to acknowledge the possibility that others may take risks we think we would not, if we dismiss others' threats as mere bluster and hope for the best, the penalties can be severe. As history suggests, the main cause of intelligence failure and shock is not a deficit of information but rather prior disbelief in the possibility of a bad thing happening.[21] When Vladimir Putin mobilized Russian forces alongside Ukraine's border in late 2021, many seasoned observers and area experts forecast he wouldn't invade. Their arguments varied but shared a logic that he wouldn't because he shouldn't.[22] Their confident message—that invasions no longer pay, that war out in the open is a thing of the past, that the United States would crush Moscow with economic sanctions, that Russia could subvert Ukrainian politics without invading—implicitly assumed Russia would behave more like a brittle risk-averse economy than what it turned out to be. It turned out to be a more risk-prone and more resilient country acting in haste, fearing conditions were worsening, calculating that it must act, and underestimating Ukrainian resistance because of the very imperialist worldview that the same commentators denounced. As for war itself, where prewar futurologists forecast an era of war in the shadows—ambiguous, lighter, and techno-centric "hybrid" clashes—here was a war of iron and mass out in the open and in your face.[23] To be sure, those who forecast that Putin wouldn't roll the dice might respond that Putin's gamble has failed. But it took determined large-scale warfare to resist the invasion and make it expensive.

So, thus far, we have seen that realist morality builds on pessimism about what international existence is like. But who, or what, is this morality for? For realists, the main organizing basis for survival in this world is *groups*. Contrary to other worldviews, the starting point of reference for realists is the *primacy of the group*—organized units of people whose security is supposed to be ensured by the state. Groups want different things and must help themselves. To work as groups of primary allegiance for their members, such units will be larger than the individual or province, large enough to carry weight and do more, but smaller than regions or multinational institutions, like the European Union, small enough to maintain cohesion and build loyalty. They lie somewhere between larger universalism and smaller particularism. Most of the time today, that arrangement takes the form of the nation-state—a territorially bounded sovereign polity organized around an idea of the "nation" and claiming a monopoly of legitimate force.

The polity—whose interests realism prioritizes—does not have to take the form of the nation-state. Much of history is a history of empires, whereby some ascendant polities subordinate others and project power coercively beyond their borders. But empires also have dominant national groups at their core. Revolts against empires in modern time have often erupted under a nationalist banner. As E. H. Carr speculates, the nation-state, in time, may be superseded by some larger unit.[24] If so, it will still likely be smaller than a global state. Human groups are too divergent, valuing different things too much, to unite under a universal authority. A single world state would either be dominated by a hyperpower, imposing its own ways that would clash with too many others, or it would be internally paralyzed.

If the most important unit in both explaining things and in advocating policy is the group, the ruler's prime duty is to safeguard the group's security, prosperity, and way of life, to create not just peace but a decent peace. What each of these means in detail varies and is open to contest. A "way of life" for many people reading this book must include liberty and constitutional government, while for others it will mean asserting a dominant confession or protecting a language. In all cases, those in power are duty bound to protect their people's safety, their material welfare, and the quality of their existence.

Realists assume that maintaining the state is wise and necessary for those within it. Opponents of realism often argue that realists' attachment to the state as the central focus of security is perverse given that the security of the state is at odds with the security of people, or "human security." For some critics, the state itself is the problem and the principal source of violence. For some observers, realism obliviously promotes a form of power "over" and against women, ethnic minorities, and/or the working class.[25] After all, states historically are guilty of oppression, including over those they govern. Therefore, they reason, it must be dismantled or subordinated to something else and yield to some other more enlightened form of governance.

Yet because of the power they wield, states are also a vital step in the effort to limit chaos and create order. They are both provider and predator. As Hugh White notes, "States are both essential for the security of individuals, and also at the same time are among the biggest threats to them."[26] This problem of creating and restraining state power is a constant one we must live with as abandoning the state is no way out.

If we are bound, then, to live in states of some kind and if war is possible, old questions arise: How is that state to be governed? Can a ruler be good? For centuries, lively minds have disagreed. People who think about foreign policy differ not only over whether those who wield power can be benign or virtuous. The disagreement runs deeper. What do we mean by "good," anyway? "Good" by what standard? Should those who hold power be bound by the same morality that governs or should govern everyone else, those who aren't in authority? Must a ruler consider doing things that would ordinarily be unconscionable and with all the burdens that brings? Most realists don't believe power should be heedless of morality. They believe power should be guided by a different kind of morality, often known as "reason of state."

In realism, there is a sharp divide between the world "out there," beyond the gates and the writ of the state, and life within. The pressures that apply to polities and the requirement to guard the flock mean that ordinary ethical duties are superseded by something else. Thucydides, like the Florentine diplomat and thinker Niccolò Machiavelli, called it "necessity." Reason of state is contentious because it is situational (adjusting itself to the details of circumstances and constraints), consequentialist (oriented more to probable outcomes than pure principle), and built around a prior acceptance of separate groups competing for security. In the realist tradition, the sovereign in an anarchic international system owes their first duty to their own citizens—or subjects—and, in descending order of obligation, to peoples beyond. As Reinhold Niebuhr formulated it, their duty is "to do justice to wider interests than their own, while they pursue their own."[27]

The idea that morality must be adapted both to the ruler's duty to the ruled and to the harshness of the environment finds echoes and earlier expressions in theology, as does much of IR.[28] In the tradition of Augustine of Hippo (354–430 AD), the fallenness of creation and our species' inclination toward evil imposes duties on the ruler to take up arms. However reluctant, "it is the iniquity of the opposing side that imposes upon the wise man the duty of waging wars."[29]

Such pessimism moved Niccolò Machiavelli, who survived banishment and torture after he got on the wrong side of rulers. In his time, the marketplace of ideas also featured a competitor—namely, a kind of Christian universalism espoused by the papacy. Machiavelli wrote partly for self-advancement to pursue the patronage of the dominant Medici family. But he also wrote as a citizen, blaming princes for their inattention to power, making their city-states prey for invasion. At the base of his hard-edged appraisal of politics as it really is, there was a civic idealism, a commitment to his city and its liberty. He didn't show the same horror of Thucydides at atrocities and had a crueler detachment at times. Yet both men had suffered exile from their city-states and had tasted the fragility of things. For both, there was still civic purpose. The experience of desolation and the cruelty of power were no excuse for a descent into nihilism. Machiavelli was impelled partly by a "passionate sense of unnecessary loss that resulted from the irresponsible conduct of political life in the city states that so easily succumbed to invasion."[30] He valued republics because they unleashed their citizens' energies to achieve "glory." And glory was not reducible to imperial expansion but linked also to a state of creative freedom. Strength and its acquisition matter vitally, but they must be a means to an end. His work *The Prince*, written to advise rulers and dedicated to the Medici family, ends with an exhortation to liberate and unite Italy.

This version of morality, centered on the welfare of the group in an adversarial setting, stresses the consequences of actions and the constraints of the circumstances more than the justness of the cause. In the film *Lincoln*, the pragmatic, calculating US president mounts an argument to the more inflexibly principled Congressman Thaddeus Stevens in terms that borrow from realist ethics: "A compass will point to true north from where you're standing. But it's got no advice about the swamps and the deserts and chasms that you'll encounter along the way. If we're heedless of obstacles and sink in the swamp, what's the use of knowing true north?"[31] This is all the more so given the ruler is not a solo autonomous actor but decides on others' behalf and must regard the welfare of the flock. For Hans J. Morgenthau, "Universal moral principles cannot be applied to the actions of states in their abstract universal formulation, but . . . they must be filtered through the concrete circumstances of time and place. The individual may say for himself '*Fiat Justitia, pereat mundus* (Let justice be done, even if the world perish),' but the state has no right to say so in the name of those who are in its care."[32] Therefore, prudence, rather than principle, is the supreme virtue of statecraft—a kind of practical wisdom that weighs the consequences of righteous decisions and guards against moralistic excess.

For realists, therefore, the question is more fraught than "How should rulers rule?" It is, "How should rulers rule given the condition of anarchy?" Realism, at one level, is a critique of moralism.[33] Moralism is the vice of making judgements in an unreflective, excessive, and imprudent way and pursuing absolute values without due consideration of limits or consequences. It is an attitude that all questions must be reduced to issues of "right" and "wrong" in a strict, absolute sense, with morality defined by a similar standard to what is good and honorable in everyday life, with pragmatic calculation and compromise a form of moral cowardice. Moralism became attractive especially at the height of Western power in the interregnum after the Cold War when people fancied that moral and strategic interests had become one and that what was good for the West was good for everyone. To be a moralist is to be like the village scold who is more interested in being right than being effective, thereby being ultimately impotent. The word "tragic" is overused, but it points to a hard truth that realists embrace, while others resist. The world is a conflicted place. Our choices at the hardest times lie between lesser and greater evils. If the system cannot be overhauled but only managed, a favorable balance of power, without protracted war, to ensure a way of life is about the best we can achieve.

Consider the predicament facing Prime Minister Winston Churchill in July 1940. After Nazi Germany overran France, Churchill had to decide whether to attack and sink part of the French navy and its crew at its naval base in Mers-el-Kébir, Algeria.[34] The stakes were high. We can be too romantic about the heroic days of 1940, exaggerate Britain's vulnerability to invasion, and forget that it was not simply an isolated island but still a large empire, naval power, and technological leader. Yet with all that priced in, Britain still faced fearful odds. France, Germany's then-largest adversary, had fallen. Nazi Germany had conquered continental Europe. Beyond the Dominions, London had few significant allies. Joseph Stalin's Soviet Union was Adolf Hitler's de facto partner, and the United States remained then aloof, still nine months away from authorizing Lend-Lease aid.

Under this darkening sky, the War Cabinet in London feared that the European Axis powers Germany and Italy would seize the fleet of Vichy France. They feared this would further tip the balance of power at sea to Britain's disfavor. Britain may not have faced the realistic prospect of invasion. It could realistically be starved and broken via naval blockade. A larger enemy fleet would have further stretched Britain's own, making it harder to apply its weight effectively. There was to be no trusting the führer to keep his word and abide by the terms of his armistice with France and not to make demands of the navy. Indeed, under Axis control, a category of ships was maintained, only partly disarmed, with its crews aboard and capable of being reconverted to military use at one week's notice. Britain lacked enough ships to mount a blockade instead. It failed to persuade the French to scuttle the fleet, defect, repatriate crewmen, or demilitarize the ships and sail them to Martinique. A stark choice remained: fire or not fire. Churchill fired.

The assault killed 1,387 men of the crew in their ships. It was a brutal order, distressing and enraging to British admirals who had to do the sinking of recent comrades in arms. It injured long-term relations with France, for whom it was a murder and a betrayal. Churchill himself recalled it as a "a hateful decision," "unnatural and painful."[35] It was also a sound judgement. Given the high stakes, Britain's isolation, and the precarious military balance, Churchill did not want to risk Hitler gaining custody of the second-largest surface fleet in Europe. In the realist tradition, the sovereign must not only be prepared to do such things when circumstances require. They should be able to decide, then carry on, not allowing the magnitude of such acts to overwhelm them. "*Virtù*" is the term for this capacity for ruthless measures in extremis. Churchill was no saint, but he exercised *virtù*.

Moralists might have made different choices over the Vichy fleet and beyond. Earlier in the war, principled internationalists urged the British and French governments to intervene militarily on Finland's behalf against the Soviet Union during the Winter War of 1939, when Britain was already at war with Hitler, in the name of defending the principle of sovereign self-determination. Such a principled stance in the world as it was may have had the calamitous result of putting Britain and France at war with both Nazi Germany and the Soviet Union at the same time. At the end of the war, blanket opposition to totalitarianism led some to argue for an offensive against the Soviet Union or even preventive nuclear strikes on it afterward. Virtue run amok results in war without end, courting defeat and ruin.

Realism, therefore, is not synonymous with the unrelenting projection of force. Note that the same instincts that led to the sinking of the Vichy fleet led to standing back over Finland and bargaining with Stalin at the war's end. While realists regard military power and the threat of violence as the ultimate currency of international life, they do not believe all violence is bound to work. Power, depending on conditions, should be husbanded or unleashed.

Beyond defending, destroying, and deterring—essential processes for survival—violence in a realist world has few other reliable uses. Indeed, many realists in the US-led West often criticized and/or outright opposed some of the most consequential military interventions of the postwar period, from the enlargement of the Korean War in 1950 to the Vietnam escalation in 1965 to the invasion of Iraq in 2003 and the intervention in the Libyan Civil War of 2011.[36]

Most major acts of peacemaking and negotiated settlement, no matter how celebrated as higher forms of statecraft, involve a betrayal or dark compromise. This is true of the 1972 Nixon-Mao rapprochement that reinforced the division of the communist world and of the 1998 Belfast Agreement that ended hostilities in Northern Ireland. The 1972 Shanghai Communiqué, signaling the opening to China and the realignment of Mao Zedong's revolutionary state against Moscow, was purchased by the interests of abandoned Tibetans, Taiwanese, and (to get Pakistan's brokerage of the deal) the victims of massacres in Bangladesh, over which the White House was silent. And the Belfast Agreement involved commuting the prison sentences of convicted murderers.

So virtue as exercised in the harsh world of international life involves a more intense weighing of evils than in ordinary life. Even a ruler setting out to be benign will, sooner or later, confront choices in serving their polity that would be unthinkable in other settings. Power must always be accompanied by a humane conscience—realism cannot just be an alibi for barbarism. But that humaneness must work from an acceptance of the world as we find it.

Indeed, realist morality is more serious than moralism, which casts judgement on human affairs from a loftier, more absolute plane. To treat intentions and inner righteousness as all-important and to insist that strict principles must determine state behavior always, that states should never compromise or trade off valued things or deceive, spy, or dissemble or never bargain with evil and only conduct diplomacy with friendly countries, where it is least needed, or always bow to international law in a world where hostile states hold veto powers or only fight wars that never target civilians even indirectly is to lose sight of the actual hard choices states historically have faced. The environment agents must pick their way through is more unforgiving and more tangled than moralists allow. International Relations is not croquet on the vicarage lawn.

For a morally effective realpolitik in action, take the case of Egyptian president Anwar Sadat, who ruled Egypt from 1970 to 1981. Sadat was one of the most hard-nosed prudent leaders in modern time, who had to deal with a difficult set of cards dealt to him. He studied the capabilities of his own and other countries closely, with a keen sense of what was possible and an instinctive distrust of great powers. He used military force in a surprise attack to achieve what diplomacy had failed to accomplish: to seize back lost territory from Israel and break an unfavorable deadlock that would get Washington to support a better peace settlement. He wrong-footed his coalition partners by independently negotiating a ceasefire with Tel Aviv. He then defected from his fellow belligerents, recognizing the state of Israel. And he carefully cultivated two onlooking superpowers to get their backing. The CIA (Central Intelligence Agency) profiled "his realism, political acumen and capacity for surprising, courageous and dramatic decisions."[37] His 1977 memoir, written as Egypt was orbiting closer to Washington and further from Moscow, was a realist act in itself, emphasizing his disenchantment with Egypt's former Soviet patron. Sadat blended the use of military force with well-judged boldness and the discipline to pursue only achievable goals. Above all, he realized self-help and negotiating for oneself was a better route to Egypt's survival and prosperity than the elusive pan-Arabist movement—more an ideal to be invoked than a solidarity to be relied upon.[38] In the terminology of the casino, he knew when to hold and when to fold.

Sadat's adroit diplomacy came at a price. It meant the abandonment of the cause of a liberated Palestine, the betrayal of pan-Arabism, and the breaking of ranks with Arab allies. Note that he practiced deceit, violence, abrupt policy shifts, and the selling out of the interests of other parties—none of which is behavior we would commend in daily life. Yet applied internationally, his statecraft recovered the Sinai Peninsula, strengthened Egypt's hand, and created a pathway to the Camp David Accords and peace with Israel and the United States. Had Sadat behaved differently, Egypt may not have recovered the Sinai. Israel-Egypt-US relations would have remained fractious. And the cause of Palestine would probably still not have advanced given the ongoing cynicism of other Middle East regimes toward Palestinians. All this effort got Sadat assassinated for his trouble. Not even realist rulers are guaranteed a long or quiet life. But the point stands. Peacemaking that supports the national interest and the common good also requires cold calculation.

ALTERNATIVES

In this section, I pit realism against alternative worldviews that regard realism and realpolitik as part of the problem. Some of these traditions look to transformation, even to a utopian degree, and reject realism's premise of anarchy. Others, especially the family of liberal theories, are less ambitious. They share realism's starting point—that ours is a dangerous anarchic world. Only they are more optimistic about the possibility of progress so that anarchy can at least be strongly blunted if not overcome.

Realists' critics object to the idea that morality must be forged in the fearful apprehension of conflict and to the image of power seeking as the natural order of things. They point out that there are multiple forms of power beyond coercive violence and that modern International Relations are layered through overlapping institutions of global governance. Other kinds of power—diplomatic, commercial, or the "soft" power of cultural attraction—can have effect.

To an extent, this has to be true, of course. Only, force remains the ultima ratio. It can trump and overwhelm other forms of power and influence if left unchecked. Underdefended states that radiate soft power and exert spiritual awe can still be plundered. Indeed, treasures can attract rather than restrain predators. The greatest libraries on earth in medieval Baghdad, then the epicenter of scholarship, could not stop the Mongols sacking the city in 1258 AD. Half a century earlier, the opulence of Byzantium did not dissuade but pulled in crusaders, who pillaged the city. Revered international institutions, intended to tame their members' behavior, don't do much taming against determined aggressors. As Stalin remarked, possibly on several occasions, when pressed about the rights of Roman Catholics in Poland and relations with the Vatican, "The Pope? How many divisions has he got?"[39] The United Nations (UN) is full of good people doing good things, but the organization only achieves significant breakthroughs in security matters when conditions are permissive to begin with, and those conditions are atypical. At the time of writing, the UN has done little successfully to liberate Ukraine and terminate its war.

Ultimately, antirealists object to realist pessimism about the possibility of transformation or major change to the workings of the international system. For realists, there is no imagining, legislating, or designing our way out of anarchy. There is no disinterested benign higher force outside human power politics that we can create on earth that will command deference and keep the peace. There is no architecture, neither already wrought or not yet invented, that can somehow subject power politics to disinterested global governance or tame countries under the force of rules. The world remains too large, power too dispersed, and aspirations too different and conflicting to create a monarch or authority with unlimited writ that would enforce contracts and regulate the system. The coming of such a thing would in itself overconcentrate power in a human entity of some kind, thereby constituting a threat to sovereign states and prompting balancing efforts against it. There is no achievable order, no universally recognized legal authority with teeth that would effectively and consistently defend norms against interstate aggression and get powerful states to forgo the use of coercive threats of violence. Rules and institutions may offer benefits, but they are supplementary to the main act—more the product of power than vice versa.

In turn, this is a disagreement about the relationship between human agents and the international structure they inhabit. Indeed, it is about knowledge itself. For antirealists, the world is more malleable, changeable, and socially constructed. If anarchy is what you make of it, it can be acted upon and made significantly more benign,[40] whereas realists assume the world has objective properties—dark properties—that exist independently of whatever optimistic things we choose to believe about it.

What's more, attempting transformation may do more harm than good. Doing so may lead to the neglect of defenses and false trust in international institutions or the kindness of others. Or it may lead in the opposite direction—to the unfettered embrace of violence and unending war in the name of universalistic doctrines that overideologize international affairs, like creating a world without war or extending democratic liberty across the globe, whereas recognizing the constraints of anarchy encourages a more self-restrained sense of limits and the pursuit of more achievable ways to mitigate human suffering.[41]

To anticipate an objection, some might argue that a truly realist foreign policy would seek to make the world more secure via universal emancipation and repudiate great power competition since it threatens peace and democracy. There are many versions of this argument, but I'll focus on Van Jackson as one of the sharpest contemporary progressive voices.[42] Jackson argues that we should forge a world around equality since that is the only viable route to true security. This echoes the logic of the revolutionary Vladimir Lenin in 1920—that, for the Bolsheviks, only "international victory" would deliver "true security."[43] For Jackson and others, pursuing real security would involve the redistribution of wealth via an international minimum wage and cracking down on tax havens, a clean-energy transition, the dismantling of an oppressive, extractive capitalism, the dismantling of patriarchy, the rejection of empire, reparations to the victims of empire and their descendants, and the creation of an antimilitarist culture. It would also entail the rejection of state centrism in favor of international solidarity. Those arguing this need not be wide-eyed utopians. They may recognize the difficulty in achieving such an order and don't suppose that perpetual peace is within reach. But in an age of multiple interlocking crises that travel across borders, they argue that our international system must be overhauled in order to make any particular country, or people, fundamentally more secure.

Why do I disagree? The argument here is not about whether emancipatory policies would be good or bad. Rather, it is about the perceived linkage between overhauling an unjust system and security, between justice and peace.

All revolutionaries must operate within historical time and the reality that humans are not a unified collective under a universal authority. No revolutionary project can operate independently of the power politics that persists around and through it. In the absence of a fully formed and self-conscious international revolutionary proletariat, who is to be the agent of revolution? This is a conundrum hard to get around—that revolutionaries must contend with the state. Conflicts and crises come sooner than convenient. One may wish to transcend the militarized state and interstate conflict. Communists may be committed to struggle against classes and "isms." But history poses threats that come in more specific and embodied forms. Direct threats to all you value will arise, and they will be hosted in an organized polity. And when they do, it will be hard to reject all compromise and bargains with other states or one's own. How far should one work with a flawed regressive state against greater evil? That was the flip side of Lenin's statement in 1920—that revolutionary Russia needed to normalize relations with hostile regimes to achieve breathing space.

Some might be tempted to take a rejectionist line. A true leftist, argued the likes of German socialist Wilhelm Liebknecht, gives their own bourgeois state no support. As Liebknecht urged in 1871, "Not one recruit, not one penny will we approve for this ruling class state."[44] Stirring stuff. But where does that put British communists in June 1941 when Nazi Germany invaded the Soviet Union—in their eyes, the indispensable workers' state? Great power war, like great power competition, threatens peace and democracy, but Nazi hegemony over Eurasia would be vastly worse. Under that compulsion, communists rallied around the cause. Less than a decade before, the Oxford Union famously voted that it would never fight for king and country. But when war broke out, no matter how much they wanted to be fighting for a higher cause, those who enlisted did so under the banner of king and country. In order to battle fascism and serve the ultimate cause of peace and equality, an armistice with and service for the British Empire was a necessary evil given it was the only accessible and plausible vehicle of resistance through which to aid the embattled Soviet Union. A similar problem confronts contemporary revolutionaries: opposing the arms industry while supporting the arming of Ukraine, say, is like loving apples while hating the orchard.

What's more, even if we somehow achieved a genuinely egalitarian world, it would still be a realist world, subject to the insecurity of anarchy, and would thereby become less egalitarian and less peaceful before long. Imagine a just and egalitarian international order created overnight, a group of internally egalitarian, postpatriarchal, and nonimperialist communities. In that alternative universe, there would still be absent a supreme authority to enforce the peace, underwrite everyone's security, and maintain the status quo. In that unprotected condition, even if every country had benign intentions, the basis for alarm would remain. There would likely be multiple pathways toward change, instability, and strife. Different countries would produce wealth at different paces, undergoing differential economic growth. To use the language of Leon Trotsky, there would be "uneven" and "combined" development.[45] Both realist and nonrealist scholars have picked up this logic too to suggest that a historical materialist emphasis on differential economic growth explains patterns of power politics and conflict, reflecting an overlap between realism and Marxism.[46]

Historically, variations of economic growth are the basis for power shifts. And power shifts tend to make rulers nervous, raise security fears, and trigger competition between those doing the growing and those falling behind. Accordingly, even in a thoroughly egalitarian world, there would be growing ambition induced by wealth. By getting richer, several countries would assert themselves more forcefully. They would start to think of themselves as special and historically destined to lead, entitled and obliged to lead, in fact, and to steer the destinies of other countries; they would start to pursue glory, but above all, they would fear losing their place at the top of the pecking order. Such ambitions could also appear threatening. Even if the leading states enjoyed absolute gains, they would increasingly fret about relative gains. They would increasingly want different things. Some of those differences—over human rights, say, or state authority or drug trafficking or trade—would exacerbate suspicions and rivalries.

The history of relations among communist states points to a similar problem. Nations that go communist are still nations, and they still seek to survive in space and time. Solidarity yields to rivalry. As between Communist China and the Soviet Union or China and Vietnam or Vietnam and Cambodia, there would emerge power struggles between states that were supposed to be ideologically kindred. Regardless of how far those splits were driven by ideological fallout or geopolitical differences, each came to regard the other suspiciously as outgroups. Until the revolutionary project supplants national loyalties and memories and the pressures that lead nations to insure against others' uncertain intentions recede, it is hard to replace a commitment to particular groups with a commitment to a universal class—and this, in practice, is a hard allegiance to maintain.

No one could ever be certain about others' intentions. As some states pulled away from others in their size, population, and capabilities, anxiety about those intentions would increase. There would be either anxiety that others' claims to moderation and benevolence were false, an anxiety about current intentions, or fear of intentions changing and ambitions rising if material conditions swung in others' favor. The shadow of the future would descend. Amidst this gathering instability, at least some actors would decide it prudent to arm themselves. And once they did so, it would be hard to persuade others that their intentions were peaceful or would remain so. It would simply be too difficult for some countries to avoid inadvertently appearing threatening. And this is only the least bad scenario, where everyone really has good intentions. It would only take one or two greedy states, especially growing ones capable of threatening harm, to make the scenario more turbulent. Imagine, say, an unscrupulous revisionist power arising that also tried to revise what other nations regarded as a noble order of egalitarian states. The order would need protecting. That is not to suggest that it is impossible to make foreign policy more progressive—up to a point. To coin a phrase, radicals can make a more progressive foreign policy. Only, it will not be under conditions of their choosing.

Another way to test this issue is to turn back to history. The past and what we derive from it is our only possible source of information, suggests the limits that fall on any attempt to transform the world. We have been here before. Famine, epidemics, wars, and economic collapse have prompted efforts before to create institutions or forms of governance to replace anarchy with something else. That "something else" usually boils down to hierarchy, under which cooperative solidarity can take root. How have these efforts fared thus far?

Attempts to abolish armed conflict have a disappointing track record, as we will see in the next chapter. Likewise, attempts to tame war strictly under humanitarian principles have also proven fragile, as rising pressure tends to relax the force of taboos. Before World War Two, countries condemned unrestricted submarine warfare and city bombardment. Yet when they took up arms against first-order threats, they applied those methods unapologetically and in detail. At the time of writing, Ukraine in its supreme emergency and grinding attritional war receives cluster munitions and antipersonnel landmines from Washington. There is a larger historical pattern here. Moral restraint tends to loosen under existential pressure. We can all be high-minded during the good times.

The fate of the League of Nations, as compared to the United Nations, reveals the dilemma at the heart of supranational international organizations that are supposed to protect common security. Designed by lively minds, the league nevertheless faltered because it could not abolish self-seeking power politics. It could not live up to its own vision. It could not inspire states to make the sacrifices necessary to intervene in violent crises from Abyssinia to Manchuria. And unlike the United Nations, as it did not "lock in" a veto power for the strongest states, it failed to survive. Nazi Germany walked out in 1933 over the question of disarmament.

The United Nations, by contrast, has at least survived by creating veto powers for a permanent five. But in exchange for greater survivability, this makes the institution self-paralyzing at critical moments, or it is just bypassed by determined members when it suits them. Hypothetically, a veto system would have enabled Germany to block the disarmament policy and press on, preserving the institution but making it marginal to real politics. To persist, such institutions must reflect the existing distribution of power but then defer to it. Thus, major powers who violate norms and rules also exercise determinative votes. That is not to deny any value to such institutions. As coordinating mechanisms for agreed-upon and decent measures, such as the United Nations Children's Fund, and as debating and bargaining chambers, it is better to have them than not have them. Rather, it is to say that such institutions cannot supplant the core pattern of competitive power politics under anarchy.

If institutions can, at best, soften at the edges but not fundamentally change the patterns of anarchy, what about other kinds of long-term change that alter the human condition and outlook? Some argue that a series of macrolevel "globalizing" changes—economic, institutional, and normative—since 1945 have made the world less warlike and more civilized, bringing out the "better angels of our nature" and driving what Nils Petter Gleditsch describes as "a clear, albeit erratic, decline of organized violence."[47] Or, in the terms of English school theorists, if we cannot get rid of anarchy, we can at least create a moderating sense of "society" within anarchy, generating more cooperation than realists would expect.[48] If these claims are right, realist morality weakens because its explanatory power weakens. It builds its morality atop a set of conditions that have passed.

How true is this, though? As we will see in the next chapter, the claim that forces of globalization, economics, and progressive thought have made the world significantly less warlike is overblown on closer inspection. Regarding economic interdependence as a source of peace, the literature debating this is overwhelming. While I can't do justice to it here, a realist response might go as follows. Economic ties can certainly be an obstacle to war making given the potential costs of war's disruption to trade and investment. But they cannot reliably be a decisive barrier. They were not, after all, in 1914, when there were comparatively high levels of foreign direct investment between Britain and Germany. Recall that in that fateful summer, "the bankers and industrialists were the last people in Europe who wanted a war. Capital's overwhelming desire was for peace and continued globalization. It was Lord Rothschild who entreated the *Times* of London to tone down the belligerence of its articles, and right up to the end the governor of the Bank of England was begging the Liberal cabinet minister Lloyd George, 'with tears in his eyes,' to keep Britain out of war."[49] Before February 2022, German chancellor Angela Merkel insisted that trade with Russia would be a source of both peace and Moscow's moderation, invoking the slogan "Change through trade." The results were disappointing. Moreover, third parties and neutrals in global economies can adapt or even profit from the disruption of war, while the belligerents themselves also can in a globalized economy.[50] Trade relations within states, too, are also often extensive, yet that does not reliably prevent civil wars. Again, economics can impose some constraints but not to the extent that states can assume conflict has passed to the fringes.

There is an important relationship here between the "is" and the "should," the explanatory and the normative. It matters a great deal to what degree realists are correct that narrower material interests tend to trump norms when the pressure is high, that international institutions, statutes, or promoted humanist values tend to be weak constraints at best, that the spread of democratic capitalism is unlikely to cause general peace, and that there are no true "friends" abroad.[51] If all this is true, countries are well advised to take these realities into account when deciding on their own policies. From the "is"—the treacherousness and brutality of international politics—flows an "ought"—that for the sake of the ruled, countries must assume war is possible and that they cannot rely on international society or even on long-standing alliances to safeguard them and must look to their own ramparts.

Some critics of realism question the centrality of military power. They insist preparing the means of violence to counter violence is neither effective nor necessary and that other forms of civil resistance are more effective.[52] This may hold in cases where adversaries are relatively tolerant. But as a response to those who are intolerant of dissent or resistance, nonviolent resistance is no substitute. Mahatma Gandhi, for instance, able to denounce the British Empire, would likely have disappeared in the Soviet Union. Even cases celebrated as triumphs of nonviolence against tyranny—the revolutions in the Philippines in 1986, South Africa in 1990–1994, and Serbia in 1999—were really only partly nonviolent. They depended on complementary violence from the civilian-supported military coup in Manilla to the repression of saboteurs and dissidents in the African National Congress and its victory in the Natal Civil War. The North Atlantic Treaty Organization's (NATO) coercive bombing campaign discredited Belgrade tyrant Slobodan Milosevic and encouraged the US-funded opposition to abandon their nonviolence, riot, and topple him.[53] The fact remains that history is violent and that the prospect of violence informs decisions over what or who prevails. True, most states, most of the time, do not take the risks of launching hostilities. Most people, most of the time, don't rob banks or commit murder either. Yet it is the distressing minority of cases that define our world and motivate our defenses.

Since 1945, there has been one significant change: an absence of major war. Major wars are direct clashes between the leading powers in the international system and sufficiently intense to threaten the survival of those actors, involving full mobilization and direct conflict at scale (more direct and more intense than peripheral skirmishes and the proxy battles of a cold war). And as wars of systemic significance, they can alter the distribution of power and the structure of the international system itself.[54] The conflicts important enough to earn an international "before-and-after" status include World War Two (1939–1945), World War One (1914–1918), the Napoleonic

Wars (1803–1815), the Great Turkish War (1683–1699), and the Great East Asian War (1592–1598). The absence of major war is attributable to a novel development that, while not abolishing power politics, created a powerful new constraint based on a lethal capability—namely, nuclear weapons. To this and other contemporary problems, I now turn.

REALISM IN OUR TIME

So far, maybe so good. But now for the hard part. What is to be done? We need to consider how the logic and ethos of realism can help us tackle current problems and guide judgement. Here, I'll try my hand at three large ones: nuclear weapons, climate change, and dictators. Not all realists would agree with the policy approaches adopted here. Rather, it is *a* realist response to three issues for which the stakes are high.

Nuclear Weapons
The most momentous development of the twentieth century was not the creation of international institutions, the rise of humanitarian norms, or the invention of the internet. It was the nuclear revolution—that is, the ability to manipulate nuclear reactions to generate force, an innovation that became weaponized. For the first time, humans have been able to not only inflict large-scale swift destruction with deliverable bombs but also, once they had sufficient strike range, fire those bombs in ways that are extremely difficult to stop. And once they made their arsenals secure via quantity, concealment, and other protective measures, nuclear states developed the ability to retaliate—a "second strike." This has created a stalemate. Conquest of nuclear-armed states have become vastly more difficult, costly, and therefore unattractive. I'll argue in the next chapter that this development is the main reason why we have had no major wars since 1945.

Here, I offer the moral case for retaining nukes rather than seeking to abolish or eliminate them. Realists' relationship with nuclear weapons—and their occasional dalliances with world government as an answer—is a complex story, already superbly told.[55] Realists dispute many things about nukes. They differ over how far nukes have revolutionized politics beyond the baseline of aversion to major war. They disagree whether increased proliferation would do more to stabilize or destabilize the world and how far countering hostile proliferation is worth the costs of high-stakes coercion or even war.[56]

But most realists, most of the time, judge that whatever other policies we consider, we must learn to live with the bomb. Indeed, if realists are right that the nuclear revolution is the political reality we must live in, like it or not, that is the only morally responsible course.

Critics beg to differ.[57] Nuclear weapons, they argue, are morally wrong for several reasons. They are intrinsically indiscriminate and often genocidal in their yield, making any use unconscionable. They are immoral as homicidal devices used against others. And they are immoral because they threaten omnicide, bringing about the self-destruction of humanity via either accident or deliberate exchange. The ultimate weapon not only might inflict unimaginable direct harm, but it also could unleash an unsurvivable climate catastrophe—a "nuclear winter" that could block out the sun's rays, alter the temperature, and cause mass starvation. The necessary flip side of living under the nuclear shadow is obviously that humans engaged in brinksmanship are fallible and that mutual deterrence can fail. Just because deterrence has held doesn't mean it will always. It could fail by miscalculation or, according to some, mishap. Critics cite historic cases of "near misses" where dangerous detonations or fatal misperceptions almost happened from the Cuban missile crisis in 1962 to the Able Archer incident of 1983, from the midair crash of nuclear-armed planes to false alerts of bomb detectors. Skeptics also point to the fallibilities of human minds and bureaucratic organizations, their propensity to filter information, fall prey to false assumptions, or overlook risks, and their imperfect record of keeping nuclear materials under lock and key. The very success thus far of nuclear stalemate, they add, could embolden some actors to take greater risks, deciding that they can elect not to be deterred while assuming they will deter adversaries.

Skeptics are surely right that eventual use of nuclear weapons of some kind and at some scale is probable, if not certain. Realists, to be consistently pessimist, cannot coherently assume that mutual deterrence is bound to last forever. The disagreement lies in what conclusions to draw. Skeptics may concede that nuclear weapons have deterred and can deter, yet they reject the conclusion that nukes should be retained. Even if nuclear weapons have helped cause the relative stability and peace among great powers, they offer us a dark wager of keeping us safe now until they destroy us or others tomorrow. Because eventual nuclear use endangers everyone, the reasoning goes, to retain them constitutes a moral failure of intergenerational form, purchasing stability now for holocaust later. Therefore, they reason, the only responsible course is abolition via disarmament, whether unilateral or multilateral, or at least extensive reduction, as well as treaties outlawing the weapon and perhaps the creation of taboos, a morally driven disinclination to use or build them in the first place. From another and more hawkish direction, some infer from nukes' horror that the best response is not disarmament but the creation of a supershield to render nuclear attacks useless by erecting missile defenses not so much to scrap nukes as to make them undeliverable.

Yet it is more prudential to accept and manage nuclear weapons than seek their eradication. This is primarily because abolition is impossible and probably undesirable. Why? First, the power of nuclear destruction is here to stay. Disarmament is not the same as abolition and will likely not achieve it.[58] The nuclear revolution that was consummated with the atomic strikes on imperial Japan in 1945 is irreversible and permanent. A denuclearized world would still contain the materials and expertise to make them again, as it did in 1939. Intellectually, it is a bell that cannot be unrung. Except for the unusual case of South Africa, nuclear-armed states not only tend to retain their weapons but also don't even consider scrapping them. No matter how much lambs vote for veganism, the wolves remain unmoved.

Even if we could magically guarantee the elimination of all nukes forever, the effects would probably be pernicious. With their main insurance against aggression removed, former possessors would remain insecure and probably feel more insecure. Unchecked by the threat of overwhelming return fire and unacceptable damage, aggressors would go back to an old and sometimes accurate calculation—that they can attack and win at an acceptable cost and perhaps annihilate others while shielding their own population. Without the weapon that uniquely serves as an equalizer, the elimination of nukes would empower the strong at the expense of the weak, using their size and wealth to lock in their conventional advantages. After all, the constraining effects of nukes are a prime motivation for superpowers, like the United States, to try to limit proliferation given weaker adversaries can use nukes against the strong to limit their freedom of action.[59] In sum, a postnuclear world, if such a thing emerged, would be more frequently unstable, violent, and genocidal, more dangerous to the weak rather than less, and more open to aggression, not less.

It would also, in the end, not even be postnuclear. General disarmament, hypothetically, would far more likely lead to conditions where countries must consider rearming. This would increase, not reduce, the dangers of nuclear use. Without a powerful enough international agency or body to enforce general disarmament, no one could be confident that disarmament was complete or that an opportunistic aggressor was not clandestinely rearming. Therefore, every international crisis in a disarmed world would be aggravated by an awareness of potential proliferation, adding further time pressure to the given crisis. In conditions of everyone else disarming, the rewards of having a small number of bombs would look large and tempting. Given the problem that "other minds" might wish to race for the bomb and seize an advantage, states would have a strong incentive to prepare the ability to regenerate nuclear arms. Ex–nuclear powers and new aspirants would likely retain the hair-trigger ability to proliferate and would be primed to strike against any nuclear breakout by others, whose targets they would have in their crosshairs.[60] International politics would still happen in an atomic shadow but with greater volatility. This danger reflects an uncomfortable reality—that there isn't a linear relationship between the size or number of stockpiles and stability. Smaller arsenals mean greater vulnerability to a first strike, putting a premium on haste.[61] By the same logic, preparing the ability to build the bomb at short notice in these circumstances would likely make others more nervous and hastier. In this way, disarmament would sow the seeds of rearmament. In the "zero" future disarmers call for, there would be fewer bombs but greater crisis instability, stronger incentives to strike first, and therefore graver danger.

Regarding the apocalyptic nuclear winter fear, to judge from the debate by scientists closer to the issue, the hypothesis that even limited nuclear use would be the equivalent of a widespread natural catastrophe is contentious, often politicized, and hard to resolve.[62] We have detonated nuclear weapons more than two thousand times, including hundreds of times in the earth's atmosphere. The largest ever nuclear detonation, the fifty-seven-megaton Tsar Bomba in October 1961, was three thousand times as powerful as the bomb dropped on Hiroshima yet, according to one physicist, "one-thousandth the force of an earthquake, one thousandth the force of a hurricane."[63] At the least, to blot out the sun may require hundreds of devices being detonated in a short time. With further refinements of modeling the impact of detonations on climate, some argue that the effect would more likely approach a "nuclear autumn" than winter.

We should not be sanguine about this. Such fallout would still be catastrophic. But that must be measured against the risks attached to nuclear disarmament—namely, the increased chance of a thing that we have avoided in the nuclear age: conventional war among major powers that would also kill millions, disrupt supply chains, devastate agriculture, and unleash famine. It is not a choice of nuclear holocaust versus peace. It is avoidance of holocausts through the threat of a worse one. To be consistently realist—and pessimistic—one must concede that deterrence is unlikely to succeed indefinitely.[64] Sooner or later it is bound to fail, as one realist observes.[65] The wager, after eighty years of nuclear weapons existing, is that prudent handling and crisis management will buy us another eighty years of no major war, if not more. If we could achieve approximately one hundred and sixty years following 1945, therefore, of human life before suffering either world war three or a more localized nuclear war that would be a significant gain. It would be terrible for those who suffered the subsequent catastrophe. But the alternative is more and earlier holocausts before a return to proliferation and the hard-to-avoid nuclear disaster eventually landing anyway. We do not have a plausible third option of returning to the prenuclear world.

Regarding the question of accidents and near misses, the risk unquestionably exists but is not a decisive argument against retaining weapons systems that are likely to reappear even if we get rid of them.[66] Thanks to increased safety measures with regard to design and handling and the technically demanding nature of mechanisms needed to set off an explosion, accidental or unauthorized detonation is less likely than before. And again, the realistic choice is not between running the (low) risk of an accident triggering a nuclear explosion versus removing the risk and therefore being safer. It is between the risks of accident and the risks of disarmament (see above). With regard to near misses, one assumption disarmers sometimes make is that we were a mere hairsbreadth from nuclear launch, judging from earlier cases of false alarms and alert sequences. Initially mistaking a flock of birds or a satellite launch or a military exercise for being an imminent nuclear launch is obviously a serious thing, but that does not mean decision-makers historically were on the brink of assuming the worst and retaliating. Just because some officials warned that signals may be false and classified them as errors does not mean that decision-makers would have otherwise unquestioningly launched before seeking confirmation. Again, technical mechanisms do not stop decisions for war being a momentous choice.

What, then, is to be done instead of pursuing abolition? One achievable step is to restore or bolster nuclear deterrence to where it once was as the backbone of security—that is, creating both the capability and the credible message that one might be able and willing either to defeat an attack or to inflict unacceptable damage by firing nuclear weapons if one's core interests are attacked. Emphatically, this does not provide deterrence for every menace or contingency, like cyberattacks or terrorist attacks. Taking out car insurance does not ward off catching a virus, but that is not an argument against car insurance.

To make the retaliatory threats at the heart of deterrence credible, realist advice might be to become both more restrained and yet more robust. On the "robust" side of the ledger, those who wish to deter should abandon the fiction of eventual disarmament and the restriction of arsenals only to the most maximal city-targeting nukes. This posture risks weakening the credibility of the deterrent by making oneself appear too reluctant. Determination to show others that one thinks that use of the ultimate weapon is unthinkable makes one look too unwilling ever to use it.

This isn't just about words or doctrines. It also means developing capabilities whose potential use is believable. Bolstering credibility in order to deter also suggests going back to a logic that informed NATO's Cold War strategy, developing tactical lower-yield nukes for battlefield use. In an actual crisis, only having the option to back off and keep one's nukes holstered or proceeding directly and suicidally to Armageddon can make adversaries too confident that you would be unwilling to escalate, especially if that same adversary already possesses other coercive nuclear options.[67] Western nuclear powers should do what their adversaries are doing—develop the ability to threaten intermediate use when defending core interests in order to shock an aggressor into backing off by more credibly threatening to take the crisis onto a dangerous slippery slope. The need to ensure credibility is especially important now that revisionist powers, like Russia and China, are already enlarging their arsenals and delivery systems.

On the "restraint" side of the ledger, responding to the realities of the nuclear revolution in an age of greater competition also means putting a priority on creating stable mutual deterrence. For one thing, this means avoiding making nuclear threats over noncore interests. The prospect of escalation is only credible when one has the balance of resolve in one's favor. Making guarantees beyond that might not be believed and might be tested.

Committing to stability in order to prevent major war also means avoiding backing nuclear-armed adversaries against the wall and making them desperate. Fomenting regime change or attempting "maximum-pressure" coercive disarmament or mounting regime-threatening military operations in search of absolute victory can tempt adversaries to reach for their trump card—coercive nuclear escalation. In crisis zones, like the Korean peninsula, a de facto acceptance of their nuclear arsenals would help create space for easing other areas of dispute and finally turn the armistice into a formal end to war. On the policy menu, there would also be constructive things that have already happened from establishing crisis hotlines to providing technical help to newer nuclear states in securing their arsenals under command and control through additional safety measures. Most of all, strengthening deterrence entails a paradoxical mix of looking willing to go over the edge if pushed but exercising more self-restraint in order to avoid driving the other side over the edge prematurely. For the threat of retaliation and punishment to make sense, one's target should be persuaded that you won't try to destroy them even after they comply.

There are some more policy choices that will divide realists in the nuclear realm not merely on theoretical grounds but also regarding national perspectives. Realists agree that nuclear weapons prudently handled are a fundamental source of stability but disagree on what counts as prudent. Most realists, most of the time, oppose measures that seek security in more ambitious forms than stable mutual deterrence, like waging preventive wars or forcibly rolling back the nuclear program of "middle powers," like Iran, North Korea, or Saddam Hussein's Iraq, since realists generally prefer to maintain deterrence at the core of security rather than risk the hazards of starting a war in search of favorable transformational change.[68] American realists generally will prefer any nuclear proliferation by friendly or unfriendly states to be rare and slow, though there has always been a strain of proliferation optimism in the tradition of Kenneth N. Waltz that more proliferation and the emergence of more nuclear-armed states *may* be better.

This is not just about America. Australian realists, to take another example, might argue for building a latent nuclear capability given increased instability in a more multipolar Asian neighborhood and the possibility that the country might one day have to stand alone.[69] Israeli realists will favor maintaining the ability to retaliate in extremis while fearing that bombing

Iran would raise the "Osirak dilemma" of suppressing Tehran's capability to sprint for the bomb now in exchange for increasing its determination to acquire that capability, further accelerating its nuclear and missile program. An Iranian bomb may well spell further instability, but a realist logic would suggest that ultimately if forced to choose, it is more prudent to live with the possibility of an Iranian bomb in the belief that a nuclear Iran can be contained and deterred, especially given Iran's regime has not yet decided to build one, rather than to keep bombing Iran. All these policy debates for realists will take place against the assumption of an enduring nuclear reality since it cannot be extinguished.

Climate Change

What should realists think about the present climate crisis? When I say "crisis," I don't mean the end of the planet or ecological collapse. The world has endured multiple physical upheavals before, from catastrophic asteroid strikes to severe shifts in temperature, and has a way of enduring. The problem is rather the survival of our species. While this is not the place for a detailed policy breakdown, some guiding judgements are in order. In particular, realists ought to have something to say about an underlying disagreement over how to respond, whether to *overhaul* our relationship with the environment or *mitigate* its bad effects, and whether the climate crisis is best approached as the overriding issue or as a relative one.

If there is a common threat to humanity in the form of a climate shift that is primarily human induced, this does not mean that sustained collective action or transnational solidarity is possible. Nor does it mean that prioritizing the pursuit of such collective action is the most prudent step forward. The emergency is not bound to bring us all together in the face of a shared threat—to the contrary, a realist logic suggests.

If anything, climate change will create more vital interests to be fought over and defended. It will place a greater premium on territory and territoriality. Even if nations "should" drop everything and make carbon-emission reduction the supreme and shared objective, they have not and show little sign of doing so. The myriad problems that come with climate change—resource scarcity, the upheaval in human movement and migration, food insecurity via shortages of arable land and fresh water, and energy-driven demand for precious materials, such as lithium—are more likely to drive competition than cooperation. This will be especially the case if the change is abrupt rather than linear and gradual.

With the coming of the climate crisis, competition, if anything, is intensifying. More to the point, the pursuit of a greener and more sustainable future is proving competitive. In policy areas directly linked to climate policy, the drive for clean energy is stimulating rather than reducing geopolitical rivalry. Take lithium, the mineral critical to green technology from electric vehicles to the storage of wind and solar energy. Lithium is not evenly distributed across the world, is deposited mainly in four countries only, and is in spiraling demand. Against incentives to pool resources and coordinate action, European Union (EU) nations and the United States seek to check China's lithium dominance—and counteract one another—by reducing their supply chain vulnerabilities and intervening with industrial subsidies and rule loosening to strengthen their own domestic green industries. This is part of a wider pattern of fracture, partial economic decoupling, and industrial reshoring.

Yet a continuous theme runs through much commentary about the climate crisis. The crisis, observers note, *should* be inspiring collective action in the face of a common threat. As Marina Yue Zhang argues, "Lithium shouldn't be the center of a competition between the great tech powers but, rather, a key component in a *collective* battle against climate change. The world is in desperate need of collaboration."[70] Well, tough. Regardless of what the world needs, the disunited inhabitants of it will only get limited and partial collaboration. They will not suspend power politics, with all the real vulnerability that would create, in the name of longer-term security even if they should. Any practicable steps to reduce and buffer the effects of the climate crisis will have to take place within that constraint.

If history is any guide, such growing competition is bound to become militarized. Recent history certainly points in this direction. Note the prevalent behavior of powerful states in the face of the pandemic of 2020–2021.[71] They hoarded vaccines, launched travel-restriction policies unilaterally, and, in the case of China, punished other countries for suggesting Beijing was at fault. Not only was international collaboration hard, getting agreement on the source of the problem was bound up with politics. Even under an unusually high stimulus for collective action, national egoism trumped collaboration whenever there was a clash between the two.

The alarm over the climate has been raised now for decades, but this has not dissuaded major powers (Russia, China, the United States) from rearming or modernizing their armed forces and nuclear arsenals, rising powers (like India) from industrializing and arming, or middle powers (such as Iran) from making significant sacrifices to invest in military capability or to fund and arm militias across a given region. Major powers still covet disputed territories or unilaterally seize them from the South China Sea to Crimea. Moreover, states with the capability to project power would be unlikely to care exclusively about climate change as the overriding priority. There will always be attention split in other directions—namely, toward nearby competitors and potential threats over borders or toward distant ones who continue to infiltrate, spy, and steal intellectual property. These are not conditions hospitable for creating a global "we."

Even if concerted Western action with perfect concord and efficiency were possible, this would barely arrest climate change. If all wealthy Western nations went back to the output equivalent of the Bronze Age tomorrow, completely curtailing all emissions, it would not be enough to arrest the change given the high likelihood that other large growing countries will not curtail their industrial revolutions. Even if all the declared net-zero goals reported by the UN Environment Program were met, temperatures would still rise by approximately 1.5 degrees Celsius.[72] If this is the range of outcomes—from Western states' all-out net zero only achieving a slight reduction to more partial worldwide reduction still resulting in a destabilizing temperature rise—they are modest ones indeed given the expense and economic regression of forcing through rapid change for rapid enforced decarbonization will be expensive. It will likely inflict suffering on communities that depend on agriculture, heavy industry, or the fossil fuel production of consumable fuels. It will also place great strain on state finances. Inquiries friendly to the net-zero agenda suggest so. In the United Kingdom, for instance, the Climate Change Committee estimates that to get to net zero will cost approximately £50 billion a year over twenty years—the equivalent of over a quarter of the annual health budget.[73] It will also impose more indirect hardship on the unlucky in other ways—for instance, by foisting low-emission zones on areas where there is little public transport. Even taking into account possible economic benefits of energy transition, these are more speculative, while the up-front costs are known, and their burden is heavy.

Some will reply that these difficulties only underline the need for a more global response and for more political will. But the absence of political will is not primarily due to the wickedness or shortsightedness of leaders or human greed. In a realist account, it flows from the problems of living in competitive anarchy, the fear of incurring losses compared to others, and thereby becoming more insecure.

Attempts to create a global response are also likely to meet disappointment. The unequal development of countries makes it very difficult for established wealthy states to persuade heavily populated states climbing out of mass poverty to sacrifice their growth or living standards. Bluntly, the West will not persuade India or China to forgo having their industrial revolutions. No matter how much those insurgent states invest in green technology and promote themselves as exemplars of a more responsible environmental policy, they will willingly continue to grow and pollute.

If this is the case, pursuing net zero by an imminent date would be to undergo a profound dislocation of human life for only limited gains, leaving most temperature increase unreversed. Achieving sustainability may be an imperative, but so too is poverty reduction, and there are real tradeoffs between the two. Net zero would divert effort and energy away from other pressing issues, such as preventable diseases or providing access to clean drinking water. To cover the full spectrum of emissions reduction, nor would it spare military forces, which would be required to eliminate emissions so quickly it would effectively amount to partial disarmament. In a world where others refuse to decarbonize to that extent, some states would therefore effectively weaken while other states maintain and grow their arsenals. In other words, an overhaul strategy would amount to imprudent waste—an irrational misallocation of resources. This may not feel good to the liberal conscience. But the priority for climate policy should not be therapeutic, designed to make concerned people feel better or assuage their guilt, given the material burdens it entails.

This is not an argument for fatalism or passivity. It is an argument for adapting to an inexorable reality rather than attempting systematic transformation. There are active measures short of transformation that the logic of realism commends. A "mitigationist" strategy is an alternative.[74] It still seeks to reduce emissions and lower pollution gradually. But it focuses more on what states can do unilaterally and in cooperation with smaller groups of states that have already had their industrial revolutions. It is more concerned with shielding populations from the oncoming extreme-weather threats and their disruption to habitats, energy supplies, and food and water. This entails things like bolstered flood and fire defenses and more resilient infrastructure, ranging from storage of reserve-energy power to reservoirs to investment in a skilled class of technicians to better-funded and more capable emergency services and to technological innovation geared toward the processes of food production, packaging, and distribution. If implemented, a mitigationist strategy would invest in nuclear power—by far the most powerful source of clean renewable energy. And generosity to the smaller island states most threatened by rising seas would take the form of strengthening defenses or assisting relocation rather than the false promise of lowering the tides.

The alternative case—making climate the overriding and supreme policy objective and forming a worldwide united front on the issue—will not only run up against formidable political barriers. It will also come at a great price even if the species could achieve it. As we have already seen, it would entail large-scale Western disarmament given that advocates of net zero typically see defense as a waste of precious resources and a contributor to environmental degradation. And what concessions would it take, say, to achieve Beijing's full cooperation on carbon emissions? At a minimum, going by China's own recent demands, it would mean suppressing domestic criticism of its policies. It would mean conceding to its wishes over everything from Taiwan to the first island chain of the Pacific. It would mean tolerating any and all investment in foreign infrastructure, thereby increasing its coercive power. And probably, the more China rises on these terms to unopposed dominance over Asia's trade and economics, the more it would have a free hand to do whatever it liked with regard to climate policy. So conceding ground to China—even literally—in the hope of a climate payoff would probably not even work. Given what's at stake, therefore, and the potential to waste precious capabilities, debate will benefit from less demands for concerted global action and more pragmatism in focusing on what can be done.

Where does development, aid, and generosity—three overlapping but distinct things—in general fit in this picture? Again, this is not the place for a detailed policy blueprint. But a realist foreign policy would temper the missionary urge with a healthy skepticism about Western ambitions to remake the world in our image. "Developing" other nations—to tilt them toward policies one wants them to adopt—runs up against the misalignment problem. That is, while richer nations can technically help poorer states to govern, no amount of effort can easily make one country harmonize its interests with another. As experience from Afghanistan to Pakistan to Iraq to Egypt to Niger suggests, strengthening a poorer nation's armed forces or police can increase capability, but those forces can be used to do things like reward domestic allies and repress opponents or launch coups, commit atrocities, or sponsor an armed proxy abroad, expanding the disorder such policies are supposed to reduce. If generosity is a laudable part of foreign policy, there must first be order, without which it is hard to do good. First doing minimal harm and distinguishing the technical from the political would be a prudent alternative, focusing help on the immediate alleviation of suffering—a more modest goal, perhaps, but more achievable.

The general pattern of donor-recipient behavior throws doubt on the optimistic idea that development aid generates soft power for the donor, creating a cultural attraction that then translates into meaningful influence. While giving help may make the donor feel important, it doesn't reliably induce the recipient to be gratefully compliant with the donor's wishes in other policy areas.[75] Billions in aid over decades to Afghanistan did not get the government in Kabul to do what donor countries wanted—to address issues ranging from corruption to narcotics. Billions in military and economic aid to Pakistan didn't prevent Osama bin Laden hiding out there, whether actively tolerated by the host country or left alone by neglect, less than a mile from the national Military Academy. For development aid to have the effect of realigning the recipient's behavior, there would need to be a credible threat of withdrawing help in the future—a corollary that would horrify most advocates of development. That doesn't mean there is no place for generosity, only that generosity in itself is not a source of power unless the provider is ruthless.

Dealing with Dictators

How should democracies deal with dictators? This question marks a major point of polarization in debates over realism and morality. In our time, there have been fierce disputes over how far the West should pursue security via a policy of regime change, from the abattoir regimes of Iraq's Saddam Hussein and Syria's Bashar al-Assad to Russia's sinister tyrant Vladimir Putin in the wake of his invasion of Ukraine. The rationales for regime change are several. But they revolve around a view of regime type as an important driver of state behavior.

Regime-change advocates argue that secure coexistence is not possible between free peoples and autocracies. The regimes that practice repression and genocide at home are also belligerent and risk prone and will also likely menace the rest of us abroad. Regime changers hold up the 9/11 attacks by a terrorist network hosted by the Afghan Taliban as proof of this linkage. And they point to the lack of fighting between democracies as proof of the democratic peace and the merits of democracy promotion. In the stark words of liberal internationalist G. John Ikenberry and colleagues, "Autocratic and militarist states make war; democracies make peace." For him, this is the "cornerstone" of the "liberal international tradition."[76] This is quite a claim given decades of democratic war making this century, almost routine drone-assassination campaigns in recent times, and armed interventions by the US-led West. But it goes to the heart of that worldview that democracy is inherently peaceful, whereas dictators embody the belligerent spirit.

From an assumption about security—that replacing dictators with democracies makes us safer—flows a moral conclusion that, in the words of the bellicose President George W. Bush in his second inaugural address, "the survival of liberty in our land increasingly depends on the success of liberty in other lands. The best hope for peace in our world is the expansion of freedom in all the world. America's vital interests and our deepest beliefs are now one."[77] To regard security as dependent on the continual expansion of one's own model of governance is a messianic view of security, one that lends itself to a kind of innocent militarism, waging war often while persuaded that one's essence is peacefulness.

There are good reasons to doubt this worldview. Look first to the distribution of power. War is not first and foremost a force that flows externally from malignant powers. It is generated by unstable interactions, often a power shift of some kind. The most intense wars break out when power hierarchies are unsettled. Realists and others debate how exactly this works, whether it is the status quo or the revisionist challenger that does most to bring about hostilities.[78] Either way, an incumbent and an economically rising state grow mutually fearful and collide. Major powers under certain conditions are war prone, even as their internal political arrangements vary, whether democratic, semidemocratic, or all-out absolutist. America's brief chapter of unipolar dominance suggests so.[79] As for a related claim—that democratic expansion is good because democracies rarely fight one another—this also loses sight of the critical variable of power. Democracies under America's protective wing in the Euro-Atlantic and Asian theaters may not fight one another much. But democracies in other less hierarchical and more multipolar settings have fought a lot. I will return to this problem in the next chapter.

As for regime change, realists counter that bringing about regime change abroad does not reliably enhance one's own security interests, that the sources of war are not primarily regime type, and that therefore a presumption against sponsoring revolution is more prudent. This is not an iron law. There are circumstances where toppling an adversary regime and replacing it with a friendly one, perhaps under military occupation, can work. West Germany and Japan in the midcentury are the usual examples for optimists. But these circumstances were atypical, involving a war that had exhausted both countries whose populations and elites under postwar occupation feared another state more.[80]

Most of the time, the creed that we must supplant dictators with friendly democracies as an organizing principle of foreign policy is flawed and dangerous. It underestimates just how wrenchingly destabilizing the act of toppling an existing political order is. Overthrowing the state creates winners and losers who have recent historical memories to drive fear of one another, with all the added fear of being threatened at home and having nowhere else to go. By definition, the countries that powerful states choose to overthrow are internally troubled enough to concern them in the first place. Revolution therefore tends to spawn violent chaos to the regime changer's disfavor.

We learned this the hard way through the recent experience of wars that were supposed to both make us safer and liberate victims—note Iraq, Afghanistan, and Libya. In Iraq, a brutal but shackled and deterrable autocrat fell. Saddam Hussein's Ba'ath rule was replaced not with liberty but anarchy as the country suffered mass bloodletting, sectarian conflict and repression, mass criminal activity, and mass displacement. Geopolitically, it empowered a larger rival in the region, Iran, also with a nuclear program, while it accelerated North Korea's determination to develop its nuclear capability. In Iraq and then beyond, Islamist terrorism in the form of al-Qaeda and then the

Islamic State took root, opening up a whole new front of the war on terror. In Afghanistan, a theocratic regime was replaced by a two-decade war, fought against both the Taliban and the Pakistani security services as their patron, in a failed defense of a corrupt kleptocratic order in Kabul, which was guilty of systematic abuse, including child rape on a large scale, all before NATO withdrawal and the return of the Taliban. Advocates of the adventure in Libya in 2011 heralded it as the "model intervention" and demonstration of the new principle of "responsibility to protect." Yet with Colonel Muammar Qaddafi's cruel regime overthrown, it descended into anarchy, with a collapsed economy, rival parliaments, militias and Islamist groups running amok, open-air slave markets, and a surge of migration out of the vortex.

One answer to this from liberal interventionists will be "Syria,"[81] coding it as a disastrous nonintervention. But the West did intervene in Syria. Led by the United States, it provided just enough arms, cash, and encouragement (via demands for regime abdication) to prolong the war and inadvertently strengthen the hand of Islamist rebel factions. Had the West applied a more maximalist policy and achieved regime change, a similar but worse fate than Libya may have been waiting given the heavy presence of Islamist forces, the fractured character of Syrian politics, and the contiguous geography whereby neighboring and regional states vied for influence throughout. Full measures took effect in Afghanistan, Libya, and Iraq. Half measures took effect in Syria. There is a pattern.

This is not an argument that constitutional democratic government is only for white Euro-Atlantic Western liberal people. Any culture can democratize, only not at the hour or in the manner demanded by interveners. Nor is it an argument that intervention is never prudent. There have been successful interventions, in East Timor, say, or Sierra Leone, and an absolute "no" would do violence to realism's emphasis on the changeability of circumstances. Rather, it is to say that realism counsels a presumption against expeditionary campaigns to make other countries become more like "us."

In truth, it is hard to organize foreign policy consistently around a stark division of democracy versus dictatorship or even a more calibrated policy of attempting to influence and reform dictators while enlarging the sphere of democracies. It is hard, first, because overthrowing states does not typically move those societies by default into the kinds of democracies that suit the

West. Doing so is just as likely, if not more so, to elevate to power groups that use the state to repress opponents and reward allies.

Even other democracies will not reliably do what powerful democracies demand, who calculate their interests differently and focus on narrower and more pragmatic material interests. At the time of writing, NATO democracies are distraught that many states in the rest of the world, from South Africa to Brazil to India, are hedging their bets with Russia despite appeals to democratic solidarity and internationalist principle.

It is hard, too, because international politics is conflicted, and when hard interests are at stake, there will be authoritarians that democracies turn to as partners or allies. In the mid-twentieth century, the United States helped defeat the Axis powers by allying with the totalitarian Soviet Union. It prevailed in the Cold War by actively dividing the Soviet Union against Communist China, and it strengthened ties with China by cultivating a genocidal regime in Pakistan. It defeated al-Qaeda in Iraq by realigning with former Sunni insurgents. The international community, or parts of it, may wish to prosecute some rulers for war crimes or crimes against humanity, like General Augusto Pinochet of Chile. Yet the same Pinochet played a crucial part in helping democratic Britain defeat authoritarian Argentina in the Falklands War of 1982 by providing radar intelligence. Creating an order where we arrest and prosecute such regimes may result in less assistance. The United States may declare foreign policies of supporting democracies against authoritarians, yet it cultivates corrupt and/or authoritarian regimes in the Philippines and Vietnam in order to build a coalition against China. On each occasion, a painful compromise was required—the kind of compromise liberal visions say little about. To make the world more inhospitable to some authoritarian adversaries, one will need to accommodate others.

It is also hard to organize foreign policy around democracy because even having democratic government in common does not overturn a longstanding pattern—namely, the impermanence of alliances and partnerships and the fluidity of coalitions. If, as Lord Palmerston said, states have not permanent friends but permanent interests, then alliances and partnerships are a means to an end, not ends in themselves and certainly not objects for reverence. Even some of the bitterest enemies become tomorrow's allies and vice versa. In turn, this often makes realists more willing to empathize with adversaries and put distance between sometime friends to the outrage of antirealists.

The question of democracies, dictators, and right and wrong restages the wider ongoing argument between the moralist mind and the tragic mind. The moralist mind is content to settle on high principles, denounce others for falling short, and presume that pursuing elevated values will serve one's interests and the interests of all. It is more confident that history is directional and has an "arc," that foreign policy can put an end to evil, and that one's own side is history's central agent of progress. The tragic mind resists all this. It doubts more because it is mindful of the limits on knowledge and the problem that we can only achieve approximate control, and it fears that history does not have a predetermined destination. Democracies are not bound to win. Historically, the great republics and democracies have not always prevailed against more authoritarian rivals, whether classical Athens, medieval Venice, or the early modern Dutch Republic. To recognize these constraints yet not fall into paralysis is the hard part—to live in a tension between fatalism and struggle.[82]

So a prudent statecraft will accept the reality of the nuclear revolution while working to maintain stability, will seek to mitigate the effects of climate change and gradually curb emissions without a more wasteful attempt at system overhaul, and will respond to dictators with a mix of deterrence and bargaining rather than crusades for regime change.

A common thread in all these issue areas is that realism is skeptical of "solutions" and views of foreign policy as problem solving. Benign and detailed formulas are unlikely to correct deep-rooted and tangled problems because they rely too much on sustained good faith and cooperation and presume too much of institutions that depend on their members' will and because even successful measures tend also to produce inadvertent consequences. We will not "solve" or even marginalize nuclear weapons, climate change, or authoritarianism because we cannot eradicate power politics.

RESPECT, DON'T LOVE, POWER

For realism to be realistic about how things are and yet to maintain moral integrity and some sense of limits, it must also turn its critical lens upon itself. Like any body of ideas, any "ism," it is prone to excess. Realism's central fallibility, its kryptonite, is the closeness of two distinct things: respecting power and fetishizing it. It is one thing to discern the insecurity that is hardwired into the globe and prescribe policies to cope with it. It is another to treat power only as an end, not as a means, and for students of power to feel exhilaration at their closeness to it as they whisper in the ears of princes and take pleasure in wielding it. Yet in practice, the former can corrupt itself into the latter. Realism has a perverse cousin—namely, amoral machtpolitik. This thing is bad because it is hollow, pursuing power as a mere end, heedless of limits, regarding strength not just as a necessity but as something to be worshipped.

The temptation to revere power, emptied of any wider purpose and permitting and providing an alibi for the ruler to do whatever they like, is why, for some decent souls, the word "realism" calls to mind something darker than acts of constructive statecraft. They do not think first of Anwar Sadat or Golda Meir making peace, John F. Kennedy skillfully blending confrontation and bargaining to navigate through the Cuban missile crisis, or Nelson Mandela steering South Africa into its postapartheid era without a postrevolutionary bloodbath. When they hear "realism," they think of the murderous Borgia dynasty of the fifteenth and sixteenth centuries or the unrestrained aggression of Indonesia's annexation of East Timor. In more recent times, they think of the darkly comic figure of Dr. Strangelove, a parody of the nuclear theorist Herman Khan, and Strangelove's maniacal pursuit of nuclear deterrence via an automated irreversible doomsday machine, which reacts to threats by obliterating all life, as a caricature of overmilitarized fanaticism. Or they think of John Bolton, a hardline veteran US official who regularly advocates escalatory armed confrontation or preventive strikes from overthrowing Saddam Hussein to launching a "blood-nose" attack on North Korea's missile installations.

They think in particular of Henry Kissinger, an exemplar of machtpolitik.[83] Kissinger pursued closeness to power even to the point of putting himself above his state via his complicity in the sabotage of peace talks between his country and North Vietnam and his later willingness to play paid counselor to China, a large and wealthy peer adversary.[84] As well as being a mercenary who craved intimacy with whoever was in charge, his response to the 9/11 attacks was imprudent and presumptuous of Washington's strength. He supported the invasion of Iraq because "Afghanistan wasn't enough" and "we need to humiliate them"[85]—"them" being the Arab-Islamic world in general, beyond Islamist terrorism.

In other words, some people of good conscience equate realism with an unchecked, unhinged belief in the utility of force, applied maximally and early. But that isn't proper realism. It is its negation, a refusal to acknowledge the limits or inadvertent effects of one's own power.

In truth, proper realism has a more fraught relationship with violence and conflict. While Strangeloves and Boltons overlap with realist pessimism, they also find realists irritating. Contrary to some caricatures, the attitude of realism to force is not casual. Because being at peace and securing a way of life are both vital things and because they can come into tension, realism's relationship with force is paradoxical. At its most prudent, realism, in its pursuit of a decent peace, draws on an acceptance of the need for preparedness but also a fear of war itself and a recognition that compromise, sooner or later, is part of effective diplomacy.

Not being prepared for war can spell extinction. The pacifist, otherworldly, unarmed monastic community at Lindisfarne was sacked and destroyed by Viking raiders in 793 AD. That doesn't mean the monks were wrong to pursue the life they were committed to. But it had costs. To deter and thereby prevent conflict, one's forces must be capable and credible, prepared and minded to fight if called upon. To persuade others that one can and will be willing to fight is hard to do without looking threatening. Yet we cannot responsibly abandon the task. Disavowing military power and preparedness also leaves a polity vulnerable to aggression, living in the hope that adversaries won't turn up rather than being prepared if they do.

There is a flip side to this coin. History also demonstrates that the embrace of war, untempered by political limitation, can also debase or destroy the state. Imperial Japan's bid for power in Asia from 1931 to 1945 ended in catastrophe. Landing a decisive blow to eliminate or neutralize a rival, like the United States, proved difficult and ended up generating counterpower and brutal retribution. More successful overdogs, who built longer-lasting empires, like the Western Roman Empire, provide warning of a different kind. Having wiped out or neutralized all peer competitors in the Mediterranean, carrying out the annihilation of cities, Rome's continual aggrandizement and plundering campaigns intensified and coarsened its politics to the point that warlords effectively wielded private armies, culminating in the republic with a mixed constitution and some political liberty becoming a de facto despotism. Hans J. Morgenthau regards Rome's practice of power as driven by the pure expediency of a technical rationale that permits no moral restraint.[86] Not only was it thus, but, in the long term, its promiscuous expansionism boomeranged back onto its own political life.

On a more contemporary note, the United States, on its worst day, does not get near the annihilationist scale of Rome. But the effect of its hard, grinding, and costly wars in the Middle East was not only to waste blood and squander resources but also to create a disillusioned distressed veteran community that contributed—possibly decisively—to the election of Donald Trump, an authoritarian demagogue who promised to end the establishment's futile war making and restore peace through strength but who would also show contempt for the constitution.[87]

The military ideally is an instrument of policy applied surgically. But in real life, war is a wilder thing when unleashed. It is hard to control; it is unpredictable and potentially subversive or revolutionary. Hence the need to respect and prepare for war but be wary of overvalorizing it. War is a hazard that can ruin the state and thereby ravage the people in it. Its purpose is to serve policy, but its nature is to serve itself. In the realm of war and its possibility, realism is useful as an antidote to two imprudent worldviews: the worldview that repudiates war in the belief that disowning it and enacting laws against it can make its shadow go away and the worldview of some muscular nonrealists who treat war not just as a necessary evil but a positive good, somehow redemptive despite all evidence to the contrary.

The problem of power and morality leads sooner or later back to Thucydides, the Athenian admiral, exile, and historian who wrote of the cataclysmic Peloponnesian War (431–404 BC) between the city-states Athens and Sparta and their allies. Thucydides's history of the ancient Peloponnesian War is a layered and rich work and was not a work of modern IR theory with systematic propositions, so careful interpretation is needed. But at its core is a humane realism, a capacity to look at things sympathetically yet without euphemism.

Recall that in 416 BC, Athens, with its naval-commercial supremacy, demanded the allegiance of a polity that was formally neutral, the island city-state of Melos, and massacred and enslaved the population when it refused to submit. In Thucydides's set-piece exchange, whereas the Melians, in defiance, placed their hopes in the gods, in their kindred Spartan allies, and in appeals to justice, a swaggering Athens spoke in the stark language of dominance. Their words, that "the strong do what they can, and the weak suffer what they must" became infamous. A point often overlooked here is that the Melian disaster involved an atrocity that happened because the weak were abandoned by their ally in whose protection they placed too much faith. As Fouad Ajami notes of the Melians, "Besieged by Athens, they held out and were sure that the Lacedaemonians were 'bound, if only for very shame, to come to the aid of their kindred.' The Melians never wavered in their confidence in their 'civilizational' allies: 'Our common blood insures our fidelity.' We know what became of the Melians. Their allies did not turn up, their island was sacked, their world laid to waste."[88]

As far as we can tell, Thucydides was not simply aligning himself with the Athenians' unchecked inhumanity. Indeed, in his telling, Athens became morally corrupt and predatory, becoming what the aggrandizing Persians were. Like a dramatic figure, Athens fell through overreach, hubris, and domestic moral and political breakdown. Athens, in Thucydides's account, lost its sense of self-restraint and was then torn apart by factionalism and demagogues who lost their heads. It suffered defeat against cold self-interested powers that better held their nerve and moved in when Athens faltered. Melos's plight foreshadowed Athens's own later fate, praying fruitlessly to the gods for salvation after their disastrous expedition to Sicily.

But nor was Thucydides writing a morality tale where the virtuous triumph over the wicked. He also chronicled atrocities by Athens's adversaries: the doomed appeal of the defeated Plataeans to the Spartans, who raze their city, Syracuse's slaughter of Athenian soldiers on the banks of the Assinarus River, coups backed by murderous oligarchs, and the secret slaughter of two thousand Helots through a false promise of freedom by a Sparta preoccupied with "security." The Persians, who decisively intervened, were coldly calculating. Thucydides's very explanation of the war is not one of innocents versus wrongdoers. Structural pressures tilted rivals toward conflict. Spartans were the "aggressors," but their main motive was structural rather than greed. An unfavorable power shift—"the growth of Athenian power"— drove them to war. In Thucydides's account, it is most often power shifts, not atrocious behavior, that triggers the revolt of tributary allies. Thucydides's very notion that overreaching hubris leads to downfall implicitly assumes a wider world inhabited at least partly by merciless states, willing and ready to abandon or to pounce. Rather than aligning himself either with the Melians and their "expensive" hope or with the Athenians and their abandonment of limits, Thucydides was portraying the world as it was, the fragility of things, and the brutal realities that descend once war strikes. So easily, the "common laws of humanity" can be ripped apart. He pitied the innocents slaughtered in the sacking of cities; captured troops, who pled in vain for mercy; and soldiers, about to be slain, struggling to drink from a river polluted with blood. Humans struggle to exert judgement and agency against extraordinary impersonal forces. In his portrayal, there is a constant tension between the brute force of necessity and the need for ethical restraint in politics—a tension that can, at best, be managed rather than resolved.[89]

Under the brutalizing pressures of war, in Thucydides's telling, both the strong and the weak should be wary of placing trust in higher authorities or principles or a sense of their own specialness or in the benefits of their shared ancestry with others or the protection of geographic insularity. Fear haunts and overshadows Thucydides's history. The word for "danger" occurs over two hundred times.[90] After all, the physical destruction of city-states was frequent enough. In more than forty cases in the classical period, the poleis suffered this calamity. And if not the destruction of city, defeat could mean the destruction of city walls and the curtailing of independence. Fear, for Thucydides, can take both useful and deadly forms, and his hero Pericles nerves Athenians against blind, unreasoning panic while at other times bringing them back to a "sense of their dangers." Leading up to the Peloponnesian War, Athens and Sparta had acquired their capabilities only through a "hard school of danger." Danger, ill prepared for or mishandled, could mean losing everything. Earlier generations faced "constant pressure" and were either constantly taking flight or had to put up with being dominated by the strong. External dangers bear down, sooner or later, on all polities, while human responses to danger, if governed by reckless urges, can then make the world even deadlier. A state of fearlessness—thinking one is secluded or separate from danger—can be fatal. When Thracians massacred the small city Mycalessus, the assault succeeded because "the inhabitants were caught off their guard, since they never expected that anyone would come so far from the sea to attack them. Their wall, too, was weak and in some places had collapsed . . . and the gates were open, since they had no fear of being attacked."[91]

Thucydides matters because he holds on to an austere view of life but also a sense of limits. He portrayed a cold harsh world of interstate relations that demanded humans help themselves without allowing recognition of the world as it is to become an alibi for nihilism or unfettered barbarism. As one classicist notes, Thucydides "recognized that men generally act in accordance with expediency and advantage. But it does not follow that he looked upon those acts with cold detachment."[92]

So realists must be on their guard and never relax. They must hold on to their tragic sense, which emphasizes the limits on power and knowledge and the possibility of both self-destruction and destruction at others' hands. They are engaged in a losing struggle, the ceaseless pursuit of an elusive thing—the right balance of war preparedness and war avoidance—against the alternatives of wishing or legislating conflict away or fatalistically embracing it. Realism is concerned not only about war and preparation for war but also about what these are for and the need to give power a purpose that justifies its use. Realism is moral because it is concerned for peace.

2   Realism Is Realistic

CRITICS OF REALISM are fond of putting shudder quotes around the concept ("realism") or branding it "so-called." They suspect realism and realists of having a poor grasp of reality and for being unduly self-flattering in the label they give themselves. This complaint about *nomenclature* can be ironic. Many of those critics call themselves "liberal internationalists," "critical theorists," or "area experts," and these are also aspirational and at times self-congratulatory descriptors. That is not a rebuttal, however. What follows is.

In this chapter, I defend realism from the accusation that it is too removed from the experience of international politics. There is a persistent charge that realists mainly just tell stories, many of them tall, that bear only a slight resemblance to history, serving primarily as an ideology that offers little insight.[1] If the critics are right, realism is more a normative expression of how things should be, not how they typically are, and really is more an ideology than a map. I beg to differ. Realism is a decent starting point, the least bad one, for navigating and surviving the world as it is.

First, let's clear up some assumptions. To be a "realist" is to look at the world from a pessimistic starting assumption about what is inexorably "real" about the human condition. It is not to claim a monopoly of wisdom about reality. Anyone who claims to possess that is hubristic. The world is a conflicted difficult place and human minds cannot comprehend all its complexity, especially as those who rule countries have some agency and do not function like mere billiard balls. From time to time, there are events and shocks that just plain surprise us. No theory—or at least no good theory—

promises to capture all the nuances or anticipate every contingency. A map that did represent the world with full accuracy would have to be to scale and therefore would not be useful. Theory can only be useful via simplification. The question is which tradition offers the most useful mental map without falling prey to oversimplification as we open the tent and walk out into the blizzard.

To say realism is realistic is not to suggest that realism is a cookbook with clear recipes for all occasions. There are varieties of realism, and realists sometimes draw different policy conclusions from the same principles. The "cookbook model" asks too much of any general theory. It sets tests that every macroaccount of human political behavior would flunk. Political science is too imprecise a craft, its subject too hard to pin down definitively, to match the precision and replicability of the hard sciences. Beware of physics envy. If something resembling hard science is the yardstick of a paradigm's value, it effectively would condemn us to leave the tent with no map at all. At best, IR theory can account for general patterns. It will struggle to make consistently accurate point predictions.

Conversely, realism, to be valuable, can't just be a set of intuitive "vibes"—a broad sensibility about the importance of power and the recurrence of conflict. The "vibes model" makes realism unfalsifiable. For realism in its different permutations to claim it is realistic, there must be a minimum of specific claims and general predictions that can be tested against history. Realism's core propositions may be austere but must still be demonstrated.

For instance, one of the sharpest realist minds in Washington today, Emma Ashford, notes that realism is an antidote to delusions that "moral principles or values can override all constraints of power and interest."[2] Amen, but this should be treated not as a self-evident point. It is an empirical claim worthy of scrutiny. Antirealists argue, from different angles, that interests *are* values rather than objective things, that the constraints are not given but constructed, that changing identities can override or redefine the imperatives of selfishness and alter how countries define their interests, that values are in fact significantly reducing war's frequency, and that deep change via changing norms or economic interdependence or technology is possible. Some argue that the realist premise of anarchy is an unwarranted construct, not an objective reality, and that the idea is itself part of the problem.[3] Others argue realists underestimate how far humans can overcome anarchy's incentives via benign forces, such as international institutions, democracy, capitalism, or normative change.[4] So realists must get their hands dirty with evaluative probes. Otherwise, the paradigm must abandon its main claim—that it best fathoms how the world is. To hold up, realism must account for patterns of international behavior not everywhere in every case, but in the aggregate.

In this chapter, I sketch out a brief taxonomy of realism in several varieties, identifying areas where they agree and where they diverge. I then apply some stress tests: the problem of hierarchy and "underbalancing" behavior, the problem of cooperation and international institutions, and the problem of explaining peace. Lastly, I'll revisit some puzzles that critics suggest confound realist expectations. While these cases may score some peripheral hits against realism's outposts, its core holds.

TAXONOMY: REALISM AND REALISMS

There is a baseline of assumptions that unite realists before they diverge on the full implications of those assumptions. Regarding how they explain the world, there are several main variants of realism.

A typical starting point is to draw a sharp line between "classical" and "neo-," or "structural," realism. This view of the tradition contrasts classical realists with their emphasis upon human nature and historical context and variety against more social scientific IR theorists in search of universal patterns.[5] And, the story goes, whereas classical realists offer rich history and emphasize the inner drives of human nature, their neorealist counterparts prize parsimony over richness and privilege the international system as the driving force of world politics. In this story, the more humanistic Hans J. Morgenthau, who warned against "scientific man" and the reductionism of social science, is contrasted with the more scientist Kenneth N. Waltz.[6] Waltz's *Theory of International Politics* and its treatment of states as functionally similar things propelled along by a system serves as an inspiration for some who wish to make realism a systematic account of politics and as a target for others who believe realism took a bad turn toward junk science and should return to its classical roots.[7] Self-described "classicals" and "structuralists" divide mainly over how far the study of politics can be rendered systematic. Classicals accuse structuralists of mistaking politics for economics and crude rational-actor models of economics at that. Structuralists accuse classicals of being too anecdotal and casual.

Along with some others, I beg to differ with this prevalent account of realism's history.[8] It's a contentious point, but classical and structural realists are not as substantively different as they both claim. The Waltzian turn is not as radical a break from the realist tradition as many assume. As I argue in the next chapter, anarchy is an old idea within realism, not a recent invention. To be sure, disagreements amongst realists are nontrivial regarding how to translate realist principles into sound policy. But the principles are broadly common. Realists use different language and are sometimes rude about one another, but they share a common set of starting assumptions about the world: that polities exist within anarchy and that this lack of central authority pressures them to help themselves and struggle for security, defined as relative power, especially material power. In describing such a world, they also prescribe the rational exercise of competitive power politics. Other factors may intervene, but the external environment gets analytical priority. In contrast to approaches that assume foreign policy builds inside out, or outward from a polity's inner life, realists, both classical and structural, see it as outside in and regard the international and the distribution of power as the main source of the domestic.

The true disagreement amongst realists is over the implications of anarchy.[9] Offensive realists, most famously John J. Mearsheimer, argue that in a pitilessly dangerous world, all polities are bound to maximize their power positions by grabbing what they can while they can, seeking security via expansion—or at least long-range power projection of some kind—and trying to dominate their regions.[10] Defensive realists, by contrast, like Charles L. Glaser, have a less bleak and more reflexive worldview. That is, they allow more room for stable interactions within anarchy and stress that rational power politics also requires a level of self-restraint and that sensible security seekers are (and should be) wary of avoidable spirals, as the bad fate of many revisionist states pursuing regional hegemony suggests.[11]

There is also another and overlapping version: "dynamic" realism. This realism, advanced in particular by Dale C. Copeland, pays particular attention both to the shifting economic and military balance and to states' expectations about their relative position tomorrow. Regimes fear an adverse power shift—or, in other words, being eclipsed by rivals who are growing at their expense—and may initiate crises or preventive wars.[12] The shadow of the future haunts even polities in a relatively tranquil present, and if they don't take it into account, they court punishment. Unequal growth and the economic base of military power—investment, trade, access to raw materials—are central in this account, alongside other metrics of power, such as alliances, strategic territory, and arms.

The offensive-defensive realism argument is really a disagreement about the relative weight of different kinds of self-regarding behavior and whether seizing as much as you can or holding back for fear of overreach, or self-encirclement, is more common and more efficient. It has important implications for the competition between the United States and China today.[13] American and Western realists mostly agree that China, a large and wealthy adversary, needs some containing. Who precisely should shoulder most of that burden of containment divides realists more, especially over the load that the United States should carry. In general, though, China needs containing because, while it cannot overrun or conquer America or the wider Indo-Pacific region, it can subordinate its region and threaten others' liberty by turning Asia into an exclusionary economic sphere with its oppressive techno-authoritarian mode of rule and by demanding deference in return for market access.

Realists also agree on the main cause of the current competition between China and America. As with realists' general assumptions about conflict, it is primarily a clash of interests born of a power shift rather than being a misunderstanding born of mutual incomprehension.[14] China and America both want primacy in Asia and beyond. They both act like it by demanding deference, seeking military preponderance, and competing for clients, bases, and access. And they tell us frequently (the Sino-centric world order versus the US-led "rules-based" international order, which presumes American preponderance). There is a rivalry because Beijing and Washington estimate one another's basic intentions accurately.

Realists mostly agree that the United States should manage this competition not as an absolute ideological conflict aimed at "victory" and regime change but as a more measured bid to check China's bid for dominance now to renegotiate the Asian order later. Realists are wary of crusades, in contrast to liberal hawks and neoconservatives, and caution against treating the contest as a principally ideological contest of democracy versus despotism in pursuit of absolute victory.[15] Rather, Washington should be more flexible and pragmatic, speaking more softly and carrying a big stick, and forge coalitions of different states, free, partially free, or unfree, who share a minimal wish to avoid China's dominance.

Yet realists disagree about how to contain China without getting into a major war. Offensive realists argue that Washington must draw a line in the ocean, so to speak, around the first island chain, build military capability strong enough to deter China via the threat of defeat, and reduce dependence on China's economy and indeed do what America has recently done—act to kneecap China's economic strengths, like the microchip and semiconductor industries. The way to contain China, in that logic, is to take all steps possible to weaken it and, by establishing deterrence via strength, avoid a direct clash.[16] Those realists who take this position tend to argue that the coming of a peer competitor as large, wealthy, and determined as China is means the United States ought to prioritize the Indo-Pacific theater and conduct a significant burden shift to allies in other theaters. Otherwise, to defend everything is to defend nothing.

Other realists agree on the need to generate counterpower but take a different view of the economic front and how best to contain China without fighting. China is highly dependent on seaborne trade. That dependency can be a constraining factor for peace or war if its expectations darken.[17] The threat of economic closure and future strangulation could tragically make Beijing fear that time is against it and bring on the clash. For what it's worth, I'm somewhere in the middle on this one. Washington should prioritize Asia and its ability to deter and fight there, and this will mean allies must do more elsewhere. At the same time, it should avoid adding excessive haste to Beijing's calculations by inducing dangerous economic expectations that would raise a "better-now-than-later" temptation to strike Taiwan.

Much of this debate gravitates around a disagreement about the United States. Given its splendid position—enjoying a continental sanctuary, protective moats guarded by a strong air-maritime shield, a large nuclear arsenal and unthreatening neighbors—how much should it project power beyond the water's edge to secure itself? How much should it do the heavy lifting abroad, or should it pass the buck, and how far can it rely on other states mutually balancing in its absence? American realists disagree with one another on these questions. There are "primacy" realists, who advise that Washington should hold on to its international dominance, albeit more efficiently. By contrast, there are "offshore balancers," who would pull back and only intervene abroad in extremis. And there are "prioritizers," who would focus American power on Asia and shift some of the burdens of defense onto allies elsewhere. America is a strange case, given its unusually advantageous circumstances and the sheer breadth of its commitments. But realism is not just an American paradigm designed by and for Americans. The question of whether realism's fundamentals are reliable is all the more pressing for less powerful states in more dangerous neighborhoods in every continent, spanning Ukrainians, Taiwanese, Somalis, Israelis and Palestinians, Armenians, and Finns.

Offensive, defensive, and dynamic realists agree on some fundamentals. Strong states, whether they are greedy or security seeking, tend to be sensitive to shifts in material power and look to help themselves even at others' expense, since things change and we can never be certain of others' intentions. Shifts in relative power are the main source of friction and war. And lasting cooperation and trust building is difficult, precisely because of these dynamic uncertainties. States do not have essences; they have circumstances, and shifting circumstances alter their behavior.

With our brief taxonomy of realism on the table, let's pose a question to guide the test cases below. Simply, what would a nonrealist world look like? How would we know, what observables would we recognize, if the main assumptions of realism don't hold up?[18]

In general, in a nonrealist world, polities, including the strongest, would put the international community and the common good first even at their own expense and even where expedient self-interest pointed in a different direction to a more cosmopolitan "other-interest." Cooperation would not be impermanent, fragile, and difficult but long lasting and robust, even natural. Heads of great powers or their officials could be arrested and tried at the tolerance of their own governments without first losing a war or being overthrown. International justice would be, if not constant, at least consistent and formidable. States of the world would cooperatively reduce carbon emissions in good faith, trusting that others would keep their word and trusting that any losses they suffer from others' relative gains would be worth the payoff for the species as a whole. Nuclear-armed states would sign the treaty to outlaw nuclear weapons, confident that others would cooperate and confident they would be safer in a postnuclear world of "zero." Collective security would be a real, continuous, and shared commitment, even to the point of great inconvenience. Direct intervention at scale would be frequent and directed against the strong as well as the weak. When aggressors flouted international rules, other countries would not only put up their hands to condemn them at the United Nations; they would band together to exert material coercion and punishment, doing what they could to isolate the aggressor. Aggressors would become pariahs. Alternatively, critics might argue that darker developments might replace the realist world (of states under anarchy competing for security) with something else, such as transnational oligarchies supplanting state power.

Are any of these developments coming soon or at hand? Critics of realism need not argue that these things have already arisen. But if their dismissal of realism is warranted, such things must be manifestly capable of emerging and within reach. Bear in mind these questions as we sort through some test cases below. I now turn to three problems for realists: the problem of hierarchy, the problem of cooperation, and the problem of (explaining) peace.

UNBALANCED? THE PROBLEM OF HIERARCHY

According to critics, realism is unrealistic about how groups behave. In practice, they say, states frequently do not compete for security, and in particular, they do not do so by balancing via the formation of alliances and coalitions. They do not even do so, allegedly, under conditions where realists would most expect them to. In other words, this is the challenge of hierarchy—a form of political relations realists allegedly are insensitive toward.[19] Realists, so the argument goes, presuppose that we inhabit an anarchic world in which power generates counterpower and human groups often seek to check and thwart one another's bids for dominance or launch their own. Yet critics counter that much of history has been a world not primarily of balancing toward equilibrium or constant interstate power contests but of longer-lasting pecking orders or, at times, of peaceable international societies.[20]

Historians like Paul W. Schroeder charged that the absence of balancing in significant times and places is fatal to realism.[21] Schroeder argued that bandwagoning was a more frequent move than balancing in the European state system over three hundred years and that the ideas of rulers mattered and altered systems, thus rendering realism "unhistorical, unusable and wrong."[22] Post-Napoleonic Europe, for him, shifted from balance-of-power politics to a pattern of concerts between major powers and equilibrium. As we will see, though, like so many historians and area experts critical of realism, Schroeder denounced realists for imposing IR theory onto history yet also brings along an implicit IR theory of his own.

The "hierarchy" critique of realism suggests that if there is an equilibrium to be found, it is not the equilibrium of balance, of states interacting reactively and regularly to guard their autonomy or to prevent any one actor achieving preeminence. For these critics, the true pattern is rather an equilibrium of superiority, laid down by the strongest, who don't always get their way but who set the conditions, police the commons, offer patronage, limit their clients' choices, and keep order on their terms. In such a universe, middle or smaller polities often choose not to resist or to resist so starkly. They prefer to bandwagon with the strong because they are strong, and they prefer to negotiate their own conditions, albeit from relatively weak hands. Others emphasize the equilibrium of mutual restraint via shared norms and identities. The historically minded scholars of the English school—a strain of liberal thought with state-centric and more radical wings—argue humans can build international society and tame the force of material power structures because discourse—the way "we" (as states or civil society) conceive and narrate the world—shapes practice.[23]

For some realist political scientists, too, the balance-of-power dynamic fails comparisons with history.[24] Randall L. Schweller examines the problem of underarming and underpreparing in the face of growing threats. He argues that failures to balance mean realists must further fine-tune their theories to account for anomalous behavior, incorporating domestic politics into the equation.[25] For Susan B. Martin, we should adjust expectations of general theory about outcomes and particular theories about the making of foreign policies. As she says, general realist balance-of-power theory better accounts for *outcomes* (rough balances of power) and the incentives and constraints generated by the system in general rather than balancing as a state strategy, which requires more fine-grained explanations.[26] The realist-friendly Brian Rathbun argues that the very practice of realpolitik and the knitting together and manipulation of alliances and agreements, both expected and advocated by realists, may be too much to ask from fallible humans given most rulers are not psychologically attuned to be successful, disciplined practitioners, like the Prussian Otto von Bismarck (1815–1898).[27]

Yet for most nonrealists, that balancing behavior sometimes goes missing in action is less a basis for further refinement of realism and more a basis for its repudiation. If states don't reliably do what realists expect them to do and if realists add in other variables to explain behavior that doesn't fit the paradigm, this is a manifestation of realism's degeneration, failing the cumulative test of theory appraisal as set out by Imre Lakatos.[28] A recent case, the lack of serious balancing against the United States as a unipolar hierarch in the post–Cold War period, suggests to some either that balancing is a dog that mostly doesn't bark or that US behavior as a unipole did not particularly threaten its potential rivals beyond a small number of regimes or that American preeminence has sources of durability that generic realist theory fails to account for.[29] Alternatively, realists may be looking in the wrong places for how they measure power and identify balancing given polities can resist via nonmilitary means by appealing to the idea of legitimacy.[30]

My response to this challenge is threefold. Let's walk through these points one by one. First, while balancing is obviously not the only mode of behavior in history, or even the most frequent, there has still been enough of it to shape our security environment profoundly. Consider Europe from the eighteenth century onward—Schroeder's main focus. While European polities may not have consistently balanced or may have only done so at times late and reluctantly, the failure of power bids from the Habsburgs (Charles V and Philip II), France (Louis XIV and Napoleon), and Germany under both the *Kaiserreich* and Adolf Hitler were cases of overreach that triggered countervailing resistance. Further back, Philip II, according to the evocative description of his biographer, was an "imprudent king," relentlessly seeking expansion in a lifelong state of zeal, thinking of himself as the agent of God's will.[31] But it was only imprudent because he tried this in a resistant world and met strong pushback, straining the state's capacity in order to project power and suppress all theological deviancy and independence from the Ottoman Empire, the Low Countries, and England.

In turn, resistant behavior or counterbalancing is hard to explain without the force of threat in this anarchic world. To deny the Axis powers command of Eurasia beginning in 1939, it would take other major powers to act, even if that brought together ideologically strange bedfellows, like Winston Churchill's parliamentary constitutional monarchy and colonial empire, Joseph Stalin's communist totalitarian state, and Franklin Roosevelt's capitalist republic—all of whom had imperial designs. And there was much balancing within that alliance. The Churchill-Roosevelt correspondence, where both parties made demands and expressed grievances, was one bitter "front" of the war, just as Stalin coerced Roosevelt and Churchill by exploiting Britain's fears of a separate Soviet-German peace.[32] It is hard to see what brought these misaligned regimes together if not a common fear and a desire to balance against it.

Historians complain that social scientists impose concepts and rhetoric from later eras on other periods who thought and spoke differently. While the vocabulary of balancing and even "diplomacy" may have been absent in antiquity, balancing behavior was not. In the Near East of the late Bronze Age, for instance, a place stereotyped as the cradle of oriental despotism, the leading powers—Egypt, Mitanni, Hatti or the Hittite state, Babylonia, and Assyria—worked with and tried to maintain an equilibrium. Various city-states emerged within the varied geography of the Levant, with mountainous regions and separated river valleys and forests so that none of them were strong enough to dominate. They jostled for advantage, brokered compromise deals, and used proxies as surrogates while often avoiding high-stakes clashes, and traditional adversaries, like Egypt and Mitanni, realigned to counter potentially threatening rising states, like the Hatti, just as the Hittites reconciled with Egypt to counter Assyria. While the total picture of motivation was likely complex, it is hard to understand these changing postures without rulers' sensitivity to power shifts—a sensitivity born of an urge to survive.[33] In modern IR terms, systemic conditions arose that prompted interaction and balancing. The rulers did not deploy the same terminology as political scientists now. But this is about behavior, and things do not have to be named—or named in the same way—to be practiced.

Balancing need not always take a comprehensive form of utilizing all means or be externally oriented toward coalition or alliance building. There is a long history of *internal* balancing whereby polities tend to amass military capabilities and imitate others' military doctrine and technology. Much of the debate is too preoccupied with alliances and external formations as yardsticks of balancing. As Joseph Parent and Sebastian Rosato argue, to a realist mind, it is prudent to rely foremost on one's own arms if you can, to exercise militarized *self*-help, and to avoid overreliance on help via cooperation with others.[34] This indeed is what most states historically tend to do. Parent and Rosato estimate that internal balancing has recurred in approximately 80 percent of cases since 1816. There are instances of major powers underarming—arguably today's Germany is one such case—and we will return to this problem.

Internal balancing can also happen without being absolute. To balance against a perceived threat and to anticipate adversarial shifts in overall material capabilities, polities may act without engaging in a comprehensive buildup of all their instruments. As Steven Lobell argues, they may balance in more targeted form by disaggregating their appraisal of threats and the capabilities needed to check them and arm selectively to neutralize specific threatening elements of an enemy's arsenal.[35] They do so not only to focus on where they are most vulnerable but also to address the problem that major powers often have limited capacity and must take more than one potential adversary into account in their plans. Thus, cases often coded as instances of "underbalancing" in fact feature targeted-balancing measures: Britain and Russia may not have consistently balanced against all the elements of revolutionary and Napoleonic France, but that was not due to neglect or naivete. It suited Russia to let Austria and Prussia take the brunt of land fighting given they, too, potentially threatened Russia, while Britain opted for concentrating its resources on maintaining naval supremacy given that it made cross-channel invasion impossible and for subsidizing continental land armies against France.

If we recognize that balancing is a spectrum rather than necessarily a binary, Prime Minister Neville Chamberlain's Britain in the interwar period did not simply "screw up." Trying to avoid economic dislocation while rearming and maintaining domestic political support, London faced multiple potential enemies in continental Europe, the Mediterranean, and East Asia. It engaged in "granular" balancing, prioritizing its airpower system with extended radar, air defense, and strategic bombers, as well as maintaining naval strength, which would prove critical to its survival against the Axis powers. It didn't get everything right: it presumed too much of French land power and neglected Singapore's defenses in its prioritization, but arguments about whether it would have fared better in an earlier war in 1938 are hard to resolve decisively. Yet its preparations did enough to help it survive the first and deadliest round of the war.

There are also other, less overtly adversarial forms of balancing to be observed. As the World War Two–alliance case suggests, competitive behavior takes place within concerts and within alliances and coalitions, as well as among them. Allies may be content to be allies for the time being and to cooperate for now. Yet they are frequently mindful that intentions and capabilities can change and that allies and partners can become economic and geopolitical rivals. After all, so-called friends still spy on one another. This behavior accompanied the formation of the United Nations itself in San Francisco, as US spies bugged international delegates' conversations and provided intelligence reports to President Harry Truman over breakfast.[36]

Balancing between so-called friends also happens within the transatlantic relationship today, organized through the NATO alliance, a US-supported European Union, and a much-heralded shared commitment to peace and solidarity. Using their embassies as an arm of espionage, they gather intelligence—security or industrial-economic related—in the knowledge that allies or partners today might be neutrals or adversaries tomorrow. A notorious recent example is the surveillance by the National Security Agency of millions of politicians, officials, and even the German chancellor's mobile phone. And while they claim to be offended, even US allies, like France and Germany, who reprimand that allies don't do this, do exactly the same thing, with their senior ally and one another, on their ministries or arms firms.[37] And anyone who thinks the European Union is not also a stage for fierce competition, coalition forming, and balance seeking needs to study it more closely. Institutions, if anything, facilitate the act of checking and balancing rather than reducing the need for it. The veto—including, more discretely, the threatened "closet" veto—is an important part of the workings of the United Nations Security Council.

Nor is balancing or ruthless competitive behavior more broadly confined to modernity. Ancient republican Rome, for instance, ruthlessly fought and expanded its empire, often balancing and checking against rivals and emerging rivals. The more powerful it grew, the more willingly it sought to suppress threats or potential threats. There are several nonrealist explanations for Rome's behavior that look inward to its pathological warlike culture as a wolfish killer breed, as reflected in its domestic constitutional arrangements and its ideological self-regard—all of which rewarded martial glory.[38] Yet Arthur M. Eckstein, synthesizing classical history and IR theory, makes a structural realist case as to why.[39] Romans lived in a harsh Mediterranean world amongst other similarly belligerent communities, who also ruthlessly fought and expanded their empires. When it was weaker, Rome had almost been wiped out by invaders and wrecked by local revolts. The international domain incentivized the city on the Tiber to embrace and channel violence as it otherwise faced extermination. The Romans who survived early crises made war often, but so did others, and Rome did not conspicuously love it more than its rivals. Rome happened to be the most efficient, developing the sharpest military instruments while co-opting the conquered into its system. Even after waring down others, the city-state-turned-empire faced multiple rebellions on its frontiers. Determined adversaries appeared and reappeared on its most vulnerable peripheries, the Rhine/Danube and the Euphrates. Even after Rome became the dominant power in the Mediterranean, it effectively reconquered parts of its domain again and again. If that isn't a realist world of power meeting counterpower, what is? Two aspects of antiquity exacerbated anarchy's harshness: the lack of a developed system of quiet background diplomacy so that negotiations between states took place in public assemblies as contests in resolve and the profitability of loot from conquest, upon which Rome increasingly depended.

"Hold on," some skeptics will respond. That was then, in the starkness of antiquity where there was little "international community" to speak of, when republics, like Rome, and kingdoms, like the Persian Empire or Chinese dynasties, thought they were mandated by heaven to take over the world, and when autocratic conquerors, like Alexander of Macedon, thought they were gods. Very well. Consider other historical worlds where alternative, less competitive conceptions of international order were more apparent. What about epochs where common identity and common norms could alleviate such competition, creating fundamental change? Consider the Middle Ages. It turns out that, yes, medieval Christendom had a different, more communitarian discourse and spoke a more cooperative language. Yet the same monarchs, principalities, and papacies that preached lawfulness and deference to authority also played the game hard. As Marcus Fischer finds, they "behaved like modern states. Outwardly professing adherence to such legal institutions as vassalage, fief, feud, and peer court, they really strove for exclusive territorial control, protected themselves by military means, subjugated each other, balanced against power, formed alliances and spheres of influence, and resolved their conflicts by the use and threat of force."[40]

One of the most important test cases is Europe's earlier concert system, founded in Vienna in 1815 after Napoleon's defeat. In literature critical of realism as an account of history, the concert, with its institutionalized summitry and common effort to maintain the territorial status quo, is a poster child for the possibilities of institutions fostering cooperation between great powers.[41] Its members certainly talked a good game, with elevated diplomatic discourse. But intraconcert interactions were also suffused with competitive behavior. With regard to the "Eastern question," as Korina Kagan observes, the "security regime" of the concert proved to be a fair-weather system, unable to constrain the interaction of powers over the war-threatening disintegration of Ottoman power in the Balkans, North Africa, and the Levant. The major powers of the concert—Britain, Russia, and France—played hardball, distrusted one another, and exploited opportunities for short-term gains at the others' expense. Periods of initial self-restraint, as over the Balkans and the Greco-Turkish conflict between 1821 and 1825, yielded to distrust and competition. In violation of concert norms, the concert powers worked to delay initiatives, competed for exclusive advantages in Greece, divided parties against other parties, excluded others from agreements, and acted unilaterally and ignored the concert where they believed their interests were paramount, as when Russia presented an ultimatum to Turkey without consultation with the others and later made war against it over allies' objections. Austria, the weakest member, argued in vain for more adherence to the concert's protocols and was rewarded with exclusion by Britain and France. Rivalries and disunity also prevented effective joint crisis management over successive crises. And the concert parties threatened and counterthreatened one another with force to alter policies, withdraw protectorates, or otherwise back off, resulting in 1840 in Europe's worst war scare since 1815. When there was restraint, "the chief source of restraint," notes Kagan, "was countervailing force, cooperation was tactical and instrumental . . . and norms were violated to the point of irrelevance."[42] Sound familiar?

There's a further answer to the charge that realists overstate power balancing as a central dynamic of world politics. The core proposition of realism, regarding how polities typically respond to systemic pressures, is not *balancing* but *self-regard* and *self-help*. An absence of external balancing does not mean an absence of hardheaded, egoistic power politics. Balancing is only one part of a wider repertoire of security seeking. That self-help flows from a self-seeking power politics, driven by the insecurity of anarchy. The logic is straightforward: neither earthly global institutions nor heaven can be counted on to put down others' attempts to impose dominance, and even allies can be unreliable. What form this self-help takes varies and shifts with circumstances. There is a legitimate criticism of realists on this point. Like their critics, some realists have too readily conflated self-seeking behavior with "external" balancing—that is, the pursuit of security via coalitions and alliances.

States generally prefer to achieve a balance so that they are unthreatened, all things being equal. Yet often, things are not equal. Realists expect that in periods where power is lopsided, balancing efforts may well fail. The very option of balancing may look too risky. Domination by hardheaded powers may be so strong that accepting this state of affairs, at least for the time being, can look less dangerous than confronting it. This applies especially when the weak face up against the strong and are denied another strong party to balance with. Hardheadedness, therefore, is not synonymous with blind aggression. The overprevalence of the European balancing era of 1495–1815 in the literature can overshadow other historical cases of lopsidedness and hierarchy in non-European systems.[43] As Colin Elman and Miriam Fendius Elman note, self-help behavior in conditions unpropitious to external balancing can take the alternative forms of hiding and hedging, buck-passing, chain-ganging, or bandwagoning.[44] The opposite of self-help is not nonbalancing but other-help, just as the opposite of outgroup fear is not outgroup cooperation but outgroup nonfear.

To be sure, some nonrealists, such as liberal internationalists, also begin with the premise that human groups are primarily self-serving. Only, they are more optimistic that groups can develop an enlightened self-interest and build cooperative trust over time via one or more benign mechanisms, such as institutions, markets, or the spread of democracy. For realists, by contrast, cooperation is never deep or ultimately sustainable. Cooperation itself may even just be a delaying strategy. China, for instance, delayed its challenge to the United States and held back from openly challenging US primacy in Asia until America weakened, and its "hide-and-abide" strategy was consummately power-political. Like George Washington's advice to the young US republic, to become a great power, China needed time and space to grow. It was not hiding and abiding just to make money and enjoy the good life or because it repudiated power politics, trusted in international institutions, or because globalization altered its identity to make it more regardful of others. Its rulers were preparing consciously for the hour of power transition when they could become a revisionist state and succeed. As we know from Rush Doshi's study of China's internal decision-making, it consciously decided, in the wake of the global financial crisis (and the power shift it portended), to end its posture of laying low, now looking to challenge and displace American primacy.[45] In the quiet of night, adversaries wait for their moment.

So there are other self-help strategies. And this point is a corrective to arguments that treat nonbalancing in non-European systems as a puzzle for realism. An example I will consider more closely in the next chapter is Ming China, which dominated Asia for over two centuries, with most of its tributary client states not putting up much resistance. Sophisticated ideational and cultural arguments suggest that this nonresistance flowed from a shared preference for peaceful commercial hierarchy—an idea still voiced in the region today. Yet a more austere realist account would suggest that this idea makes a virtue of necessity. Even if the likes of Korea, Vietnam, or Cambodia wished to balance, they could not. There was rarely any power strong enough to balance with. The one state that was plausibly a candidate, Japan, was too often fractured and preoccupied with internal struggles.

As for the "unipolar moment" of nonbalancing against the Pax Americana, a moment was exactly what it turned out to be. Unipolarity is a particular condition whereby the leading state has an outsized margin of relative strength to the extent that there are no peer or near-peer competitors, making counterbalancing impossible, and where there is a stable equilibrium that can be expected to persist for decades at least. America's place at the commanding heights was a brief historical interregnum. For a time, optimists argued that the United States would not encounter serious resistance apart from fierce localized resistance in peripheral wars in Iraq and Afghanistan, and some even suggested that the distinctive attractive qualities of America meant that its hegemony was especially durable.

Yet even optimists will now concede that even if Washington still holds many cards as the most powerful state, it is hard to argue there is not now balancing, both in terms of intention and outcome. As we have seen, a group of "central powers" is forming and hardening: Russia, Iran, China, and North Korea increasingly cooperate, more as nonaggression-pact partners than allies but with a shared commitment to blunting American power in the three overseas regions Washington cares most about: the Middle East, continental Europe, and northeastern Asia.[46] The United States struggles to project power in those regions while also managing its own society and dangerous levels of debt-deficit load, with its shipyard capacity, defense industrial base, and even presidential bandwidth stretched to the limit. And while the behavior of US allies in this time of contestation is a complex topic given many seem conflicted about how far to help themselves and how far to maintain their dependency on Washington, we are in general seeing an increase in their efforts at both internal and external balancing, with an enlarged NATO and an increase in defense spending in Europe and Asia. A number of realists, such as Christopher Layne, forecast during the interregnum that the levels of US ascendancy would be impermanent and that China's growth in power and ambition would reduce the gap significantly, if not close it.[47] It's true that counterbalancing took longer to get going than some realists expected. But if we can identify China as balancing in earnest from at least 2008–2009, Russia, from at least 2014, Iran, from the moment it began helping insurgents bleed US forces in Iraq beginning in 2005, and North Korea, during either its defiant development of the ability to strike the United States with nuclear weapons in the face of Washington's pressure or at least from the moment it sent troops into Ukraine to help Russia in 2024 and with the quartet increasingly coordinating to counter the United States and its allies from 2022 onward, it's fair to say balancing predictions were imperfect on the details but right on the main point.

What about cases where regimes commit blunders and fail to balance enough or well? In a realist world, when states do not take steps to counter, contain, avoid, or suppress threats or when they take such steps incompetently, they court punishment. This is an important point as some argue that realism cannot deal with cases of self-defeating behavior since it unduly assumes polities are rational, sober, and sensible. How, they ask, can realists explain why Athens launched its gratuitous expedition against Sicily, underestimating the difficulty of the task and derailing its own military command through internal political disarray? Or why the thirteenth-century Mongols, already possessing a vast continental empire, wrecked their naval power by launching multiple seaborne attacks on Japan? How can realists account for Vladimir Putin invading Ukraine, assuming it would be swift and decisive given Russian supremacists thought too highly of their capabilities and dismissed the force of Ukrainian nationalism? How can realists deal with economic hubris, such as the Euro-Atlantic policies that allowed for reckless and corrupt financial practices, in turn leading to the global financial crisis of our time?

To answer such questions, one variant of realism, "neoclassical" realism, delves down into domestic, unit-level explanations. It is less a general theory of realism and more an approach to explaining particular historical cases. This approach is more sensitive to the multiplicity of things that shape rulers' decisions, but by trading generality for precision on particular historical cases, it opens up a problem. If realism must dilute its main analytical priority—the system level—to explain anomalous behavior, its explanatory power weakens.[48] Moreover, it makes a concession to antirealist theory that it might not have to make—that international behavior is a product of domestic forces—when a more consistent realism regards the domestic condition of a state as primarily rooted in its international circumstances.

A better realist answer is a blunter one. Look what happened to them, to the Athenian military adventurers, the Russian invaders, and the Wall Street market fundamentalists. Athens suffered a catastrophic blow to its navy, army, treasury, and its very self-belief. If Russia prevails in Ukraine or gets the better end of a negotiated settlement, it will still be a Pyrrhic victory in that the invasion has stimulated the growth of the NATO alliance and depleted Russia of blood and treasure, which will take years to recover from. And after the reckless behavior that triggered the global financial crisis, European and American economies have not been the same since 2008. One recognition, common to the ancient realism of Thucydides and modern structural realism, is that polities can err. They may not behave according to the dictates of rational self interested behavior. Only, they invite punishment. Deviations from realpolitik, flouting limits, and overextending power raise risks against them at the hands of opportunist, predatory, or fearful onlookers.[49]

Importantly, it is not enough just to assume that almost all behavior reflects a realist logic. That would be cheating, making realism indeterminate and unfalsifiable. If a polity chooses not to resist or balance, we must ask what impelled it to refrain. Was it adopting another form of self-help behavior, like bandwagoning or buck-passing, because of a calculation that balancing is too hard or that there is no one to balance with or toward and a bet that their security is better served by submitting to an empire? Or did they refrain because they were not self-regarding agents and, in their own minds, repudiated power politics, assumed that arms or alliances are not necessary, and just wanted to focus on the pursuit of leisure, salvation, or money as ends in themselves? Most importantly, what happened to these avowed nonrealists?

Realism looks not only to patterns of behavior by those making choices but also to patterns of reaction and outcomes, the consequences of decisions, and how the international system treats imprudent behavior. When polities fail or refuse to engage in self-seeking power politics or engage in it recklessly, this makes them more vulnerable and likelier to suffer costs in terms of relative strength in the form of invasion, loss of autonomy and/or dismemberment, or the waste of precious resources. Realists, as Robert Jervis observes, generally assume that most states are at least "fairly rational" in their pursuit of their interests and "are not supposed to do really foolish things."[50] And as he argues, there must be some theory of what makes foolish behavior foolish in the first place. For realists, it is the cumulative predatory behavior of other states that makes it stupid, because they tend to take advantage.[51] Stupid behavior—behavior that is excessively risky, lacking due diligence, and/or driven by underscrutinized "best-case" assumptions—in itself is not necessarily a disconfirmation of realism any more than a business driving itself into failure through inefficiency disconfirms the existence of a competitive market of self-serving and more astute firms ready to pounce—to the contrary.

One further objection to realism is that in its materialist leaning, it gives undue attention to other, more ideational forces that move the world—in particular, ideas of justice and legitimacy or, in some criticisms, of heroic willpower. Alternatives to realism suppose that some forces beyond realists' imagination are the engines of history. For idealists, it is moral virtue and political values. Athens, in this version, lost because it turned predatory and lost its moral authority as the Hellenic leader, just as America lost in Afghanistan because it killed too many people and propped up a corrupt government.[52] For the ideationally minded, ideas are critical and causally prior to capabilities: "You cannot kill an idea," they often say, especially about counterterrorist or counterinsurgency campaigns.

By contrast, for thinkers of the machtpolitik school, the key is willpower, heroic greatness, and unapologetic overwhelming violence. Athens, in this version, lost because it was irresolute, distracted, and not committed enough to victory. Likewise, to machtpolitikers, America's modern defeats, whether in Vietnam or Afghanistan, were rooted in failure of will and spine. Washington didn't want victory enough to endure the hard slog. It was strategically impatient and feckless in its desire to end its longest wars.

In a realist view, being smart and being good (by the standard of ordinary morality) are more likely to be different things. The imprudence of behavior is not the same thing or parallel to the injustice of behavior. Sometimes, states behave in a predatory fashion but calculate correctly that they can get away with it. At other times, they launch aggression or bid for expansion on the basis of faulty assumptions that it will be easy or easy enough. That does not mean that we should not care whether they are doing the wrong thing. It means, rather, that there is no inherent justice woven into things, and we, like the Melians, should not count on there being so. China, for instance, calculated that it could quickly suppress opponents and strengthen its power position against Vietnam in 1978 and Hong Kong in 2020—a calculation that was wrong in the first instance and correct in the second.

In general, a prudential worldview centered on hard power, self-interest, and limits does a better job in accounting for who wins and who loses, whether in Syracuse or Kabul. Realism is not primarily a predictive model of battlefield outcomes given its most acute minds fear war and its contingency, volatility, and disruptiveness. It cautions, though, against worldviews that treat either virtue or brutality as decisive variables or morality as a precondition of relative strength. Pitilessly brutal campaigns sometimes succeed by grinding down less united, less resilient, and less supported opponents: Maoist China in Tibet, Vladimir Putin in Chechnya, Sri Lanka when warring down the Tamil Tigers, Francisco Franco's fascists in Spain, and, indeed, the United States when it suppressed the revolt in the Philippines. The Taliban and the Viet Cong were crueler toward civilians they subjugated than Western forces were, yet they seized Kabul and Saigon, respectively. Most insurgencies, victorious or failed, commit atrocities. Only some enjoy other advantages of capability and supply that correlate more closely with success, like international support, cross-border sanctuaries, and higher resolve. International politics is not a fairness contest. Nor is it a Platonic trial of ideals. While you cannot literally wipe an idea off the face of the earth, inflicting defeat and reversal on an idea can damage it greatly and lower its appeal. The queues to join the Islamic State of Iraq and the Levant (ISIL) are lower now than they once were, and French colonialism never recovered from defeat in Algeria.

Against machtpolitikers, realists respond that international politics is not primarily a drama about heroic will summoned up from virtue. It is more about capacity, competence, and the balance of interests in a conflict. That a country is willing to sacrifice greatly in one cause but prefers to limit its liability in another, to defend NATO but abandon Afghanistan, is best explained not by varying levels of virtue but by the fact that some interests are essential, some, peripheral. Brutal campaigns can fail too for the very reason that they encounter determined adversaries who believe they can prevail, such as the Soviets in Afghanistan and Nazi Germany on the Eastern Front and in its unrestricted submarine warfare. No barometer of gentleness or roughness, moral authority or moral barbarism, provides a reliable formula for winning. People will care about who is committing atrocities, but they will also often consider whether resistance is futile or ultimate victory is possible. Justice is its own reward and doesn't make the world go round.

THE PROBLEM OF COOPERATION

Another complaint about realism is that it fails to anticipate or explain increased cooperation in the world. This is allegedly so especially about the cooperation facilitated and embedded by institutions. International institutions are enduring patterned expectations of behavior that receive formal assent, usually involving rules but lacking a central commanding authority.[53] If our international life really is a bleak affair, critics ask, how do we account for increased global governance and the invention and spread of institutions since 1945? What of the attempt to create and impose global rules, laws, and norms, from laws against war crimes to trade? How do we explain self-restraint, for instance, in the taboos around chemical or nuclear weapons? If countries typically are so self-seeking and if institutions are so unimportant, why do those same countries invest effort in participating in those institutions? And in the big picture, how do realists cope with the puzzle that on core measures and in overall "net" outcomes, our world is getting more cooperative, less warlike, and more regulated? There is a "peace" of some kind, generated by more democracy, perhaps, and/or more institutions and/or more capitalism. As critics suggest, realism does a bad job with the fact that there is an increased attempt at cooperation, that signaling benign intent and eliminating uncertainty is possible, and that these efforts have achieved major successes.[54] Humans may be born in anarchy, but, in the tradition of Hedley Bull, they are creating a society.[55]

The Limits of Institutions

The underlying disagreement here is about the relationship between institutions and power. Do institutions primarily change (or transform) politics, exerting an independent effect on their members? Or do they primarily reflect or reinforce the distribution of power outside them? Are they more the instruments of state policy or its determinants? Does the United Nations, the World Monetary Fund, or the European Union make the world fundamentally more cooperative by generating more information, creating more trust, and/or instilling transnational identities? Or do they act as mere hosts that play back the power asymmetries of the world? Is the UN really the "last best hope" for our species or just a benign but peripheral thing that provides a useful setting for interactions? The realist response is that anarchy limits cooperation since even the most benign polities enjoying the fruits of cooperation fear making only relative gains against others, mindful that others might cheat. This problem is reflected in the limitations suffered by institutions.[56]

For starters, let's deal with the argument that states' efforts to create and join institutions in themselves suggests that those institutions are significant.[57] One response is that whether or not states invest in institutions does not demonstrate that those institutions are determinative rather than instrumental. They might just be a convenient way of pursuing self-interest. More simply, the fact is that those investment efforts are limited, relative to their budgets. In the 2023 financial year, Washington devoted $18 billion to UN entities. It devoted $820 billion to its defense budget. Eighteen billion dollars is not nothing, but compared to its investment in hard power, it is a rounding error. The superpower conducts itself as though the UN is useful yet supplemental. Also, the very creation of institutions does not straightforwardly mark a leveling shift toward cooperation. Cooperation there may be but on the terms of the strong, who also incentivize cooperation on their terms via coercion. As Lloyd Gruber shows, the creation of European monetary unification and the North American Free Trade Agreement, two market-opening measures, presented weaker parties with a hard choice.[58] By joining, they didn't simply benefit but also suffered nontrivial material costs.

Yet staying out would have met worse punishment given the dominant states were taking the better status quo ante off the table. In this way, powerful states strong-arm weaker powers to accept suboptimal outcomes by threatening to "go it alone."

What about arms control and active measures to defuse tensions, build confidence, and signal benign intent? These can take effect—to an extent. But they run up against the fundamental problem that others' intentions are not only uncertain but changeable. Anarchic insecurity runs through arms control arrangements: even good faith parties will insist on verification, and verification requires monitoring, which reveals information about the other parties' capabilities and supplies a military advantage, thereby rendering the inspected party more vulnerable.[59] For the likes of North Korea, "information about the leadership's locations or means of physical protection could make them easier to target by either U.S. missiles or a domestic coup."[60] Transparency is possible but jeopardizes security. Iraqi despot Saddam Hussein feared UN arms-monitoring teams because he feared they could be infiltrated by spies. They could use their inspections to obtain intelligence that would provide Washington with a target set. Even though he had scrapped most of his chemical and biological weapons arsenal, he still had this fear. And his fear in this regard was not ridiculous. The CIA *did* infiltrate UN weapons-inspections teams.[61] And "regime change" had become the official policy of Washington since it proclaimed so in legislation in 1998. Parties therefore have rational incentives to conceal, cheat, or defect. In turn, that duplicity can make them look more threatening. For similar reasons, efforts to signal self-restraint are hard to convey. Declarations of nuclear No First Use policies, which claim a commitment to nuclear use only in retaliation against an adversary's nuclear strike, are mostly disbelieved. They are only credible in instances where the relationship is already benign and/or when the declaring state lacks the capability to launch a first strike.[62] Like so much in the history of arms control–reassurance measures, they work best when they are least needed. Arms control measures more broadly are more the result than the cause of greater stability within a competitive relationship. To even achieve an agreed-upon control regime, the parties must already be sufficiently confident in their security—confident enough that implementing some transparency won't be overly threatening.

International law has some effect but mostly only so long as compliance is convenient or cost-effective and mostly in ways that reflect rather than alter the distribution of power. It works like a spiderweb: strong enough only to catch small creatures but weak to irrelevant at stopping elephants. Even states that have a preference for complying with international law will typically become more flexible when it collides with other things they care about, from economic growth to hard security.[63]

World courts may claim their writ runs far and wide. Yet they lack a supreme armed authority to enforce their writ against the strong so that only defeated rulers or leaders of small states appear before them. In 2016, the Permanent Court of Arbitration at The Hague ruled against China's territorial claims in the South China Sea and in favor of the claims of the Philippines. Hopeful observers declared it was a blow to Beijing's "moral legitimacy." Yet China has since rejected the ruling, has not changed its behavior, and continues to grab and militarize disputed atolls and islands and to terrorize fishing vessels.[64] How is that norm against conquest looking, by the way, given it is overridden by one of the world's largest states? To be sure, China has made some low-cost rhetorical effort to challenge the ruling, reflecting that it cares. But measured against liberal internationalist claims that a "rules-based order" can supplant power politics, that is weak tea. Do China's violations attract reputational costs and make it look hypocritical and thuggish? Probably, but not to the extent that Asian states are imposing any meaningful material punishment on China any more than most non-Western states have disengaged from trading and collaborating with Russia after it invaded Ukraine. If there is a common theme in the region, it is a wary reluctance of third parties to sacrifice their interests for one another and a preference for internal balancing over highly committal external balancing. Might The Hague ruling give hope to other claimants, like Vietnam and Malaysia and their supporters, that China can be litigated and shamed into greater restraint? Yes—a fool's hope.

Not only do elephant powers flout rules and norms at will, often with impunity, but also they take detailed steps to resist any attempts to create an enforceable legal order against them. The United States, for instance, helped create the International Criminal Court but argued it should be exempt, coerced states around the world to recognize Washington's immunity, and passed The Hague Invasion Act to warrant armed extraction of any American held in The Hague. To exempt oneself from rules while demanding others defer to them is part of the process of world ordering. There aren't many cases of leading states breaking with this pattern.

Institutions, then, vary in their impact and are mostly hostages to the material balance of power. How, then, do we account for peace?

Explaining Peace
Apart from the absence thus far of major war, the post-1945 world has not been significantly more peaceful with regard to lesser but still serious wars. There is a realist account for the absence of major war, which we will get to. Regarding conflict below that level, it depends on how you do the measuring. The Whiggish thesis of macro forces driving a decline of organized violence—one that is unlikely to reverse—has met with significant challenge. Optimists too readily measure war's frequency by counting the dead, assuming that a decline in combat fatalities equates to a reduction in conflict. As Tanisha M. Fazal demonstrates, this is not so. Fatal casualties are less and less a reliable measure of the occurrence of wars as they ignore nonfatal casualties and the profound impact of the medical revolution in shifting the ratio of dead to wounded.[65] Once nonfatal casualties are taken into account, the reduction is, if anything, modest, suggesting humans aren't fighting much less, just that we are getting better at stopping wounded people from dying. War's lethality is less and less a reliable yardstick of its frequency. There are other difficulties with the body-counting method too. Much of the historical record has left marginalized the casualties suffered in colonial wars, including modern ones, thereby understating the extent of wars in places beyond conventional recordkeeping.[66]

From another direction, Bear F. Braumoeller shows that rates of war initiation and escalation have not changed much over two centuries. Larger political units ruling larger populations send fewer people to fight, telling us more about demographics than about belligerence.[67] To be sure, there has been some reduction in some places. But it is attributable less to some civilizing normative or economic process and more to patterns of political order that can change. Swift destabilizing power shifts still can and do trigger catastrophic wars: the often-neglected disaster of Africa's Great War (1998–2003) in and beyond the Democratic Republic of the Congo, the multiple wars in the Balkans (1992–1999), and the civil war in Syria, which was also internationalized (2013–2023). This is, then, not nearly enough to constitute evidence of a lasting paradigm shift in International Relations and not enough to rule out a regression to high intensity or even major war. And if war's shadow has receded less than optimists claim, this has important policy implications. The proposition that war is increasingly obsolete may not only be wrong but also dangerous if those who exercise power believe it.

As for major war, the best explanation for its absence is not the coming of the United Nations or other institutions. We have had international institutions designed to prevent or limit all-out conflict before, like the League of Nations and The Hague Conventions, not to mention the Concert of Europe. We have tried to outlaw war itself in the Kellogg-Briand Peace Pact of 1928. Two lively minds, Oona A. Hathaway and Scott J. Shapiro, valiantly argue that the pact was really a success because it marked not the end but the "beginning of the end" of interstate war and the rising norm against conquest.[68] It is hard to see how a radical plan to abolish war in 1928 that was unable to prevent the eruption a decade later by one of the bloodiest genocidal conflicts in history, in which one party successfully conquered much of Eastern Europe, should get credit for causing the progress achieved afterward in radically reducing interstate war and making conquest a taboo. To look for the sources of peace in noble-minded blueprints is to look in the wrong place. Also, the supposed norm against territorial conquest is overstated. Postwar states are less inclined to take a run at swallowing large real estate, but they still grab and bite smaller pieces of territory—a more measured form of aggression that suggests not a norm-driven mindset of restraint but a calculation about what they can get away with.[69]

Even if the world has not gotten nearly as peaceful as optimists believe, some will maintain that realists fail to account for peace between democracies. What about the alleged "democratic peace"—the thesis that democracies are generally disinclined to fight other democracies, making regime type a pivotal historical force?[70]

First, this argument depends heavily on convenient coding, classifying Wilhelmine Germany in World War One as "nondemocracy"—a difficult case given its free legislature voted for war credits to make the whole adventure possible. A semiauthoritarian state whose democratic parts willingly supported one of the largest major wars in history may not fatally wound the general thesis, but it's awkward.

A more general difficulty is that democracy has not been a free-floating thing for at least eighty years but rather closely linked to and (often, not always) under the superintendence of US hegemony. Democracies, if narrowly defined as rule of the citizens, more removed from the modern US orbit and less subject to its ordering and coercion have fought one another plenty: Israel and Lebanon, India and Pakistan (during Pakistan's democratic periods in 1947 and 1999), Turkey and Cyprus, Ecuador and Peru, and the American Union and the Confederacy. At the very least, the fact that democracies under different conditions are more likely to fight one another suggests that the democratic-peace theory could be a theory not of democratic peace but of *Atlantic* and *Pacific* democratic peace in a certain historical moment.

A useful test case lies in antiquity, when there was no global democracy-promoting hegemon to keep democracies in line. Ancient democracies, by our standards and in some ways, weren't very democratic, owning slaves and marginalizing women. But in other respects, they took radical direct forms. And these democracies fought one another with relatively high frequency. Even some democratic-peace theorists concede that while fragmentary sources mean we can't be confident about a large group of cases, amongst "clear" democratic pairs, if anything, the frequency has been higher.[71] Other democratic-peace theorists, like Spencer Weart, resist this finding, performing intellectual gymnastics over the case of Athens and Syracuse in 415 BC.[72] This was the premier ancient case of interdemocratic bloodshed. Syracuse had been a democracy for half a century, at times, a raucous one, with mass citizen assemblies passing laws, deciding on foreign policy, and appointing and sacking generals. Both Syracuse and Athens, at times, sponsored friendly aristocratic against popular ones abroad, and Syracuse was one of several Sicilian democracies that fought one another in the mid-fifth century BC. To try to disqualify the case, Weart claims others didn't regard it as a true democracy (even though the main contemporary source for the conflict, Thucydides, unambiguously did). To make this case, he relies on the language of Aristotle a century later (ambiguous at best), the power wielded by oligarchs (yet the assemblies denounced and exiled them), and the fact that there was disunity. On that artificial standard—that democracies aren't democracies if they have social inequity and division—many countries in democratic-peace datasets would be excluded, reducing it to a theory of why modern Denmark and Sweden don't fight much. Instead of straining to force facts to fit the theory, we should recognize the fundamental point. Athens and Syracuse were established democracies by any reasonable definition, yet they waged a draining conflict.

The democracy-war debate restages the disagreement between "outside-in" versus "inside-out" views of the relationship between the domestic and the international. If we recognized democracy as a thing "caused" rather than as a thing "causing," it could be the result of something international and power-political related. As Patrick J. McDonald suggests, the very rise of democratic regimes is partly attributable to the fact that ascendant great powers shape them and manage them within hierarchical orders.[73] If democracies do indeed engage in less conflict with one another, this may not be because of their internal qualities as democracies but because ascendant great powers help lock in a democratic-regime type. Thus, it is not so much a "democratic" peace as a peace of the "great power hierarchy." Even if West Germany and France had wanted to fight a war in the 1950s, the United States wouldn't have let them.

Some will respond that even if the main pattern is Atlantic democracy, that's still an argument for ongoing democracy promotion and spreading the Atlantic system and thereby increasing peace. Perhaps that could be one result. But it would involve a direct challenge to dictatorships and semiauthoritarian regimes, amounting to a revolutionary subversive project that sacrificed medium-term stability for ultimate liberation. Michael Doyle, a leading theorist of democratic-peace theory, says as much: today's liberal states cooperate with one another while they gear up for a "long twilight struggle" so that, "with respect to autocracies, they are ready for war."[74] In real life, it is murkier than that. The Atlantic democracies collaborate with undemocratic states from Turkey to Saudi Arabia to Vietnam, and some democratic partners are increasingly illiberal and less free, like India. Yet Doyle's admission tells us a lot. The vision of a democratic peace, achieved via a great struggle between the free and the unfree, if taken up, would lock its subjects into ideologized and perpetual crisis, making practical diplomacy much harder. And as with revolutionary France, this process promises to create a tilt toward militarized autocracy. There comes a point in prudential foreign policy where attempting to spread peace generates more violence, not less, and where you must coexist with things that offend you—especially in a nuclear age.

A Nuclear Peace

The most powerful explanation for the absence of major war since 1945, thus far, is neither institutions nor interdemocratic concord. It is the innovation that most distinguishes postwar conditions from what came before: nuclear revolution and the resulting stalemate. We're back to nuclear weapons since we are now talking about the sources of peace. Here, I'm making just one point: that the weight of evidence suggests nuclear weapons are the most important cause of the absence of major war between World War Two and now.

Alternative explanations of the absence of major war are weaker. International institutions can help encourage cooperation, but we had them before nuclear weapons were invented, and they did not prevent the recurrence of major wars. The Concert of Europe and the League of Nations are ultimately stories of temporary lulls, disappointed hopes, and institutional frailty. Similarly, economic interdependence can create obstacles to conflict, though this depends upon how the countries involved see their future. Ultimately, it has not proved to be strong enough to prevent interdependent countries coming to blows. We should recognize that such polities are not narrowly just economies but are political communities that care about things beyond just tomorrow's trade figures, that historically, at times, believe they must run risks and use force to survive, and who often prove resilient in adapting to the disruption of wartime sanctions, embargoes, and lost markets. So why are nukes different?

Let me explain. Nukes are novel but not simply because of their raw destructive power. The capacity to inflict genocidal violence has always been with us. Humans have waged wars of annihilation and inflicted rapid and extensive slaughter from the earliest recorded massacres to modern genocides in Bosnia and Rwanda. As the economist and strategist Thomas C. Schelling remarks, "Against defenseless people there is not much that nuclear weapons can do that cannot be done with an ice pick."[75]

Nuclear weapons are different, rather, because along with their violence, their small size and ease of deliverability makes it very hard to stop enough getting through to lay waste to capital cities or whatever population or asset that the target holds dear. Few political goals are worth suffering that harm or significantly raising the risks of it. This change has had a profound effect on the calculations people make during conflict. In the nuclear age, so long as the "losing" state retains the ability to retaliate by getting one bomb through their adversary's defenses, they can still hold at risk that adversary's country even while losing every clash on land, sea, and air. And with the ending of America's atomic monopoly in 1949, nuclear retaliation to nuclear strikes became possible. Compare this with the prenuclear world where a strong side prevailing in the battlespace could attack knowing that its population and cities were either safe or could be defended against bombers who could be hit back by an air defense system. In other words, nukes break the link between combat domination and security. Because a weaker side can inflict unacceptable harm on a stronger side, the presence of nukes makes meaningful victory between opponents so armed just about impossible. Humans range widely in their tastes, way of life, and values, but the bomb focuses the mind.

In this condition of stalemate, major war itself became a far less attractive temptation. Nuclear weapons tend to deter major war and direct threats to a state's vital existential interests. That is, at the highest level of potential violence, the ultimate weapon, if deployed and controlled with restraint, tends to dissuade countries from tipping over into hot war. Whether we like it or not, in the relations among major powers for generations now, we have lived in a nuclear peace.

The overall pattern is undeniable: nuclear-armed states have almost never been invaded on the ground as most aggressors confine their attacks to disputed territories.[76] A rare exception is Ukraine's cross-border offensive into Kursk in August 2024. That anomalous attack on the motherland, though, was a response to being invaded, and in the eyes of Kyiv, they were only counterinvading a country that was trying to destroy them anyway. Consistent with the broader point, no all-out direct conflict between major powers (the largest and richest states) has taken place in nearly eighty years. In comparable time periods, there were multiple wars: two dozen within the seventy years following the Treaty of Westphalia (1648) and several after the Vienna Congress (1815). There were three India-Pakistan wars before both neighbors got the bomb, yet since, there have been crises and skirmishes but no clashes reaching anything like the same scale.[77] Do the math.

Some argue that this is just correlation and that we should remain doubtful about deterrence because the absence of major war and the coming of nuclear weapons may be unrelated. Leave aside the fact that the correlation between nuclear weapons' arrival and absence of major war, thus far, is perfect. There is also positive historical evidence that the correlation is no coincidence and that we are entitled to greater confidence in the power of deterrence. We know from the historical records that decision-makers in crises, from Berlin to Cuba to Kashmir to Kargil to Damansky Island, worried about the dangers of nuclear use. We know from Soviet archives and oral evidence that the US arsenal played a major part in persuading Stalin not to resolve the Berlin airlift crisis (1948–1949) by attacking.[78] Washington's cautious, calibrated steps in the 1958 Berlin crisis drew partly on President Dwight Eisenhower's increasing risk aversion, his well-founded belief that the coming of the Soviet Union's thermonuclear capability would mean, in the event of escalation, tens of millions of immediate fatalities. We know from India's former army chief that after terrorists attacked Mumbai in November 2008, Pakistan's nuclear weapons dissuaded India from an all-out military retaliation.[79] In recent time, hawks in the Trump presidency advocated a "bloody-nose" limited preemptive strike on North Korea only for the executive branch to conclude "no attack plan could confidently preclude escalation or collateral damage." Now compare the reluctance to attack North Korea, which successfully advanced its nuclear program, with the fates of Libya's Colonel Qaddafi and Iraq's Saddam Hussein, who abandoned theirs. There is clear unignorable evidence that nuclear-armed rivals do indeed carefully weigh the consequences of escalation in crises.

In historical crises, decision-makers knew they were struggling within the nuclear stalemate, that escalation risks were real, their potential consequences grave, and that some reciprocal restraint was needed to avoid being incinerated. This moved them far more than the opinions of the United Nations. We know from the deliberations of the secret US Net Evaluation Subcommittee in the 1950s that policymakers and their advisors grasped the potential devastation that a maximal nuclear strike could inflict and understood the elusiveness of achieving victory in nuclear conditions.[80] The debate the West is having today about how far to intervene in Ukraine is overtly conducted with the possibility of nuclear escalation in mind. These patterns also provide reasons to expect that nuclear regimes will not transfer their devices to terrorist proxy groups in an effort to launch attacks deniably. Would-be martyrs who ache for heaven may not be easily deterrable, but the governments that support them have much more to lose. To expect or hope for deniability would also be foolish. An act of nuclear terrorism would highly motivate the targeted state to identify and punish the culprit and their supporters, there wouldn't be a long suspect list to begin with, and large states have an impressive record of attribution.[81]

Some argue that nuclear weapons failed to deter interstate attacks in the past, citing in particular the Yom Kippur War of 1973 and the Falklands War of 1982. In fact, in both cases, the aggressors limited their war aims to disputed territories rather than targeting their adversaries' heartlands. Argentina's Falklands attack was against a territory geographically peripheral to Britain, and the Galtieri regime calculated that Britain wouldn't defend it at all, let alone with nuclear weapons. Thus, it was more a case of disbelieving the threat of nuclear and conventional escalation than proof that Britain's deterrent would be disbelieved everywhere. And in 1973, Israel's arsenal constrained both Egypt and Syria's war aims and put a limit on their risk appetite. Egyptian sources suggest that Anwar Sadat insisted on a limited territorial objective, calculating that Israel would not convey a nuclear threat below a certain threshold, and that its arsenal motivated Egypt not to advance toward the line of the Gidi and Mitla Passes in the Sinai. And while we lack, so far, positive testimony about Syria's calculations, the limitation of goals and escalation risks are the most plausible account for their decision not to advance beyond the southern Golan Heights and seize the bridges over the Jordan River despite opportunities to do so.[82] None of this is absolute: there are intermediate cases of extended deterrence where miscalculation is possible. Deterrence is never automatic and depends upon the deterrer convincing the deterred that their threat to retaliate is believable. Deterrence also depends on showing restraint in order for threats of retaliation to be meaningful. For instance, Russia has failed to deter Ukraine from bombing it in retaliation largely because Russia is attacking Ukraine anyway, trying to seize control of its capital and kidnapping children, making its punishment threats carry less weight.

It is also unclear how a postnuclear humanity, if such a remote thing were somehow realized, is supposed to sustain general peace between leading states. We have much evidence for what international life can be like without nuclear weapons: the last long era of nuclear "zero." The historical record is not encouraging. Why should those with nuclear weapons or under the shield of extended deterrence, especially relatively weaker states facing larger adversaries, be confident that next time it will be different? Why should they trust that giving up the ultimate weapon will not lead to a bloodier future, similar to the bloodier past, where those who mean them harm are less constrained? Serious disarmers, such as Ward Wilson, concede that the prenuclear world was also lethal but maintain that nuclear deterrence is too volatile and unreliable to bank on.[83]

As we've already seen, reasonable people can disagree about whether it is ultimately worth it to maintain the bomb or at least try for its elimination in whole or in part. It comes down to a choice of evils. Nuclear deterrence is not infallible. It does not reliably deter activity and aggression below the threshold of major war, though it does deter a hell of a lot. Nor should we deny the arithmetic probability that at some point, there will be nuclear use, accidental or deliberate. We shouldn't be blind to the risks involved at lower levels of violence, where nuclear arms embolden some possessors to be more aggressive, not less, in lower-intensity skirmishes or standoffs.

While deterrence may be fallible, it is demonstrably achievable. General disarmament is not. Better instead to focus on making deterrence work, on rationally choosing to be deterred from threatening others' most core interests, as well as securing stockpiles and fortifying systems of command and control. One benefit of accepting the bomb is to make possible the intensive study of how to make deterrence work, helping decision-makers be mindful of the risks and what is at stake. Accepting and managing nukes is a lesser evil—and more prudent—than trying to abolish them given the extreme unlikelihood of general multilateral disarmament and the paradoxical danger that the reversibility of disarmament would make nuclear crisis and nuclear use more likely.

The argument about cooperation and realism flows from an older, deeper dispute over the possibility of transformation. American diplomat and realist George F. Kennan cautioned in 1951 against a strain of thought that is still especially active in the Euro-Atlantic world. He called it the "legalistic-moralistic approach to international problems"—"the belief that it should be possible to suppress the chaotic and dangerous aspirations of governments in the international field by the acceptance of some system of legal rules and restraints."[84] It was and is an effort to transpose a concept of individuals living under the rule of law and apply it to governments abroad. Yet as thousands of years of history suggest, the international domain cannot replicate the system of the domestic sovereign domain, and each attempt, at best, ends up circumscribed, compromised, and weak when it is most needed. That's our permanent condition. Institutions may have a value, but we should not expect much of them.

HARD QUESTIONS

On hearing that I was arguing the case for realism, the scholar Nina Tannenwald posed some puzzles that she believes confound realism, or, in her words, "some things realism doesn't explain." These include the rise of human rights, the existence of the International Criminal Court (ICC) and the rise of war crimes prosecutions, the EU, the big influence of small allies (e.g. US-Israel relations), and the creation of the Nuclear Ban Treaty.[85] Challenge accepted!

The Rise of Human Rights

To borrow a analogy from Stephen Walt, saying realism is falsified by the rise of human rights is like saying gravity is falsified by the rise of aviation. Aviators may resist gravity but must also take it into account, from designing their aircraft to refueling to liftoff. A similar problem haunts the pursuit of human rights under anarchy. Humans constrained by conditions may still act in defiance of those conditions, up to a point, and may very well entertain illusions that by doing so, they have not only acted to help others but also transformed the world. The true test is not whether collective groups, states or nonstates, sometimes try to assert the integrity of people internationally. They clearly have and do. The test is how far they are willing to do so even when compliance is costly and inconvenient. Are human rights a robust global commitment or fragile and reversible? When the imperatives of universal general good collide with self-interest, which force tends to win out? When disaster or crisis strikes, do polities default first to their own interests above others, or do they band together collectively, sacrificing short-term gain in pursuit of the common good?

The global pandemic of 2009 (swine flu) and the more severe case of COVID in 2020–2021 were revealing tests of this question. The plagues' pressures induced some collaboration and vaccine sharing and much charitable public-private enterprise. But when push came to shove, narrowly self-regarding behavior prevailed.[86] Polities hoarded vaccines and stockpiled protective equipment. Ideas of human rights and human security have indeed arisen. Yet a hierarchy of commitments tends to dominate. Even an egalitarian state whose rulers wish to do good abroad will want human rights and security for its own populace first. Altruism and cooperation feature in the mix but usually get traded off for other valued things. There was early suggestion during the crisis that the COVID pandemic would challenge the tenets of realism.[87] Yet we still await the revolution.

Critics of realism hold up one revolution that did happen as a major and discrediting predictive failure on realism's part—that is, the collapse of the Soviet Union in 1989–1991 in its timing and manner, the bloodless nature of its fall, and its peaceful withdrawal from Central Europe. As the argument goes, so preoccupied were realists with material capabilities and a Waltzian bias toward the stable endurance of bipolarity that they couldn't anticipate the erosion and collapse of a regime whose citizens and elites had lost faith in. Yet material capability is central to any decent explanation of the Cold War's outbreak, as William C. Wohlforth argues.[88] The relative decline in Soviet capability is central to understanding why it gave up its challenge to the US-dominated status quo and ended its rivalry. Against the pressure of hard necessity and relative material decline, the Soviet Union reluctantly retrenched. In fairness to critics, most realists (like most Sovietologists and just about everyone) did not anticipate the timing or manner of this revolution even as it was consistent with realist views of the conditions that make change possible. But the event vindicated one realist who did most to craft the doctrine of anti-Soviet containment, George Kennan, who expected that the United States and its allies could oppose Moscow via long-term counterpressure and measures short of war.

The Existence of the ICC and the Rise of War Crimes Prosecutions

The ICC and war crimes prosecutions exist—no question. And yet how far does their writ truly run? One simple measure of the ICC's coverage—and its capacity to replace power politics with international justice and create a law above power—is who it prosecutes in the first place.

Here are the names of all those indicted, thus far, by the court at the time of writing: Joseph Kony, Germain Katanga, Uhuru Kenyatta, Raska Lukwiya, Mathieu Ngudjolo Chui, Henry Kosgey, Jean-Pierre Bemba, Francis Muthaura, Okot Odhiambo, Dominic Ongwen, Omar al-Bashir, William Ruto, Vincent Otti, Bahr Abu Garda, Joshua Sang, Abdallah Banda, Muammar Qaddafi, Saif al-Islam Qaddafi, Thomas Lubanga Dyilo, Bosco

Ntaganda, Saleh Jerbo, Ahmed Haroun, Callixte Mbarushimana, Abdullah Senussi, Ali Abd-al-Rahman, Mohammed Ali, Laurent Gbagbo, Charles Blé Goudé, Simone Gbagbo, Abdel Rahim Hussein, Sylvestre Mudacumura, Tohami Khaled, Walter Barasa, Narcisse Arido, Fidèle Babala,. Aimé Kilolo, Jean-Jacques Mangenda, Philip Bett,. Paul Gicheru, Ahmad al-Mahdi, Iyad Ag Ghaly, Mahmoud al-Werfalli, al-Hassan Ag Abdoul Aziz, Alfred Yekatom, Patrice-Edouard Ngaïssona, Maxime Mokom, Noureddine Adam, Mahamat Said Abdel Kani, Hamlet Guchmazov, Mikhail Mindzaev, David Sanakoev, Maria Lvova- Belova, Vladimir Putin, Sergei Kobylash, and Viktor Sokolov.[89]

Most the indicted are Africans. Of the few that aren't, Vladimir Putin and his fellow Russian fugitives will very likely not be arrested and tried before any international court or tribunal given that they rule a state strong enough to refuse cooperation. At the time of writing, the court has issued arrest warrants for the leaders of Israel and Hamas. Since the former rules a state strong enough to refuse cooperation, we may be waiting some time. Since the latter enjoyed the patronage of a Gulf state strong enough to provide refuge from international courts and Israel took matters into its own hands by assassinating the leaders, we will be waiting longer.

What about the Nuremberg and Tokyo trials of 1945? Those were prosecutions of defeated regimes, once powerful states rendered powerless by brute force. Even then, the trials were compromised and channeled by the interests of the war-winning states that arranged them. While some war criminals and *génocidaires* were convicted and executed, Washington shielded other guilty actors as it suited, spiriting Nazi scientists, spies, and military officers away to take part in missile development or (later) NATO military command or intelligence gathering on the continent.[90] And American prosecutors helped cover up Japanese emperor Hirohito's complicity in atrocities to preserve the imperial throne as the basis for a new democratic protectorate and anti-Soviet bulwark.[91] None of this is a criticism. It is an observation about the limits of international law.

Critics rightly note that the court fixates on the world's poorest continent. They call for a more truly international court.[92] Yet the court's limited geographical effectiveness is a feature, not a bug. It cannot become international without an international enforcer. If one day a genocidal general or politician from an unsubjugated major power gets indicted and convicted, then realists will have some explaining to do. Until then, the international domain is one of victor's justice.

There is a wider point here, beyond formal institutions and rules—namely, as some argue, realists should consider the supposed effects of norms, morality, and perceptions about justice on international behavior. There is a liberal assumption that runs through much commentary on international affairs that given our world is made up of a morally sensitive audience, misbehavior undermines a state's moral authority or stature and that this in turn has material costs. When it came to light that the United States was conducting extraordinary rendition and torture in its "war on terror" and when it invaded Iraq without a final UN Security Council resolution, there arose a complaint that these policies were not only bad but strategically self-harming. Similarly, Russia's invasion of Ukraine and its subsequent atrocities, including child theft, allegedly have isolated it internationally. More recently, Israel's invasion of Gaza has prompted South Africa to launch an international lawsuit for war crimes before the International Court of Justice, with the vocal backing of other states and civil society. Some herald South Africa as a new exemplar of *Moralpolitik* for its principled stance.

But if we look closer, neither waging a war without proper mandate nor abuses at CIA black sites or Abu Ghraib nor even Russia's illegal lunge into Ukraine isolated the offending powers. When Russia invaded Ukraine in February 2022, the "Global South," nations from South Africa to Kenya to India to Brazil, responded not with virtuous internationalism or shared solidarity from a history of colonial victimhood but by hedging and trading with Moscow. As Tim Sahay argues, this à la carte behavior is all part of a larger pattern of energy diplomacy, whereby determined states pursue both resources and leverage, using their diplomatic stances as bargaining chips. "Countries like China, India, Indonesia, Brazil, South Africa, Mexico, Saudi Arabia, and the United Arab Emirates have refused to sacrifice their national interests to punish Russia. Most importantly, they believe their bargaining power in the new Cold War will result in sweeter trade, technology, and weapons deals from the West." Theirs is "a stance of non-alignment to secure the same key technologies—fighter jets, green technology, chips, submarines, nuclear, advanced pharmaceuticals, 5G mobile networks—that could power their catch-up growth. The map of countries that remained neutral on Russia sanctions is a hard-nosed security play."[93]

Regarding Israel in the wake of Gaza, it is denounced but not isolated. Most of Israel's neighbors walk a careful line, disapproving or denouncing Israel's bombardment but maintaining ties. To the extent that some other states are attempting to punish Tel Aviv, it is mostly inexpensive. South Africa is no more an exemplar of *Moralpolitik* than America. Only a week before litigating against Israel, President Cyril Ramaphosa hosted the Sudanese warlord Mohamed Hamdan Dagalo, accused by Human Rights Watch of atrocities, "including killings, mass rape, the burning and looting of villages, and mass displacement of civilians."[94] Like most leaders, only when it is convenient does Cyril Ramaphosa see human rights violations as something to be punished.

This detachment may offend Westerners. But where were Westerners when Russia brutally suppressed Chechen separatists or when Saudi Arabia bombed Yemen indiscriminately? It's not that we approved of such things. Only, like W. H. Auden's ship seeing a drowning man, we had our own interests to attend to and interests to pursue with those states and sailed quietly on. Speaking of the West, despite public protestations against Operation Iraqi Freedom, the two European nations that publicly led the charge against the invasion also privately shored up their strategic relationship with Washington. The French government gave intelligence assistance behind the scenes and soon afterward integrated its military command into NATO. Germany provided intelligence assistance in Baghdad and allowed extraordinary rendition flights from its soil. Under the outward show, it was business as usual.

That isn't an argument for an "anything-goes," morality-free foreign policy. Indefensible massacres, kidnapping, and torture are bad regardless of their utility. Only, most of the time, their badness doesn't move the rest of the world to sacrifice self-interest for principle.

The EU

The European Union, some claim, is an internationalist peace project founded on principles of openness, liberal values, and free market exchange. Its proponents argue that the EU with its pooled sovereignty, single internal market, protective outer tariff-trade walls, and liberal norms is a—or *the*—leading cause of post-1945 peace in a historically bloodstained continent.

Peace is not in itself a rebuke to the proposition that the shadow of war defines International Relations. In realist terms, peace is an (impermanent) product of power. Does the EU peace signify something profoundly different is afoot? Does it function to prevent strong members getting their way against weak members? Does it so empower the weak that it defies the distribution of capabilities and transcends traditional power politics? And doesn't its main bargain—the ceding and pooling of sovereignty in return for collective benefits—rebuke realist pessimism about cooperation?

No. The argument that institutional arrangements rather than hard power best explain peace fails to deal chronologically with the period of interstate peace in Europe that predated the formal institution, coming before the European Coal and Steel Community was formed in 1951. And it skates over postwar Europe's highly militarized condition during much of that period, being the theater of two rival armed camps. The notion of a radically demilitarized and pacified Germany, for instance, is overblown given the scale of West Germany's Bundeswehr. And emphasis on the EU loses sight of the more immediate source of internal restraint and stability, the dominance of two superpowers, one of whose dominance made a European organization possible in the first place. Put another way, Europeans were able to forge peace more easily because it was first imposed from above. Of course, there will always be the objection that Europeans regard using force against one another not only as unacceptable but unthinkable because they have forged a peaceable security community. While this is mostly true, the post–Cold War Balkans aside, it may not be a permanent condition but rather one dependent on a configuration of power. Were Europe to enjoy less US protection and patronage or none, realists would expect a similar pattern to arise that has arisen in most cases where power configurations are unsettled: a heightening of insecurity, a growth in mutual fear, and remilitarization.

The question of whether a post-American Europe would retain its profound commitment to continental peace remains hypothetical. But there is evidence in favor of realist skepticism that ruthless power politics persists. The EU is mostly a host and tool for statecraft. While there is a sophisticated debate about the extent to which the European Union was a realist initiative to begin with,[95] there are simple reasons to doubt the transformative effects of the EU. If America is still the hegemon in continental Europe, Germany and France, as the largest and richest states, still overshadow their neighbors, set the agenda, and tend to get their way. When formal rules get in the way of their immediate interests, like the budgetary limits of the Stability and

Growth Pact, they override them, mostly with impunity.[96] Even within the EU, cooperation can quickly break down and yield to competitive behavior when core interests are at risk or when groups fear others' free riding. When a fiscal crisis struck the eurozone in 2015, Germany and other creditor countries made few concessions to Athens's request for debt relief, insisting on austere economic reforms and adherence to rules. When a political crisis struck the European Union in 2016 with Britain's vote to leave it, the EU played hardball in its negotiations, determined to make an example and demonstrate the consequences of walking out. The "Brexit" documentary *Behind Closed Doors* featured Elmar Brok, chairman of the European Parliament Committee on Foreign Affairs, who argued that the EU should coerce Britain by running down the clock on negotiations "while the air becomes thinner and thinner." This reflected their strategy. Under pressure, the peace project based on common democratic values quickly resorted to coercion. If that isn't ruthless power politics, what is? It is not hard to imagine that absent the constraining effect of dependency on US security provision, the propensity of EU states toward coercion under pressure could turn more violent. Indeed, with recent signs of a nationalist turn by younger Europeans, it would be a brave bet to judge that Europe has invented internal peace for the long term.[97]

It can be argued that there is a realignment afoot whereby the increased prominence of military-strategic matters in a more turbulent era is giving more prominence to eastern EU states. "Defense and eastern enlargement," argues *The Economist*, are giving a "new voice to Ukraine's neighbors in eastern Europe," driving Germany's influence "down" and creating a new "pecking order."[98] But notice already from these very sentences about pecking orders—"who's up, who's down"—that the EU has not supplanted power politics, the main currency of interstate/interpolity power relations. At the level above, the superpower whose primacy European states accept and seek has prevented the EU from forming an army. Under US auspices, the EU has not converted its wealth into a significant independent capability outside NATO—an alliance Washington leads. At the level below, groups within the EU still regard themselves primarily as nationals first and Europeans second and behave accordingly.

The Nuclear Test Ban Treaty

States do try to institute arms control measures, as we have already seen, and one of the signature measures is the Comprehensive Nuclear Test Ban Treaty (CTBT) of 1996. The test of realism in this area is not whether people try to restrain violence but whether and why it is difficult and how sustainable it is. Do such treaties as they are made and responded to support a wider criticism that realism has little to say about voluntary nuclear restraint or the effects of a nuclear-use "taboo"?[99]

First, nuclear-weapons states still test and refine their capabilities via other means, such as modeling and simulation tools. This is odd behavior if they are in the grip of a powerful taboo against use. In recent times, China has begun an accelerated nuclear buildup. Russia has made nuclear escalation and coercive threats central to its doctrine. North Korea, despite economic pressure and overt threats, has developed intercontinental ballistic missiles that can strike the US mainland.

Indeed, a number of nuclear states—Russia, Pakistan, and North Korea—conceive of their weapons as central to their security. They don't understand them as unthinkable apocalyptic devices to deploy against civilian populations only in the event of an exchange. Rather, they value their weapons of coercive escalation for offsetting their conventional vulnerabilities, thereby helping them avoid defeat. They can credibly threaten to use them in extremis on the battlefield in ways that are distinguishable from a maximal strike on the enemy's homeland in order to forestall collapse by frightening adversaries to back off. China is a more complex case. It formally insists that its nuclear deterrent is reserved only for retaliatory use against a nuclear attack, yet it increases not only the scale but also the diversity of its arsenal, and its military documents suggest it could redefine attacks on its mainland as a "nuclear strike" in order to warrant its own use. The revival of doctrines of nuclear use is neither new nor surprising—after all, the same logic informed NATO doctrine by the late Cold War.[100] There is also survey-based research that suggests Americans, if it comes down to it, would hypothetically favor nuclear use against noncombatants at a lower threshold than in response to a nuclear attack to protect threatened US military forces in a conflict.[101] If a taboo is operative, it is a strangely permissive one.

Is the CTBT evidence of a growing international norm as well as environmental concern of fallout? It must be, to an extent, since it did attract the signatures of 187 nations and the ratification of 178, and in a minority of cases, this represented an inconvenience. The question, though, is how robust it will prove under pressure. In November 2023, Russia withdrew its ratification. This was not just one anomalous state amongst compliant states. It is a critical case, one of the states that arms control advocates most worry about given the size of its arsenal, its aggression against neighbors, and the consequent possibility that others will react by rearming and even violating rules themselves. So a central player in the nuclear arms control field has repudiated the rule, and as we saw, this has not resulted in international isolation. The CTBT is vulnerable to power politics, in other words, just like the Intermediate-Range Nuclear Forces Treaty was. The United States, by the way, also did not ratify the CTBT due to a narrow defeat in the Senate. And now, the three major nuclear powers—Russia, China, and the United States—may be preparing to resume testing in the future given "expansion and modernization work underway at China's test site in the far western region of Xinjiang, as well as at Russia's in an Arctic Ocean archipelago and the US test site in the Nevada desert."[102] Once again, arms control arrangements are most feasible when least needed and least feasible when most needed.

Other Anomalies

Having defended realism's core, a note of uncharacteristic humility is due. There are some occasional cases, some of them of wider significance, that realism just doesn't predict or explain well without inserting variables that are supposed to be of secondary or tertiary weight. In other words, there are cases where inside-out domestic politics and ideational forces really do seem to drive policy and in ways that cannot easily be attributed to outside-in systemic imperatives.

A famous example of expensive inconvenient altruism, or costly moral action, is Britain's long campaign to suppress the Atlantic slave trade from 1807 to 1867, which may have been powered by a program of domestic moral reform against sinful corruption that projected itself outwardly.[103] That kind of case—of international activism that attracts high material cost—is emphatically a minority one. It is relatively rare. To be frank, realism just doesn't handle it well. It does, however, explain its rarity, which is why we are still talking about such isolated cases.

There is a more contemporary case that realism, despite the efforts of realists, doesn't quite manage to account for—namely, the outsized influence of a small client state, Israel, over the superpower's policy in Washington. The overriding issue is that a state of Israel's smallness ought not to exert the kind of domestic leverage it apparently does over US policy in the Middle East. Any realist outlook would expect the United States to seek out and maintain alliances in theaters it cares about but should find puzzling the "reverse leverage" within those relationships. The most prominent explanation and critique of the Israel lobby, written by leading realists John J. Mearsheimer and Stephen M. Walt, relies heavily on domestic ideational variables.[104]

There is much more to say in mitigation here, but the mitigation is partial at best. Israel doesn't uniformly get its way, from arms sales to its neighboring adversaries to the Joint Comprehensive Plan of Action with Iran, so it isn't a simple case of tails wagging dogs. True, yet it still gets its way and successfully obtains far more military and diplomatic support than other small states friendly to Washington, from Luxembourg to Sri Lanka, and it enjoys America's near-automatic solidarity. Other Gulf states also receive American largesse and exert a lot of influence, from Egypt to Saudi Arabia or, indeed, the Iraq National Congress in the run-up to March 2003, suggesting that the issue is not reducible to a particular policy lobby or identification of US security elites with the Jewish state. Again, true, but that just suggests the problem is larger. Why is America deferential to those smaller states and even as they support Islamist proxies, murder US journalists, or refuse to lower oil production at Washington's request? Why is America reluctant to coerce them, and why do those states evidently feel able to defy Washington's will at the same time? As President Bill Clinton muttered after being browbeaten by Israeli prime minister Benjamin Netanyahu, "Who's the fucking superpower here?" Who, indeed?

One answer is that this unwise behavior is meeting punishment. An excessive fear of being evicted and an overvaluing of partners as ends in themselves have led Washington into a suboptimal position whereby it is too scared to exert its influence, too reluctant to coerce, and therefore finds it too hard to get others to comply with its wishes, from Israel's intransigence over everything from illegal settlements to making ceasefires in its wars from Gaza to Lebanon. And we see this beyond Israel as well—for instance, in the case of Saudi Arabia's refusal to increase oil production. Another realist answer is that unipolarity and the absence of countervailing pressure on

America's power position freed up space for all sorts of domestically rooted lobbies, ideas, and causes to exert influence and, indeed, to take on excess commitments that invited punishment. But that runs counter to the usual pattern, as we will see in the next chapter, of smaller states only exerting influence when their patron is more constrained by other competitors. In principle, a realist worldview expects states at the apex of their power to be less patient and accommodating of their smaller allies and clients, not more. If unipolarity is the condition that confers otherwise puzzling levels of influence on small states, then realists have more work to do to understand the effects of unipolarity on the unipole.

Indeed, an emerging area of realist inquiry is precisely this—the paradox that the successful accumulation of power by the strongest states can cause them to lose sight of power realities, to mistake their international preeminence for a world permanently transformed, to become imprudent, and to be taken in by the flattery, duplicity, and demands of their clients. In that sense, realists need a sharper grasp of how the anarchic world can lead major states not to husband and apply power ruthlessly and well but rather foolishly.

For every realist failure of point prediction, like the failure to anticipate the timing and nature of the Cold War's end, there are more cases of realists correctly warning against overexcited longer-term prophecies that profound change is at hand. The Arab Spring revolts did not revolutionize the Middle East. Economic interdependence did not make Russia peaceful or China deferential to Western versions of international order and what the rules dictate. The internet and technology-driven global connectivity have not diluted nationalism. Likewise, cumulative changes from the primacy of commerce to the rise of civil society did not stop another period of blood and iron descending along the edges of America's domain in Eastern Europe, the Middle East, and northeastern Asia. Older patterns have reemerged, suggesting older traditions can help.

3 Realism Is for Everyone

IS REALISM JUST FOR THE WEST? Does it only serve the strong or a privileged few? Does the realist view—of an anarchic world that pressures states to be self-seeking and compete for security—just reflect the particular historical experience of the Euro-Atlantic, the Occident, or the "Global North"? Does it fathom world politics in its fundamentals as it is? Or is it merely a construct that misleads? And does realism work as an oppressive system of "colonial" or patriarchal knowledge or class privilege, dressed up as universal insight, that should be left behind?

These questions matter. If realism is time-bound and necessarily a Eurocentric or patriarchal enterprise, if its salience is limited to a particular moment or region in history and really just serves an overclass, its value is limited. If that is the case, it can't help us understand much of world politics in the past or today, especially as the center of wealth and power shifts away from the Euro-Atlantic West to the Indo-Pacific East. If a "decolonization mood" has recently arisen in IR, realists ought to respond to the suggestion that their intellectual tradition is inherently part of a colonial undertaking.[1] In this chapter, I argue realism is for everyone.[2] Via a tour of the horizon, I defend the tradition against two overlapping criticisms: that it is just for occidentals and that it serves only the demands of the powerful.

Before launching, a note of clarification: The issue here is not whether some realists, some of the time, have fallen prey to Eurocentrism or insularity. They have. Rather, the question is whether realism is *inherently* particular to one culture or *inherently* colonial, Eurocentric, or provincial. The accusation that realism and IR theory is inherently racist, patriarchal, or classist by virtue of its origins should be met head on.[3] There's no denying that realists—like other IR theorists—at times apply their theory narrowly. Western thinkers can be preoccupied with major power struggles either within the West or against large non-Western adversaries, showing too little curiosity about the world beyond the countries and regions they know, arguing only from a limited familiar universe of cases. It's likewise true that historically, some students of international politics have devoted their craft to serving orders founded on racial hierarchy. Indeed, IR as a discipline originated (partly) with overtly colonial assumptions. *Foreign Affairs*, the house organ of the transatlantic foreign policy establishment, was originally entitled *Journal of Race Development*. To the extent that antirealist criticism highlights how scholars may practice their craft in insular ways, it is a valuable correction.

It is a fallacy, though, to infer that realism is doomed *necessarily* to be culturally specific, only for the few, complicit in racism and/or patriarchy, and inapplicable to the wider world. To show a thing's (partial) origins and historical linkages is not to show its permanent essence. Realism is no more intrinsically part of a colonial project than modern chemistry is inherently based on alchemy. There are some ideas, I argue, that transcend cultural divides.

THE INDICTMENT: TOO PAROCHIAL, YET TOO IMPERIAL?

A number of voices accuse realism and established IR theory of being insular and colonial. Consider the accusation at its strongest. Race, argue Kelebogile Zvobgo and Meredith Loken,

> is a central organizing feature of world politics. Anti-Japanese racism guided and sustained U.S. engagement in World War II, and broader anti-Asian sentiment influenced the development and structure of the North Atlantic Treaty Organization. During the Cold War, racism and anti-communism were inextricably linked in the containment strategy that defined Washington's approach to Africa, Asia, Central America, the Caribbean, and South America. And today race shapes threat perception and responses to violent extremism, inside and outside the "war on terror." Yet mainstream international relations (IR) scholarship denies race as essential to understanding the world, to the cost of the field's integrity.
>
> Take the "big three" IR paradigms: realism, liberalism, and constructivism. These dominant frames for understanding global politics are built

on raced and racist intellectual foundations that limit the field's ability to answer important questions about international security and organization. Core concepts, like anarchy and hierarchy, are *raced*: They are rooted in discourses that center and favor Europe and the West. These concepts implicitly and explicitly pit "developed" against "undeveloped," "modern" against "primitive," "civilized" against "uncivilized." And their use is *racist*: These invented binaries are used to explain subjugation and exploitation around the globe.

While realism and liberalism were built on Eurocentrism and used to justify white imperialism, this fact is not widely acknowledged in the field. For instance, according to neorealists, there exists a "balance of power" between and among "great powers." Most of these great powers are, not incidentally, white-majority states, and they sit atop the hierarchy, with small and notably less-white powers organized below them. . . . Race and the racism of historical statecraft are inextricable from the modern study and practice of international relations.[4]

That this critique appeared in *Foreign Policy*, one of the leading academic-practitioner sites where IR and policy are in dialogue, reflects the fact that these arguments are gaining ground. Such claims also have an older history.

Several crises have reenergized this line of criticism, from the George Floyd–inspired protest against the police's racist violence of 2020 to Russia's invasion of Ukraine in 2022 to Israel's war in Gaza in 2023. Before that, the global war on terror, triggered by the 9/11 attacks in 2001, inspired similar allegations. Indeed, the denunciation of intellectuals for being complicit in colonialism derives also from the era of wars in Vietnam and Algeria, which inspired the doyens of postcolonial criticism, like Franz Fanon, Edward W. Said, and Aime Cesaire.

This issue is part of an older and wider argument about the proper relationship between scholars and power. As America geared up for war against Iraq in November 2002, Said took aim at court intellectuals and regional experts who betrayed their scholarly calling by helping provide the war's rationale. What purported to be a disinterested pursuit of understanding about the world, he noted, in fact served a campaign of "self-affirmation, belligerency, and outright war."[5] Said wasn't specifically attacking realists, nor did he deny the possibility of knowledge if it sprang from a humane spirit of understanding. But others in his footsteps put realists in the frame and developed a more radical complaint, objecting not only to realism but to the whole business of formulating universal theory. "Postcolonial" literature frames realism as part of the intellectual structure of Western colonialism. For Sanjay Seth, realism, with its fixation on sovereign states, perpetuates amnesia toward the reality of empire and thus is a "parochial," not a universal, form of knowledge[6]—parochial and, for many, serving not primarily scholarly knowledge but the will to dominate. For John M. Hobson, whereas premodern realists were straightforwardly racist, modern realists, like Carr, Morgenthau, and Waltz, were subliminally Eurocentric. Their claims were grounded in a parochial account of Western politics as world politics and part of an IR tradition dedicated primarily not to discovering the truth about international life but to Western aggrandizement and self-celebration.[7]

The notion that there is distinctly "Western" and "non-Western" International Relations theory is widespread.[8] From within the discipline of International Relations, scholars argue that their craft is so defined by coloniality that it needs to be overhauled from the roots. For Arlene Tickner, beyond standard IR theory, there is a distinct "third world knowledge" and hitherto marginalized scholarship that can redeem the discipline by correcting dominant understandings in the field across topics from war and conflict, the state, and sovereignty and autonomy to nationalism.[9] In the same spirit, there has arisen a school of "global IR" to reorient scholarship around the "multiplicity of the world," assuming the diversity of experience of the international, with a normative commitment to values of inclusiveness, plurality, and globality.[10]

It is not only realism or IR concepts that more radical critics target. In positioning themselves as "postpositivists," they also attack the very notion of pursing objective knowledge dispassionately. Those denouncing realism or IR's parochial qualities typically quote Robert W. Cox: "Theory is always for someone and some purpose."[11] They then go on to extend this logic ad absurdum to imply that theory—at least in mainstream forms—is so value-laden that it can't tell us much, because it reflects little more than self-interest and power. As Tickner puts it, the pursuit of value-neutral, rational, and instrumental knowledge is "culturally specific" to the West given that "human thought has no shared foundations."[12] If so, if the very act of seeking the truth is a parochial Western activity, and if it is the struggle over power rather than truth seeking that lies at the root of scholarship, then the task is to enter that fray and emancipate the oppressed from the oppressor.

There is a glaring contradiction in this outlook. It asserts as a universal truth claim that universal truth claims cannot be made. Notice, too, an assumption implicit in the idea of non-Western knowledge. This comes close to the reductionist and essentializing argument of Samuel P. Huntington: that there are separate, almost primordial civilizations with built-in and different ways of knowing, making rational, instrumental means-ends thought only for Westerners.[13] Indeed, Tickner cites Huntington's demarcation of civilizational knowledge systems approvingly.[14] If this is postcolonial analysis, it is more "colonial" than "post."

From another direction, "strategic-culture" literature (and constructivist literature alike) finds realism too materialist. For those in these camps, behavior in the realm of security has primarily ideational and cultural sources.[15] If the concept of culture encompasses the things humans make to mediate between themselves and their environment, culturalists aver that identities and inherited ideas about security, force, or order weigh more strongly than material factors in shaping how polities interact with the world. From this vantage point, too, realism, with its emphasis on material power, on the similarity of polities, and the primary role of external pressure, is largely a Eurocentric conceit that cannot account for variations in behavior across different societies. In one historian's sweeping dismissal, culturalist literature reveals "just how little the Western norms considered universal under realist theories matter in determining the actions of non-Western states."[16]

The critique that realism is ethnocentric and therefore oblivious to important cultural differences is associated these days most often with the political Left, in particular its postcolonial and anti-imperialist wings. But there are also centrist and right-leaning hawkish versions, articulated by muscular conservatives and liberal hawks. Some "hardliners" also emphasize the central importance of cultural difference, albeit from a more adversarial perspective. They are often positioned at the intersection between the national security state and academia. They argue that realism is fundamentally flawed given that traditional identities and regime type drive state behavior. For them, realism, especially post–Cold War realism, is generally too restrained. Realism, they allege, is not only analytically flawed, overlooking fundamental differences of regime type; it is also morally flawed in its pursuit of stability over justice, too readily accommodating hostile states' imperialism and too solicitous of their security demands. Like imperial Japan, revolutionary Iran and post-Soviet Russia are better seen primarily as unstable, intrinsically aggressive, status-obsessed, and risk-acceptant regimes, not as typical nation-states that can be deterred and bargained with.

These voices include Cold War "deterrence skeptics," such as Colin S. Gray and Richard Pipes, who contended that Western policies and attitudes toward adversaries were founded on naive assumptions about their similarity. Confidence that Washington could sustain a stable state of mutual nuclear deterrence and bind the competition in the Cold War relied too much on the West mirror-imaging opponents, like the Soviet Union (and, later, Iran), when those opponents in fact thought differently. History and a tradition of autocracy, they argued, made the Soviets more predisposed to going on the offensive preemptively, more cost tolerant, more risk prone, and more prepared to fight and win a nuclear war.[17] Since they doubted the ultimate deterrability of Moscow, the skeptics therefore opposed many arms control measures, détente talks, and efforts to maintain "crisis stability" by self-restraint, from the Nixon-Kissinger realignment with the communist world in the early 1970s to the last days of the Soviet Union, when President George H. W. Bush distanced Washington from nationalists in Eastern Europe.

A coalition of "Vulcans" in the post–Cold War "interregnum" then took up the same worldview of a clash with deadly, dissimilar, and irreconcilable enemies and applied it to the "rogue states" that followed the Soviet dragon, like Saddam Hussein's Iraq. Unlike postcolonial culturalists, these culturalists were often close to power as the United States reached the apex of its global preeminence. Their ideas were embodied in the expansive "Bush doctrine" of 2002, with its vision of Washington pursuing security via sponsoring democratic regime change, maintaining overwhelming military dominance, and waging anticipatory war. More recently, they and their heirs mounted a critique of US policy toward Vladimir Putin's Russia and Xi Jinping's China. In particular, they target the caution of American presidents, whether Barak Obama's attempt to wind back Iran's nuclear program with sanctions and accords or Joe Biden's approach to limiting arms to Ukraine in its struggle against Russia and placing conditions on their use. Now, as then, hawks argue that the stability-seeking repertoire of deterrence and containment is based on faulty assumptions about enemies' values and pathologies. Instead of falling back on deterrence and containment, they insist, confrontation and rollback are needed.[18]

For this stream of antirealism, realists are wrong about the main source of polities' behavior. They believe it is not principally international anarchy and its external pressures that make the world go around. It is states' domestic inner life. Strategy is made at home. And "home" is analytically prior to the international, which emerges from the interaction of domestically rooted units. Because authoritarian regimes are inherently volatile and expansionist, they reason, to seek security through stability and the status quo is to encourage further instability and hand a dangerous advantage to unscrupulous foes. Other cultures and their regimes are different; they do not value stability like "we" do, and therefore, the West must prepare to fight and win nuclear wars. In contrast to realists, for whom war is ultimately a tragic biproduct of structure, of anarchy with its built-in insecurity, for others, war is primarily generated by the agency of warlike players and others' failure to confront them. In the words of David Adesnik, a proponent of American primacy and democracy promotion, "Great wars happen because dangerous men want them to."[19]

Hardliners share some of the realist worldview that the world is dangerously anarchic and requires militarized self-help. Indeed, they claim to be the true "realists," offering a more realistic realism than the realism offered in the academy.[20] But they reject the suggestion that most polities are similar when put under similar circumstances, assume the sources of behavior are primarily domestic, believe the world is more one of dominoes and bandwagoning than balancing, believe that prudence requires the pursuit of regime change and transformation, and have a lower threshold for striking enemies first. In that worldview, there is no substitute for shows of strength and victory, which are also the safest route to peace. Thus, the "strategic-culture" paradigm, with its stress on cultural diversity and a rejection of realism's assumption of universality, can make minds more warlike, not less.

What's at stake here? The issue is not whether those who rule have preferences that derive from memories, education, folklore, or collective experience. Of course, they do. People are not automated machines. The issue is how resilient these codes, taboos, or identities prove to be when conditions change, when pressure bears down, and when incentives for survival drive in different directions than the given culture. An aversion to arms, proliferation, alliances, or war can seem both noble and prudent until neighboring states rattle their sabers or mobilize on the border. Conversely, a predisposition toward risk-taking military adventurism can seem attractive until other powers credibly threaten to resist. Groups may have their cultural peculiarities, but are they willing to suffer high costs to maintain those cultures, or will they bend pragmatically to the imperatives of anarchy?

For culturalists, there is too much anomalous activity that realism cannot explain, like the absence of power balancing where we might expect it or the operation of stable hierarchy rather than war-prone anarchy. We cannot fathom, say, postwar German or Japanese behavior without the powerful ingredient of antimilitarist culture, as domestic and ideational variables bear heavily.[21] Similarly, culturalists argue that realism is alien to regions neglected in IR, like Africa, and that realist analysis is part of the problem.[22] We hear, too, that realism cannot cope with countries that are impelled by powerful self-identities—identities that link how they see foreign relations with who they are. Self-proclaimed Islamic republics, such as Pakistan and Iran, present themselves as instruments of faith. They claim, as do external observers, that their fidelity to Islam is the basis of their external policies, from choice of allegiance to nuclear doctrine.[23]

India, too, attracts arguments that realpolitik doesn't offer much explanatory payoff. The accounts vary, as culturalists assign different weight to various sources of India's statecraft. They emphasize elements such as its Hindu heritage, historic geographical fragmentation, civic tradition of disciplined nonviolence, sense of "morally derived self-restraint," and self-assigned role as the world's spiritual and moral tutor.[24] Taken together, they claim these influences make India averse to hard-nosed strategic thinking and theorizing, predisposed against the use of force, oriented away from the urgent short term and toward the long haul, resistant to war-prone alliances in its tradition of "strategic autonomy," committed to international institutions, predisposed toward peaceful conflict resolution, and reluctant and slow in its development of nuclear weapons even when it had the means.[25]

Such claims about India are also articulated by the country's leaders to define it against the power politics of other states, from the founder Prime Minister Jawaharlal Nehru to today's premier, Narendra Modi. While Indian commentators and participants disagree over just how much India *ought* to adopt more self-seeking realpolitik, a consensus emerged that India traditionally was disinclined to it. India is also an awkward case for claiming that a continuous coherent strategic culture operates. As a vast, ancient country of multiplicities, it also has its own tradition of homegrown realpolitik, as we will see.

Culturalists may be generally critical of Samuel Huntington's account of civilizations colliding. Yet they share his baseline assumption that the dominant source of decision-making is cultural. Whether the focus is on perceived "ancient hatreds" of blood and religion around the Caspian littoral or in the Balkans, more recent battlefields in Central Asia or Eastern Europe, or modern pacific idealism in postwar Asia, the arguments boil down to the same thing: realism doesn't get us far for it overstates the strength of material interests in shaping foreign policy. Where realists see convergence, similarity, and flexibility in state behavior, with states picking, choosing, and reinventing their repertoires expediently, culturalists see divergence, difference, and the prevalence of traditions that are hard to shake off.

The most frequent and popular case for culturalist arguments, however, is China and its perceived "Confucian" ways. China, from this vantage point, has a supposedly "unique strategic culture, which is more peaceful and nonviolent than the realpolitik Western one."[26] For many of those who claim realism cannot adequately comprehend China's international behavior, the main source of China's behavior is the legacy of Confucius, transmitted by his discipline Mencius, instilled through the education of the country's ancient civil service bureaucracy, and championed by China's governments. This historic worldview allegedly creates an aversion to force, offensive strategies, and expansion. It does so by stressing moral restraints and the primacy of defense and nonviolent measures—a preference for attracting and influencing others via a largely noncoercive tributary system, ethical governance, and the allure of its majesty. Supposedly, all this is symbolized in the defensive fortification of the Great Wall. In fact, the very construction of the Great Wall was an aggressive imperial act. It was free to build on only once Qin rulers forcibly expelled the Rong and Di tribes from their own land.[27] Irenic claims about China's strategic culture turn out to be distant from the historical record.

Culturalists argue that this "unique" culture also informs its nuclear-weapons posture—one of minimum deterrence, rarely if ever put onto high alert, optimized for reassurance and stability by separating warheads from missiles, and deployed under a No First Use doctrine.[28] When China does draw its sword, or so the arguments go, it does so only defensively, reluctantly, and in a spirit of virtuous self-control. This has important implications for today. If realism doesn't account well for China, China is unlikely to behave like a revisionist power, vying for primacy in its region or beyond, and pessimistic realist expectations that a relative power shift will trigger a collision between Beijing and Washington are ill founded.[29]

Arguments for a particular Chinese way of strategy and statecraft vary in their sophistication. Alastair Iain Johnston's more subtle account perceives a dual tradition in China's strategic culture and rich body of texts about warfare and statecraft, whereby there is room for both antirealpolitik and realpolitik. Confucian idealism jostles with a harder-nosed alternative tradition, a willingness to project power offensively. Johnston, though, still argues that Chinese realism, too, has primarily cultural roots.[30] The simpler, more selective thesis of "Confucian pacifism," or at least reluctance, is a popular one not only amongst some China-observers but also amongst Chinese officials, security elites, and commentators.[31] Cunning minds will detect why the idea is politically useful. If China is inherently nonaggressive and nonimperial and only fights to defend itself and when it is forced to, its wars must be defensive, nonimperial, and legitimate.

There is a more ambitious "macro" version of the thesis of Chinese peculiarity or Asian difference. David Kang extends the logic to Asia as a whole, past and present. For Kang, there is an Asian strategic culture that historically produced a more hierarchical, more peaceful, and more stable region. Realists' preoccupation with power transitions, disequilibrium, and resulting struggles between status quo and revisionist states in the tradition of a rising Athens clashing with a declining Sparta reflects a distinctively European experience. It is not Asia's fate to endure militarized power struggle, Kang contends, given its historical predisposition toward less volatile, less interrupted commercial relations. Kang echoes the central logic of China's tributary empire of peaceful hierarchy. As he puts it, "Thucydides didn't live in Asia."[32]

Given these self-flattering images of a state's unique culture appeal to—and are invoked by—elites of those countries, this should put us on our guard. Ironically, claiming to be essentially peaceful and uniquely benign, possessed of a longer-term wisdom and reluctant to use violence because of some cultural DNA is typical of great power exceptionalism.[33] Recall Madeleine Albright's notorious statement at the apex of America's unipolar dominance when asked about the campaign of economic sanctions on Iraq and their humanitarian impact: "If we have to use force, it is because we are America. We are the indispensable nation. We stand tall, and we see further than other countries into the future."[34] Such talk provides an alibi and a warrant for projecting power coercively. It makes rulers feel virtuous and important as they do it. It's an appealing marketing device. It is how most major powers talk about themselves even as they throw their weight around. Ancient and modern superpowers don't speak exactly the same way, but they rhyme. As Edward Said noted, "Every single empire in its official discourse has said that it is not like all the others, that its circumstances are special, that it has a mission to enlighten, civilize, bring order and democracy, and that it uses force only as a last resort."[35] If so, this holds for Ottomans as well as the Orange-Nassau, Mughals as well as Victorians, Mings as well as Bonapartes. It would be the height of methodological naivete to take rulers' claims about their peaceful cultures at face value.

Another version of antirealist criticism, the "bad-genealogy" version, has recently resurfaced. To challenge the idea that realism is ancient and universally applicable, this approach undertakes intellectual archaeology to expose realism for being relatively recent, bound up with Western empire building, and therefore redundant, unnecessary, and pernicious. Aaron Beers Sampson, for instance, argues that the central concept of anarchy is a misleading and regressive trope rather than a real state of affairs.[36] Targeting the theory of Kenneth Waltz, he shows Waltz's account of anarchy derived from an image of African politics as "primitive" that was propagated by British social anthropologists of the interwar period who wrote to guide colonial administrators. Just as the primitiveness of African politics was an invention that anthropologists had cast off, so too was international anarchy a false construct better left behind. It reinforced an offensive binary logic of primitive versus civilized, privileging power over progress, equilibrium over change, and preventive measures over curative ones.

The most sustained and sophisticated form of genealogy hunting comes from Matthew Specter. For him, realism is a relatively recent invention, an intellectual construct born out of nineteenth-century Anglo-German imperialism and the dark imaginations of empire-minded geopolitical thinkers, like Karl Haushofer, the anti-Semitic historian of realpolitik Friedrich Meinecke, and overt Nazis, like the jurisprude Carl Schmitt, then transmitted to the United States via European émigrés like Hans J. Morgenthau to be inherited and turned into a pseudoscientific ideology in our time by John Mearsheimer.[37] In this telling, realism's claims to antiquity are overblown. Realism, for the genealogy-hunting school, is a latecomer, and it is intellectually and morally impoverished because it is fruit of a poisoned tree, tainted by fascism and part of the intellectual foundations of a brutish empire.

Vladimir Putin's invasion of Ukraine in February 2022 gave added energy to this line of criticism. Some realists argue—to varying extents—that Russia's attack was not simply a gratuitous lunge by a greedy state but also reactive to Western and NATO-EU overenlargement, the brutal pursuit of a secure buffer and more or less typical of great powers fearing encroachment. The only way out, for these realists, would have been to strike an early deal with Moscow.

The political economist Adam Tooze, drawing on Specter and deploying the genealogy literature, treats Mearsheimer as representative of all realists. He deplores Mearsheimer's treatment of the Ukraine invasion as an act of mere security seeking rather than imperial aggrandizement. Not only are realists too indulgent of Russian imperialism, but also they too readily naturalize war and expansionism at a time when we should be treating war as a "radical and perilous act."[38] Tooze's generalization from one prominent realist is inaccurate, as it happens, given other realists, from William C. Wohlforth to this author, judge that Russia is both a greedy state and a security seeker, and such realists support balancing against it in Ukraine by arming and supporting the defenders. More fundamentally, Tooze loses sight of realism's other roots beyond the modern and the Anglo-German. In reality, the likes of Carl Schmidt and Karl Haushofer have been marginal at best in realist circles, rarely invoked and even less frequently debated, far less than the historical examples of British and continental European statecraft.[39] And Tooze, as we shall see, misses the complexity of realism's relationship with war. In most forms of realism, the fear of armed conflict sits alongside the imperative to prepare for it. If there are ideologues in the marketplace who need reminding that war is a "radical and perilous act," it is not realists who are most in need of the correction.

And so antirealist criticism ranges far and wide. Taken together, it becomes confusingly contradictory and, at times, unreflective. Realists allegedly are oblivious to empire and its hierarchies, wedded to a mythologized era of autonomous "Westphalian" states, making them blind to the reality of luckless peoples denied autonomy by oppressors at home or abroad. Yet they are also too imperial, apparently too comfortable with orders in which the strong dominate the weak, curtailing or crushing their sovereignty and carving out oppressive spheres of influence. Realists are said to be part of a colonial project, but why? Because in their universalist pretensions, they don't understand that non-Western cultures are essentially different and incapable of realpolitik and averse to rational, instrumental power politics, which is supposedly only for Westerners. That Westerners have cold-reasoning calculation and that "Others" have emotion, spirit, and spirituality is a "noble savage" variant of a regressively colonial worldview. Who exactly, we are entitled to ask, is being colonial here? This mess of complaints warrants cold demolition.

OCCIDENTALS ONLY? REALISM BEYOND THE WEST

Realism is not particular to the West. Its ideas and/or practices take root or travel in other parts of the world, including in cultures where it is supposedly alien and inapplicable. This is not to say that non-Western states are always calculating, instrumental, and skilled in their statecraft. Like Western powers, other things like ideology, ruler personality, and domestic politics can intervene. The point, rather, is that realism—as both a generally accurate account of behavior and a springboard to appraise policy—is mainstream and widespread beyond the Euro-Atlantic.

To get one issue straight, realists do not presuppose that sovereign "Westphalian" states are the only form of polity that matters, do not assume they were always the organizing basis for international politics in the past, are not blind to empire or its history, and don't assume the future is postimperial. Waltz, in his critique of Leninism, observes that empire is "at least as old as recorded history."[40] Robert Gilpin's *War and Change in World Politics* mentions empire thirty-one times as he argues that "a theory of international political change must also be a theory of imperialism and political integration."[41] Gilpin's central unit was not necessarily the state in the way we mean nowadays, narrowly defined, but the "conflict group."[42] Gilpinian realism, indeed, lays more stress on hierarchies and imperial orders than Waltz, who draws more narrowly from the post-seventeenth-century European system.

Realism, or intelligent versions of it, does expect aggregate similarities of behavior. It does not expect or depend upon uniform types of political organization. Tribes, city-states, nation-states, empires, or just gangs in a stateless postapocalyptic world will take different shapes, sizes, and borders, make different laws, with boundaries that are strong or porous. Rather, realists expect the underlying dynamics of an anarchic world to recast themselves in different contexts and for conflict groups to function in equivalent ways.

Errol Henderson, for instance, demonstrates that postcolonial African states practiced realist statecraft of a sort, not primarily via the formal state institutions of uniformed armies and clearly defined territorial borders but through a more informal "neopatrimonial" model of sponsoring insurgents through cross-border patronage networks—a form of conflict that reflects the legacy of empire.[43] Leaders nervous at home used their militaries to patrol or suppress within while turning to other fighting groups to project power without. Colonialism institutionalized particular political practices while anarchy created competitive pressure. Beyond racist Eurocentric versions of IR, which overlook Africa as a source of theory, there is a more transnational model to be found. As another author recognizes, to segregate Africa from what is assumed to be an essentially European realism is also to partake of a distorting essentialism, to exoticize Africa as lying passively outside the scope of theory.[44] Repudiating other work that claims realism is inapplicable to Africa, Henderson offers a "modified" African realism.

Let's now respond to the arguments of Zvobgo and Loken. They, like John M. Hobson, claim that realism is Eurocentric and colonial by design, that it almost uniformly neglects nonwhite great powers, and that its core concepts of anarchy and hierarchy are intrinsically racial. The charge of neglect is overdrawn. Histories inspired by realist logic, like Paul Kennedy's *The Rise and Fall of the Great Powers*, assign importance both to imperial Japan and its consequential bid for power in mainland and maritime Asia and to modern Japan with its potential industrial and military power.[45] Stephen M. Walt's account of power balancing makes extensive use of the alliance choices and threat perceptions of Gulf states as actors, not just subjects. Cold War realists like Morgenthau emphasize the significance of the Sino-Soviet split and Anwar Sadat's Egypt in reshuffling the deck of international politics. Hobson suggests Morgenthau naturalizes the Western empire. Perhaps so but not because it was Western. The same Morgenthau presciently foresaw the growth of Asian states and Asian nuclear proliferation, fusing nationalism with modern technology, "especially in the nuclear field," "which until recently have been a virtual monopoly of the West," resulting in a changing distribution of power.[46] There is nothing natural or guaranteed about Western preeminence here. To dismiss Morgenthau as just a Western supremacist, fixated on Europe as the global pivot, is not a radical insight. It is just empirically false. Today, American realists hardly neglect modern-day China but focus on it as a near-peer adversary. And this is to say nothing of non-Western realisms. In the mid 1990s, before China resurged as a major power, one close observer interviewed dozens of civilian and military analysts in Beijing, concluding China was the "high church of realpolitik."[47] If anything, attitudes since then have hardened.[48]

It is one thing to claim that racism influenced and influences Western foreign policy; it is quite another to elevate it into the essential determining force. The claim that race is decisive in twentieth-century US policy in Asia is distorting. While Americans, like others, have attached racist attitudes to foreign affairs, racism fails to explain some significant wartime and postwar policies. Anti-Asian hostility did not prevent Washington adopting a "Germany-first" war strategy. Incidentally, white and Christian-majority Germany was the initial intended target of the atomic bomb. And while mutual racist brutality helped define the fighting of the Pacific War, cold calculation could trump it, which can be seen from Harry Truman's refusal to bomb the sacred site of Kyoto to postconflict famine-relief efforts. The lens of race fails to explain US aid to China before the Pearl Harbor attack, its pressure on the United Kingdom to supply China during the war, or its efforts to include China as one of the "Big Four" in the Cairo wartime conference. The explanatory lens of racism does not account for the pan-cultural heterogeneity of US Cold War alliances, from Turkey's membership in NATO to the creation of the Southeast Asia Treaty Organization and US partnerships in South Korea, Taiwan, South Vietnam, and Indonesia. This suggests, prima facie, that calculations about material strength, wise or unwise, carry more weight and more consistently explain US behavior.[49]

And notice, too, the leap of logic: because racist people in the past were drawn to ideas like anarchy or hierarchy and used them to justify Western dominance and exploitation, those ideas are inextricably racist. We return to a recurrent question: Must intellectual traditions be defined by pointing out some of their historic connections? Must they be ideologically pure at the point of origin to be useful? If realism is inherently objectionable because some realists, like Morgenthau, derived some of their worldview from Carl Schmitt, does that make modern feminism objectionable given some leading suffragettes who helped create modern feminism were also bellicose nationalists and some, interwar fascists?

If suggesting that the world has a power hierarchy—that some countries are larger and more powerful than others and use that power disparity to subordinate and coerce them—is an inherently "raced" thing to do, where does that put those on the receiving end of those hierarchies, some of whom also find realist ideas useful? Missing in action here is the reception and revival of realism and realist texts by Asians, Africans, and Latin Americans, as well as the evidence of indigenous realism, whether written up or just acted out. The very study of International Relations beyond the West arose because there was an appetite and a market for academics and donors to reach.[50] For their part, Chinese scholars and policymakers translate, consume, and debate Thucydides as a prudential political thinker whose work might suggest broader patterns in international politics and yield insights into building a rising state in a hostile world.[51] China's most senior general, Xu Qiliang, recently invoked the theory of the "Thucydides trap."[52] Likewise, Chinese IR scholars have translated and published canonical realist works of modern America—Morgenthau, Gilpin, and Waltz—in a robust debate between "peace-and-development" and "war-and-revolution" camps, with a rate of publication second only to Marxist-Leninist literature.[53] As in the West, the appeal to realism is contentious, but the salience of the text in modern China throws doubt on the argument that realism is reducible to Eurocentric chauvinism. Not to consider the text's enthusiastic reception in "the East" or "the South" while declaring it irrelevant in those places reflects an unacknowledged Eurocentrism. Thucydides did not live in Asia, but Xu Qiliang does.

Likewise, attempts to isolate modern realism to a narrow recent intellectual stream of modern colonialism do not survive interrogation. Take Sampson's argument that since Waltz borrowed concepts from anthropology to formulate his version of anarchy, anarchy in realism is intrinsically "tropical" and derives from an outmoded interwar anthropology. Waltz may have been the most systematic elaborator of the idea of anarchy in modern time, arguing that the absence of a central authority both enabled and encouraged conflict, but he was not its sole founder.[54] The idea of anarchy has an older pedigree.[55] Its proponents did not all use Waltzian vocabulary or sources. Yet they advanced the same essential idea, less systemically than Waltz, and their intellectual stimuli varied well beyond interwar anthropology. If they were all galvanized by a political concern, it was not a preoccupation with colonizing the "primitive." It was the shock of world wars and the failure of interwar international diplomacy and institutions to check the rise of totalitarian threats.

Writing in this shadow, there were realists on both sides of the Atlantic who emphasized structure and the need for self-help, who wrote before or independently of Waltz's first theoretical work, *Man, the State, and War* (1954).[56] In his 1939 work *The Twenty Years' Crisis* and his lectures beforehand, E. H. Carr, a realist and socialist enthusiast for collective planning, chided idealists for supposing the League of Nations could supplant power politics.[57] Carr, in turn, was inspired partly by pastor and prophet Reinhold Niebuhr, whose account of the inherent insecurity of humanity synthesized Augustinian pessimism, Marxist structuralism, and antipacifist progressivism. While the young Waltz was preparing to be deployed as a soldier to the Pacific theater, Nicholas J. Spykman concluded his 1942 treatise on America's need to thwart totalitarian bids for Eurasian mastery by unambiguously noting the lack of an international central authority and the resulting need for states to preserve or improve their power position.[58] The following year, Walter Lippmann issued his manifesto for a coherent American statecraft linking means and ends, arguing that the inability to control other states' actions meant that the true "shield of the republic" could not be the mirages of disarmament, pacifism, or collective security but prudent and armed power politics.[59] Lippmann did not need to extract ideas from anthropologists. He drew on his own personal disillusionment with the promise of Woodrow Wilson's program for war prevention—a program he had helped author. In 1949, Hans J. Morgenthau, Weimar lawyer and Jewish refugee from Nazi Germany, drew on both early-republican American and nineteenth-century British historical examples to argue that the absence of a protecting agency to stand guard meant that "what is euphemistically called the society of nations differs fundamentally from national societies."[60]

Dismissals of "anarchy" as a value-laden construct drawn from anthropology do not succeed even on their own terms given the various pathways and influences that led realists to converge on it as a baseline idea. And the claim that the concept of anarchy is a mere construct runs up against reality. The simple fact remains that anarchy still looks like a very real condition. It is hard to argue that there is or can be a global Leviathan to stand sentry, enforce rules, and keep the peace. There never was one. And it would be wildly difficult to create one as it would require the acquisition of such a preponderance of power that it would appear very threatening and trigger counterbalancing. We can recognize that there is no supreme authority to enforce the peace without importing racist judgements about who or what is primitive. Anarchy is an absence, and that is what the concept means etymologically—the absence of an archon, or ruler. If this is wrong, who or what does or can serve as this agency?

Nor is this a point that just privileges the experience of the powerful. It is a painful reality for those on the receiving end of violent expansion. When Mesoamerica fell under the brunt of the conquistadores and the inhabitants of Tenochtitlán watched the conquerors lay waste to their city or when Australian indigenes saw British settler-colonials arrive with weapons and diseases or when Azerbaijan ethnically cleansed Armenians in Nagorno-Karabakh, the locals surely noticed no one was intervening to help. There was no committed earthly authority to appeal to for deliverance. In recognizing this simple tragic fact, were they too falling prey to bigoted "tropical" ideas about anarchy or just seeing the world for what it is?

Realism does not derive primarily or even mostly from relatively recent projects of Euro-Atlantic colonialism. Thucydides's history of the ancient Peloponnesian War is not centered on race or race hierarchy. It studies and laments a cataclysmic conflict mostly within a culture—a civil war within the Hellenic world that depleted and debased that world—one Thucydides participated in as a failed and exiled admiral. If there was a feared oriental "Other" to fixate over, it was Achaemenid Persia, but if anything, the Athenian Thucydides neglected that actor in writing up the war as a largely intramural Greek tragedy. Eighteen hundred years later, Niccolò Machiavelli developed his own realism in the context of clashing Italian city-states. The central animating concern in *The Prince*, apart from his own career advancement, was not to draw up a theory-driven manifesto for the conquest of the New World; it was to tutor Florentine rulers in the bleak realities of power, since the neglect of power had left the city vulnerable to predation at the hands of local rivals and the larger European kingdoms of France, Germany, and Spain. As Thucydides and Machiavelli plied their trade, they did so from a position of weakness. Earlier versions of Western colonialism existed, but it was well before their own polities were powerful enough to dominate parts of Asia or Africa. It was the liberation and autonomy of their cities and their power position in their neighborhood, not subjugating the globe, which concerned them.

Nor is it the case that most realists uncritically and fatalistically accept war as a policy. After all, it was predominantly realists of the time who led the intellectual case against the calamitous invasion of Iraq, as did many of their forbears over Vietnam. A group of academics, led by eminent realists, took out an advertisement in the *New York Times* in October 2002 with a prudential appeal to the limits of American power, the dangers of attacking an already fractured society, and the likelihood of insurgent resistance.[61] They were following in the footsteps of Morgenthau, opponent of the Vietnam War and critic of Nixon-Kissinger coups in South America. Morgenthau was hardly a trojan horse for colonialist sentiment at home or abroad. As a Jewish émigré and target of racial abuse himself, he defined the national interest partly as the pursuit of a more egalitarian and just social order at home through his opposition to racial segregation and support for civil rights.[62] If such realists were or are in the grip of crypto-fascism or colonial hubris, they have an odd way of showing it.

Realists often have a hawkish view of the defenses a country needs but often accompany this with a narrow and cautious view of its value and a fear of using it. The pursuit of security and an aversion to messianic and expansive views of war are parts of realism's canon. So too is a pessimistic view that large states tend to insist on maintaining their regional spheres, reasonably or not. The émigré intellectuals who regarded themselves as the descendants of ancient and medieval realists, the likes of Morgenthau and Zbigniew Brzezinski, fled European fascism and tried to educate the republic that had suddenly risen to become a colossus. Along with homegrown but worldly pessimists like George Kennan, they objected to what they saw as the naive Wilsonianism of American International Relations, with its enthusiasm for international institutions and other transformative devices, such as the outlawing of war, international tribunals, or excessively moralistic and reckless crusades to overthrow evil ideologies. They warned that this progressive optimism and its schemes could not guard against totalitarian menaces and could trigger catastrophe. Their watchword was not "war" but "deterrence" and "preparation."

Let's now assess the claim that realism does a bad job of explaining the behavior of polities outside the Euro-Atlantic orbit and that those polities are impelled by fundamentally different culturally rooted instincts. On closer inspection, this thesis collapses. It is untrue of India. Indian rulers like Nehru and Modi talk a good game about India's higher, more peaceable, and restrained statecraft in contrast with Western realpolitik. Yet for all the exceptionalist rhetoric, under pressure, Indian rulers relax the strictures their culture lays down for them and more or less do as they please.[63] As India's neighbors and more perceptive students of India's statecraft realize, even while it preaches nonintervention and the sanctity of sovereignty against interference, Delhi intervenes at will to coerce and assert its own sphere of influence. Nehru, the champion of international law and nonviolent measures, militarily annexed Goa in 1961, postwar norms against conquest be damned, while warning external powers against stepping in. India unapologetically waged a counterinsurgency campaign in Sri Lanka from 1983 to 1990 and deployed special forces in the Maldives in 1988 to suppress a coup by mercenaries. It blockaded Nepal in 1989–1990 after it decided to buy weapons from China. It fought a war with China in 1962 and four wars with Pakistan in 1947–1948, 1965, 1971, and 1999. It launched raids across the Pakistan border, whether against Mizo insurgents or its neighbors' military outposts across the inviolate Line of Control. It agitated for the overriding value of human rights in South Africa while granting special status to Jammu and Kashmir, which it keeps under martial law in defiance of UN resolutions calling for a plebiscite. Hardline power politics thrives on the subcontinent.

And these glaring inconsistencies took place when India was relatively weak compared to major powers. In the Modi era, as India got richer and more populous, it has intensified both internal and external balancing, converting its resources into hard military power while remorselessly wielding coercive force. Even while Modi emphasizes the need to decolonize his country of British names, rituals, and insignia, he exercises a prerogative to override others' sovereignty and with a more robust "offensive-defense" strategy that pays less heed to the Line of Control.[64] It has engaged in brinksmanship with Pakistan multiple times, including in February 2019 over Kashmir, when Modi threatened Islamabad with a "night of murder." India also expanded its military presence along its border with China in a confrontation that heightened in the Galwan Valley clashes in eastern Ladakh in June 2020. It has circumscribed its commitment to aloof autonomy once again by strengthening security ties with the United States on its maritime front as part of the four-power "Quad" (referring to the "quadrilateral security dialogue" along with Australia and Japan). A stronger India is more risk acceptant. According to the US director of national intelligence, "India is more likely than in the past to respond with military force to perceived or real Pakistani provocations."[65] It allegedly sponsors Baloch insurgents against Pakistan, though this is disputed. Like the American superpower whose unilateral, unmandated targeted-assassination programs that internationalists and sovereigntists deplore, India now carries out "wet jobs" abroad of its own.[66] It does so in territory across the border and beyond. In June 2023, it liquidated Sikh separatist and terrorist suspect Hardeep Singh Nijaar in Canada. And like America, India has fashioned its own permissive doctrine to support extrajudicial killings—one of contingent sovereignty, whereby India may strike a country unwilling or unable to rein in terrorist activities on its soil.[67] We are a long way from Gandhi.

India's internal and external balancing may not necessarily succeed. The country remains reliant on Russian military technology, has far to go in developing its own defense-industrial base, and contends with adversaries on multiple fronts.[68] Realists expect that countries like a growing India will try to balance even if balancing can fail. It inhabits a dangerous neighborhood facing increasingly heavily armed countries with ruthless security services and a worrisome Chinese-Russian rapprochement. In this world, none of India's more violent and destabilizing activities makes it especially wicked, just unexceptional.

As for India's perceived reluctance to acquire the bomb, even this point is contentious. This is not the place for an in-depth account of India's proliferation. Suffice it to say, a cultural preference against acquiring genocidal weapons may have exerted some effect, but it was modest and never prohibitive. Prenuclear India kept the proliferation door open and studiously kept a free hand, refusing to sign the Non-Proliferation Treaty of 1968. India's delay in deciding to go nuclear after China's nuclear test of 1964, despite having the capacity to do so, was three years. That's a delay but a brief one.

Nuclear refusal and hedging, under pressure, then became nuclear minimalism, matching China's small arsenal. In the face of external pressure from an adversary, India crossed the threshold. And in the face of a growing proxy conflict with Pakistan in Kashmir in 1998, it made its nuclear deterrent more overt with tests. Today, nuclear minimalism is yielding to nuclear enlargement. Delhi has added new delivery systems to create a triad of platforms operating from air, sea, and land. Realism doesn't account for all the twists and turns in India's nuclear evolution. But it is a stronger "first cut" than an ideational account, which, at best, is supplementary.

Cultures themselves are conflicted and multiple things, serving more as weapons than as scripts. The elephant in the room, so to speak, is the other side of India's repertoire. India has its own rich tradition of realpolitik in practice and in theory. India boasts Kautilya (375–283 BC), author of *Arthashastra*, one of the earliest and seminal realist texts, albeit a particularly pitiless and cold variety but with a "mandala" account of concentric circles of adversaries and allies that anticipated later "balance-of-power" theory. Kautilya was also tutor to the ruler Chandragupta Maurya, who overthrew the incumbent ruler, fought Hellenist invaders to a standstill, and established a dynasty. Neglected during the Gandhi and Nehru eras, this materialist, pragmatic strain of thought—one potent enough for Modi to invoke in support of his "neighborhood-first" diplomacy—was then revived in Indian intellectual life.[69] As some observers argue, the antiquity of this tradition means we should not so much regard Kautilya as the Asian Machiavelli but rather Machiavelli as the European Kautilya.[70] Indeed, there is a more historically grounded and perceptive criticism of established IR theory that insists precisely not that realism is insular to the West but that Asians got there first.[71] This case demonstrates that realism can be indigenous to non-Western cultures.

In a similar way, the history of strategic thought and practice in China, too, is copious. To depict China as intrinsically defensive minded, skeptical of violence, and lacking imperial ambition is not only wrong but innocent. It would be instructive to try that argument out on countries in China's vicinity who at times have felt the self-styled Middle Kingdom's lash in Vietnam, Tibet, South Korea, Taiwan, or Thailand. China has also felt the lash, of course, especially at the hands of predatory European empires and Japan's assault in the mid-twentieth century. Part of China's historical memory today is its sense of victimhood and, like all major powers, entitlement. This makes the question of its "diplomatic culture" politically loaded. That, in turn, demands from scholars some dispassionate care.

Let us also consider medieval China, particularly in the Ming era (1368–1644 AD), for this case is one "front" in the strategic-culture debate, as well as its linkages with modern-day China and how that country navigates the world. The Ming era is an important test case for the relative strength of material and cultural variables. China, at this time, reached the height of its preponderance over other states. Yet at the same time, Confucian discourse also reached its height as the Ming dynasty put scholar-officials reared in that tradition into influential advisory positions in the emperor's court. China had the capability, then, either to embrace or eschew militarized power politics, to opt more for restraint or expansion, to conciliate or try to destroy opponents. An important guide here is Yuan-Kang Wang's seminal study *Harmony and War*, a study that combines realist theory with deep area knowledge, closely tracking both China's relative capabilities and internal court debates about whether, when, and how to fight.[72] Wang shows that while Ming potentates ostentatiously preached Confucian values, they struck hard, far, and deep.

Consider that the Yongle Emperor, who ruled from 1403 to 1425, steeped himself in Confucian literature, ordered its increased publication, and declared it the orthodox credo of the state. Yet the same emperor also built the empire without hesitation, both implementing and exploiting newly abundant resources. He heavily garrisoned the northern frontier, increasing the provision of horses for cavalry warfare on the steppe fortyfold, and extended Ming borders to their greatest distance. When Ming China was at its strongest, from 1368 to 1449, it initiated conflict at twice the rate than in the rest of its history. It attacked and annexed Vietnam, dispatched maritime expeditions to dominate its nautical approaches from Japan to the Malacca Strait, and launched successive campaigns to reduce or destroy the Mongols.

When Ming China got weaker and the Mongols strengthened, court debates intensified about how to deal with Mongol threats. Consider the debate of January 1547 about whether to try to recapture the Ordos area, a fertile platform for Mongol attacks that the Ming state had withdrawn from. Opinion was divided on the merits of a "recovery" campaign versus the alternative proposal of increased fortification and military regeneration. The core disagreement, though, was not a dialogue between the offensively minded and virtuous antimilitarists but over the campaign's practical feasibility. Those who opposed the expedition based their arguments primarily around expedience. Projections about costs and the war tolerance of locals and prospects of fighting an opponent optimized for mobile offensive warfare formed the bulk of the discussion. Officials only occasionally nodded to more Confucian arguments for pursuing security by cultivating internal virtue. Rather than repudiating war, opponents of the scheme advocated building up strength to buy time and await a better opportunity to strike. The more static fortification side carried the day. They prevailed not through a cultural preference for defense but because they persuaded the emperor that the state was not yet strong enough and that a campaign would likely be wasteful and fail. In a written counterproposal to the Ordos venture, the governor of a border area argued that while the goal of retaking Ordos was laudable, the means were lacking. "Times have changed. The strong and the weak have switched places."[73] Spoken like a realist.

The Middle Kingdom traditionally saw itself as an enlightened civilization facing a world of barbarians who required management. Coastal pirates, Mongols, rival dynasties, and rebellious distant subjects vied for their attention, along with the threat of internal implosion. China varied in its use of tools from force and intrigue to bribes and threats. Yet those variations flowed not primarily from distinctive culture but from material power. China's rulers altered their footwork depending on their net assessments of their power position. Rather than conducting statecraft on a "constant" setting of Confucian minimalism, they were often sensitive to shifts in the balance of capabilities between themselves and their adversaries. When they were preeminent, they "power maximized" with offensive force. That tendency helps explain the frequency of wars on their mainland. When they were weaker, they would try to appease or buy off enemies or pass the buck of the burden of fighting them to others. They were flexible opportunists. Their strategies did not always succeed, to be sure, and they could fall prey to hubris. In their pomp, they also overreached and miscalculated at times. But they were not cultural "dupes." Violence drew its utility—or futility—from changeable conditions, and decisions about its use were based primarily on judgements about those conditions rather than a primordial cosmology. That cosmology appeared in debates but around the margins, fitting with a general claim that when it comes to explaining behavior, strategic culture is mostly supplementary.[74]

When projecting coercive power against threats, whether successfully or not, Chinese rulers could draw upon a body of strategic thought that played up the utility of striking first with force. Even China's most celebrated text on armed conflict, Sun Tzu's *The Art of War*, so often wheeled out by Anglophone strategists as an exemplar of a bloodless, indirect, "Eastern" way of war, did not simply advocate such methods. Sun Tzu, after all, may have personally commanded forces. He devotes most of the work to advising not how to avoid combat but how to apply violence advantageously. And as John Sullivan argues, even the famous passage about "winning without fighting," which occurs in a chapter entitled "Planning the Offensive Attack," better translates as an urge to avoid *pitched*, *set-piece* battle and instead attack while enemies are still forming up.[75] Conversely, in European history, there were periods of battle avoidance, whereby the art of generalship was more to maneuver forces than commit them. Images of conflict-shy Confucian rulers and Sun Tzu as the antithesis to a Western cult of battle have more to do with attempts to link virtue and identity with fighting styles than the realities of China's history.[76]

The point here is not to suggest that the only realist form of behavior is offensive strategies. Conceivably, another version of a realist China would be more defensive, less expansionist, and more accommodating of threats, accumulating its strength behind its Great Wall and posturing more reactively to deter rather than conquer or destroy across the steppe or the water. Still, it would be more willing to engage in war and more prepared to strike over the horizon than a stereotypically antimilitarist China. The Middle Kingdom, even with its idealistic discourse about restrained governance, didn't, on the whole, allow itself to be a prisoner of that discourse. It made its choices about dealing with foreigners based on close attention to concrete circumstances and to its level of hard-power advantage or disadvantage. "Defensive" and "offensive" realists contend that in a realist world, certain postures are more rational and effective than others. That debate matters. But here, what counts is the "baseline" agreement: that dominant actors, like China, didn't rise by adhering dogmatically to scripts.

If this is true—if realpolitik is a better guide to China's behavior than a long-term, culturally rooted, violence-averse way—that has implications for today. To the extent that there are continuities from historic to current-day China, we should expect a more powerful Beijing to be more assertive and for the wider region to become more militarized, more competitive, and more crisis prone. China will gradually shift to an offensive grand strategy when it has accumulated sufficient power, making demands of its neighbors and coercing them more frequently and intensifying its security competition with the incumbent leading power in East Asia: the United States. China will not content itself with genuflecting to a US-designed and US-led security order. And its neighbors, albeit reluctantly, will engage in increased balancing. At the time of writing, China is undergoing a buildup of blue-water-naval and nuclear missiles to project power over the horizon. It has made increasingly expansive territorial claims in the East and South China Seas. It has recently attempted to punish countries, like Australia, that criticize it with trade sanctions, and indeed, as I write, it is sailing three warships close to Australia's coastline and conducting live-fire exercises. It has subjugated Hong Kong and snuffed out its semiautonomy. It has openly declared its intent to reunify Taiwan with the mainland and increasingly flexes its muscles on Taiwan's air and sea perimeter. And it has been accelerating its stockpile of gold and raw materials. Beijing is clearly a revisionist power, actively competing in conditions where the distribution of capabilities is in flux and preparing the capabilities to deter its chief adversary and, if necessary, fight a major war.

In this context, we can better fathom China's nuclear trajectory. We do not have to rely on an image of a naturally reticent actor to understand the evolution of its nuclear posture. Its earlier more minimalist stance suited its weaker power position, and its policy to "hide and abide" and avoid conflict with the United States helped it to buy time to grow. Its later behavior is consistent with the decision to compete directly with a superpower by unshackling itself from its earlier constraints: its out-in-the-open enlargement and diversification of its nuclear arsenal, its ballistic missile tests, and its possible preparation to lower the threshold for nuclear use. This last point is contentious—we can't know how far the leaked document from the People's Liberation Army's Second Artillery Corps (now Rocket Force) reflects Beijing's thinking, stipulating conditions under which it would launch a nuclear first strike in response to conventional attacks. But even skeptics recognize that China allows limited ambiguity over first-use nuclear strikes in the event of attacks on its nuclear weapons or supporting infrastructure.[77] The likeliest explanation? Just as America's nuclear primacy in the Cold War persuaded the Soviet Union to abandon nuclear restraint and engage in an arms race, so too does a stronger Beijing seek to checkmate America's nuclear dominance by making its deterrent more survivable and useable under fire.

Another area in dispute is the Caspian region and the post-Soviet Islamic republics located around it. This is a salient case because the states of that region outwardly identify with a cultural way in the form of faith and claim that Islam binds and channels their choices, including choices over alignment and allegiance. On closer inspection, those actors prove flexible, and constraining cultural forces, such as Islamic precepts and coreligious solidarity, do not prevail when pressure arises in the other direction.[78] Iran collaborates with Orthodox Armenia at the expense of Shi'a Azerbaijan. It curtailed its support to the Islamic Renaissance Party of Tajikistan, its occasional partner, to reinforce its pursuit of closer relations with Moscow.[79] Iran maintains flexibility with regard to nuclear weapons as well as its allegiances. While it formally prohibits the ultimate weapon as un-Islamic, according to Supreme Leader Ali Khamenei's oral fatwa of 2003, it has also articulated a doctrine of "regime expediency" (*maslahat-e nezam*)—a mechanism that leaves open the rationale that drastic measures might be necessary to defend the revolutionary state.[80] Iran's regime historically has revised fatwas as circumstances change—for instance, over chemical weapons during the war with Iraq. And Iran has accelerated its enrichment of uranium and tested nuclear-capable missiles to make possible this policy shift in the future.

Similarly, rivalries persist between Uzbekistan and Kazakhstan despite their shared religion and ethnicity. Georgia seeks to shield itself from fellow-Orthodox, post-Soviet Russia by cultivating NATO ties. The state of Pakistan seems to work hard to advertise its Islamic credentials. And it collaborates with and sponsors Islamist groups. But it does so primarily on pragmatic, instrumental grounds, by turn embracing or distancing itself from radical militants as expedience dictates, like with the Taliban in the first days after 9/11. It also cultivates a close, "all-weather" relationship with colossal atheistic China on its border—a partner not known for benign treatment of its own Muslim population.[81] You don't have to be a deep area specialist to spot the patterns here.

REALISM OF THE WEAK

Realism forms the main basis and logic not only for the creation and use of power by the strong but also for rebellion and resistance by the weak. Realism applies just as much for Davids against Goliaths or Muhammad Alis against George Foremans. Two types of "reverse leverage" are available to underdogs. First, smaller "microstates" play larger powers off one another and, under certain conditions, can succeed. Second, armed insurgencies can wear down and outlast stronger occupiers. Napoleon's quip that "God is on the side of the big battalions" was not quite right and not so in the end for him. On one estimate, weaker sides in asymmetric clashes with a less than or equal to five-to-one power disparity win 30 percent of the time.[82] To be sure, both microstates and rebels must still navigate a realist world where greater material strength prevails most often. For every victorious insurgent, there are many crushed ones. The George Foremans win most battles since most underdogs aren't Muhammad Ali. Only, lesser powers can thrive if they astutely pick their moments and their methods.

Microstates have a microrealpolitik of their own. One objection to realism on both moral and explanatory grounds is that realists are preoccupied with larger states at the expense of the small. As Kenneth Waltz suggests, it is "ridiculous to construct a theory of international politics based on Malaysia and Costa Rica."[83] In this spirit, it is said, realists give too much weight and priority to the likes of the ancient Athenian empire over Melos, the small island city-state it slaughtered and enslaved. Realists, some complain, lose sight of the agency of weaker states. A whole literature debates how far Thucydides's account of the Melian dialogue was really an acceptance of the logic of brutal realpolitik or a warning against it. I can't resolve that here. But I can observe that realism, far from being irrelevant to weaker polities, is even more valuable as a guide.

The repertoires of the world's smallest countries have attracted renewed attention recently. And realist logic helps explain how "small-island developing states," the states that can hardly defend themselves against superpowers, can still exert influence of their own.[84] Consider the Solomon Islands. For long periods, outsiders treated the South Pacific archipelago as a recipient of events, a battleground, a colony, or a welfare case. In this century, remote and poor, it attracted little international study or expertise, and large or middle powers spoke of it as a needy minnow. The islands existed in a sphere under America's protective wing, with the waters framed as an "American lake," as President Dwight Eisenhower termed it in 1954. There was no rival patron to court, and the United States even closed its embassy there in 1993.

How things change. With the return of great power competition, the United States designated the Indo-Pacific the central theater for its effort to maintain international primacy. In that contest, China, the United States, its allies, and neutrals worried more about bases, transport nodes, supply chains and maritime chokepoints, access to raw materials, and the building of coalitions. The shift of the world's economic and strategic center of gravity gave the Solomon Islands a new salience. Such circumstances generate both opportunities and dangers. In September 2019, the Solomon Islands shocked Western opinion by pointedly reversing its thirty-six-year-old recognition of Taiwan's sovereignty and embracing the "one-China" principle. It began negotiating membership in China's Belt and Road Initiative. It also signed two bilateral cooperation treaties with China in March and April 2022, covering humanitarian assistance, police training, and disaster response. Only five years before, it had signed bilateral security pacts with the middle power Australia, which one prime minister claimed to be America's "deputy sheriff" in the region. A concerned Washington established an embassy in the country in 2023. Watchfully keeping a foot in both camps, the small state also demanded the United States do more to help patrol and suppress illegal fishing in its exclusive economic zone yet denied a US vessel port entry for a summit and announced a moratorium on foreign vessels in Washington in September 2022.

As a result of the Solomon Islands' adroit maneuvers and its noncommittal posture of "friends to all, enemy to none," high-level delegations from Washington, Japan, and Beijing descended on the country and invited return visits. Countries competed for a higher profile by investing in the Pacific Games of late 2023, with China investing in sports facilities and Australia sending security personnel. Suddenly, global rivals competed for the Solomon Islands' favor. As a sign of Washington's geopolitical anxiety about the "strategically located" Solomon Islands potentially hosting a Chinese base, it dispatched Kurt Campbell, its Indo-Pacific coordinator and seasoned China-watching believer in Pax Americana.[85] America, he said, had not done enough for the Solomon Islands before and was there now "to help address the urgent demands of climate change and illegal fishing."[86] Yet without using the term "sphere of influence," a thing Washington and China both deny they assert, he made clear that the United States opposed the installation of any Chinese military facilities.

The Solomon Islands played the cards that geopolitics had dealt them, exploiting fears that China would build a naval or air base within range of Australia, a US ally. while avoiding binding commitment to either side of the security competition, it maximized the benefits it received in the form of investments, bilateral and multilateral aid, capacity building, and technical assistance. It had the benefit of being a monopolistic supplier of a sought-after location of increased value and the ability to play on the prospect of shifting sides, elevating the island state "from a microstate at the receiving end of great power politics to an attractive partner."[87]

One neglected realist is especially useful here. Arnold Wolfers theorizes that certain conditions hand small states (and microstates) unusual leverage. While large states are generally more consequential than smaller states and do more to make the world, smaller states can exploit external rivalries by offering or withholding access or allegiance, opening up or denying basing rights, and opening up or closing down a resource base. Therefore, "small states are the opportunists of international relations: they are, and they need to be, alert to changing circumstances and policies of other actors that they exploit and take advantage of."[88] By triangulating, hedging, and waiting or playing hard to get, they can extract utility from their relationships with great powers without getting into trouble. Crucially, their ability to punch above their weight is not a constant. It is dependent on wider conditions. Namely, there needs to be a level of disequilibrium and competition for them to exploit and for their allegiance to matter, as with Cuba and Albania toward their Soviet patron during the Cold War or Yugoslavia and its willingness to switch allegiances when threatened. Under more stable hierarchical orders or when cold wars ease into détente, for the most part, they can't as easily threaten overdogs with defection and have less bargaining power.[89]

Large states, by being larger, more often survive their miscalculations. Weaker countries have smaller margins of error. The ancient Melians relied on an "expensive" hope that their parent city, Sparta, would honor its kinship to rescue them against invaders and perished for their miscalculation.[90] For the Solomon Islands, by contrast, there was an opening in world politics that gave them opportunities to thrive even in the shadow of the strong, provided they were hard-nosed.

One historical microstate serves as a powerful caution against reductionist attempts to demarcate "Western" from "non-Western" knowledge and a reminder of the hybridity and cross-border fertilization of real International Relations.[91] It is eighteenth-century Haiti (then Saint Domingue) and in particular its revolutionary military leader Toussaint Louverture (1740–1803), who led a slave uprising and brought his country to the threshold of independence. Louverture frequently quoted Machiavelli and ruthlessly practiced power politics. He triangulated different political forces and identities to cultivate a legend in ways that confound glib clichés about the imperial and indigenous, Western and non-Western. As a man born into slavery, he appealed to antislavery amongst the Haitian helot class and claimed descent from African kings, yet at times, he owned slaves and delayed his approval of emancipation and imported new slaves in pursuit of the support of the brutal wealthy slave-owning Haitian class, whose cruelty he had tasted firsthand. Leading an indigenous revolt, he was also a devout Catholic who tried to stamp out voodoo. Invoking French identity and revolutionary principles conveniently as he realigned with France against Spain, he dialed down that music when negotiating with France's enemies and set himself up as an absolutist with powers for life. Biographers give him names to domesticate him to Western audiences, such as "Black Jacobin" and "Black Spartacus," but that is too much like calling Kautilya "Brown Machiavelli."

The wiser point is to recognize that there is nothing either distinctively Western nor non-Western and exotic about what Louverture did or about his methods: using divide-and-rule politics, defecting from the Spanish back to the French after they abolished slavery, cunningly delaying obtaining trade treaties before declaring independence, and purging rivals even in his own family. He also blended systematic drill and military discipline with both direct-battle and scorched-earth guerrilla-fighting styles to outmaneuver Spanish, British, and (almost) French forces. He picked and mixed styles, strategies, and techniques because they seemed to work. It's a story ultimately of defeat. But with the weak hand of a small state, he shook an empire. Louverture was a realist.

Guerrilla forces, like small states, also need realism to succeed. A concern for power and material capabilities lies at the heart of successful rebellions. In our time, a superpower was outlasted and defeated by Islamist insurgents in Afghanistan, the poorest country on earth, after the same superpower was bled into a barely acceptable settlement in Iraq. Further back, the Soviet Union floundered against determined resistance in Afghanistan, Israel did so in Lebanon, and France's war in Algeria resulted in civil strife and revolution.

There is a puzzle here given that stronger sides of both more and less relative brutality can meet defeat. This is no place for an in-depth account of small wars and their complex histories. The debate about why large states sometimes lose small wars is energetic, with a wide range of variables said to shape outcomes, such as the balance of resolve, geography, levels of brutality, and selection of strategies. But in cases where weaker and determined adversaries prevail, they ruthlessly harness and apply material strength. Resolve and fighting, of course, are rarely the whole story. But without them and without the very material elements like supplies, people, favorable geography, sanctuaries, and allies, there would be no victory. As Tarak Barkawi notes, International Relations needs an "imperial turn" precisely to "deepen the insights of those realists who have long argued for the decisive role of the political military in shaping human histories, for in the final analysis imperial frontiers are won and lost by force of arms."[92]

To say this is to resist an alternative popular and liberal idea, which goes in and out of fashion: that small wars, especially in distant lands, are a contest for legitimacy, won by being more morally appealing than one's opponent and that these clashes are won and lost by appealing to "hearts and minds" via enlightened rule. Insurgencies, in this view, are not so much outfought as outgoverned. The key variables, supposedly, are less power and weakness and more ideas and norms. To defeat warlords, nationalists, or sectarian competitors, so goes the argument, the job of the counterinsurgent is to safeguard the host government by selectively killing resistors while helping the new state establish services, from schools, police, and bureaucracy to health services and dams. Conversely, rebels will prevail if they offer better governance and exploit local resentment. Failures of conventional military campaigns by the strong and the perceived need to switch to a population-centric counterinsurgency campaign that focuses on legitimacy is an idea that challenges realism.

This recipe drew upon a certain Anglo-American understanding of historical campaigns in the Anglosphere, contrasting the supposedly more benign campaign of Britain in Malaya with the misguided violence of Vietnam. During the war on terror and the implosion of Iraq, the icon of counterinsurgency practitioners US general David Petraeus insisted that you can't "kill your way out" of an insurgency. If so, how could you quell a revolt and escape? For Petraeus, it would take positive inducements, including bribery, to buy off and pacify warring factions in order to make space for political reconciliation and build legitimacy. "Money," as Petraeus argued, "is a weapons system."[93]

Money is indeed a sinew of war. But Petraeus was getting at a deeper proposition: that the path to victory is to treat the foreign population primarily as *Homo economicus*—a consumer of state offerings whose loyalty could be purchased, with political struggle fading to the background. Legitimacy via services into a capitalist modernity under the counterinsurgent's protection was the main thrust of the famous field manual Petraeus oversaw, *FM 3-24*. Such a vision assumes an alignment of interests between the well-intentioned visiting power and the local state, when in fact those states could themselves be predatory and pursue different interests.[94] And it also makes suspect assumptions about what influences popular will in embattled countries. Norms, identities, and values clearly inform decisions about rebellion and obedience. But the balance of hard power and the clash of interests is pivotal. You may not be able to "kill" your way out of an insurgency, but neither can you necessarily buy your way out.

To grasp why the "hearts-and-minds" worldview is mistaken, let us consider a film that reflects the fraught realities of small wars. In *Sand Castle* (2017), a squad of American soldiers in post-Ba'ath Iraq tries to repair a water system in a remote Iraqi village. The locals are reluctant to offer their labor to speed up the repair even in return for generous payments in US dollars and even though they suffer water shortages. They are reluctant to enter a cash nexus with the troops. Their reticence baffles and frustrates the soldiers. "Who the fuck doesn't want money?" asks one soldier, after one Iraqi driving his daughter to a pharmacy refuses cash as compensation for being held and interrogated. Asked to get men to help and assured of payment and protection, the local sheikh says if he helps, he will pay with his life given the town belongs to other people at night. "When the night comes, you cannot protect [us]. . . . When you leave, what will happen?" A local schoolmaster helps. His burnt body is found tied to a stake in the village square, and laborers stay away. After troops locate and kill some of the insurgents, the water project resumes with local labor—until a suicide bomber destroys it.[95]

Sand Castle poignantly illustrates the flaws of the "hearts-and-minds" approach. The loyalties of the host population do not obey the logic of the legitimacy contest or the economic rewards of building a new state. Rather, insurgents deterred them from collaborating. Their threats draw credibility from their demonstrations of terror and from their continual presence as opposed to the armed cashed-up foreigners, who will leave. They can't match the Americans' firepower or fiscal power, but they have enough capability to coerce and enough political will to outlast the visitors. Similarly in Afghanistan, a concurrent war of the time, the Taliban also worked on that logic, delivering intimidatory "night letters" to homes, mosques, and government buildings to remind Afghans that they would still be there after NATO forces departed, threatening anyone who worked for the "crusaders" and warning them of the reckoning to come.

Realist accounts of small wars, such as Jacqueline Hazelton's *Bullets Not Ballots*, are able to recognize better than liberal "hearts-and-minds" accounts that counterinsurgency war is still primarily a war, retaining coercive violence at its core.[96] As Hazelton argues, states defeat revolts not so much via enlightened reforms that win over populations but by co-opting elite domestic rivals, using brute force to limit the flow of resources to insurgencies and to break rebels' will and capacity to fight on. Thus, even campaigns heralded for their relative gentleness, like the Malayan emergency, were still brutal affairs. Insurgencies can defy these campaigns of repression but need favorable conditions, from international support that ensures the flow of arms and money to secure geographies with rear areas in which to regenerate. And they too apply coercion and/or terror to win. As the historian Charles S. Meier cautions, "Let us not be sentimental about resistance." Rebels "can live in a Manichean world," where "terror is the instrument of justice and no victim is innocent in the eyes of history."[97] Likewise, let us recognize the realpolitik of threatened local populations. Their calculus is often not primarily about fairness but about relative strength, working out where the power lies, and survival when the night falls.[98]

REALISM AND GENDER

What about gender? While much discussion about realism's universality revolves around a resurgent argument over empire, race, and culture, there is also a long-standing critique that realism and all the major "isms" are patriarchal at their roots. There is now a large literature on this.[99] Patriarchies are hierarchical, exclusionary, and oppressive orders dominated by men. If so, realism presumes and reinforces a world built around values coded as "masculine" that entail mass violence: belligerent, acquisitive, state centric, anti-internationalist, and status obsessed. That order not only targets and exploits women and girls, making them victims of conflict in ways that are invisible to traditional IR; patriarchies are also bad for men. Its older men send young men to kill and die. If realism is a biproduct of patriarchy and intellectually services it, there is a hard choice. One can be a realist or a feminist but not both.

There are multiple versions of gender-centered critiques, varying in their sophistication. At the less advanced end, there is a crude form of essentialism in which men fight and saber rattle, and women nurture, bargain, or collaborate, and this difference accounts for international crises. For instance, British prime minister Boris Johnson claimed that Vladimir Putin would never have invaded Ukraine if he had been a woman.[100] Similarly, former US secretary of state Hillary Clinton claimed, after the invasion of Ukraine, that the problem today is men who start wars.[101] Yet one of Putin's predecessors, Czarina Catherine the Great, added two hundred thousand square miles to the Russian empire with the sword. Her predecessor, Empress Elizabeth Petrovna, waged war on Sweden (1741–1743) and Prussia (1756–1763). For her part, Hillary Clinton's own voting record from Iraq to Libya suggests biological sex is hardly a barrier to women actively supporting military expeditions. Stephen Pinker has repopularized gender determinism. He infers that women are less inclined to collective violence from the simple pattern that "men plan almost all the world's wars and genocides."[102] This argument need not detain us long. While it is obviously true that men plan almost all wars and genocides, men dominate most of the world's governments and militaries. It is not in itself a commentary on what women do in the minority of cases when they, too, wield executive power. If women in office or power are also prone to belligerence, then gender may not be as decisive a variable.

There are more sophisticated versions of feminist IR. These emphasize the distinction between biological sex and constructed gender. They would contend that patriarchy and its gendered codes, not genitalia, shape the worldview of even powerful women and how they think about security, prestige, and force. Significant from this vantage point is not that Catherine the Great or Hillary Clinton are women but that they think and act within a patriarchal ideology, seeking male support in government and politics via "male posturing." Feminists—like realists—emphasize the importance of structure, only feminists argue that realists focus on the wrong structure. This gender critique of realism cannot be so easily dismissed.

There are several difficulties with the argument that feminism and realism are necessarily at odds, that violent power politics derives principally from patriarchy, and that a "true" feminist statecraft would abolish the need for realpolitik.

First, one does not need patriarchy, or even humans, to have conflict. Wars occur frequently amongst ants. And amongst humans, it *is* dispositive that women at both mass and elite levels have combined feminism with realism. While pursuing their own emancipation, they have also actively and resolutely supported the cause of the armed polity, whether tribe, city-state, nation-state, or empire.

Take the Iroquois Confederacy of North America from the fifteenth to the eighteenth centuries. While not strictly a matriarchy, the Five Nations, who made up this union, were some of the most gender-egalitarian polities in history. It was matrilineal. Gatherings of "clan mothers" selected each male leader and could remove chiefs at will. They wielded veto powers in foreign policy debates and decisions for war. They appointed "peace chiefs" as delegates to the central council of the Onondaga people with its conflict-resolution ceremonies. They adjudicated the fate of male war captives, whose capture, torture, and execution were religiously important to Iroquois nations' society, while women and girls were forcibly added to the villages. The nations of this same confederacy waged war vigorously. They practiced power politics vigorously too, using their strong position to play off French and British interlopers, whose arrival created both opportunities for metals-for-furs enrichment and threats in the form of disease and patronage of their rivals. As they grew stronger, they became more imperial, dispossessing, destroying, and dispersing rival indigenous groups. As trade with Europeans made fur-trapping lands increasingly valuable, they remorselessly secured access and drove off competitors. And like many patriarchal societies that grow powerful, they regarded themselves as essentially peaceful while demanding others submit. As one historian reports, "The Five Nations believed it was their duty to spread the Peacemaker's message" to other Native American nations, "and to bring them into the Iroquois League. Only then could peace exist for everyone." Those who resisted "were considered enemies, and the Five Nations warred them to force their submission."[103] It doesn't take patriarchs to start wars.

Other research also casts doubt on the assumption that patriarchy is a necessary or even a significant driver of war. Recent literature undermines assumptions that women leaders are more peaceable given they resort to force in similar frequency.[104] In one study of Europe from 1480 to 1913, polities ruled by queens engaged in armed conflict more often than those ruled by kings—for various reasons: the perception by male rulers that they were easier to attack and the increased capacity effect of co-opting their male corulers into running the state.[105] Importantly, there is little evidence that women launched campaigns to impress male audiences of their toughness. In the early phases of their reigns, when audience-signaling pressures were strongest for new rulers, belligerence was not more frequent. Nor is it likely they were just doing the bidding of bellicose male advisors given that younger female rulers (who were probably most susceptible to such advisors) show no differential effect.

In modern-era patriarchal societies, women have agency. Kurdish women suffer high levels of domestic gender-based violence yet fight on the frontline against ISIL, an Islamist organization committed to women's enslavement, one of the most patriarchal forces on the planet. World War One, often central to the feminist critique of patriarchy's oppressive violence, featured mass voluntary women's mobilization. Women coerced conscientious objectors or otherwise reluctant or conflicted men, for instance, via the shaming technique of publicly giving them white feathers. Women worked in munitions factories and organized through civil society to "dig for victory" or buy war bonds. Feminists of the age, such as the Pankhurst sisters, enthusiastically supported military recruitment and led enlistment drives. It is a strain to infer that women who were otherwise determined to overthrow straightforward gender inequality by winning the vote or the right to work or own property against the determined opposition of patriarchs were still unwitting dupes of a male world. If patriarchy was so insidiously powerful that it was the main thing that drove feminist support for the war effort, why couldn't it prevent them campaigning for the vote?

There is no certain or decisive test of these issues, of course. There will always be the counterargument that every historical case thus far is compromised because it occurred in a world where most societies are male dominated. We don't have a "control case" of an alternative universe of matriarchal "pairs" in which nonpatriarchies interact with one another. Still, the partial imperfect body of evidence we do have points in the same direction. In general, reductions in patriarchy and gender inequality or increased women's empowerment do not correlate with reductions in belligerence, coercion, or competitive power politics. If patriarchy were removed or lessened, it is more likely than not that our species would be similarly conflict prone.

What of the counterclaim that historical cases of otherwise egalitarian women willingly supporting the nation in arms are still just symptoms of patriarchy? This argument rests on a highly abstract, almost utopian concept of "true feminism." To advocate equality in a world of polities under anarchy is one thing. But it is another thing to advocate equality via the abolition of competing polities in a transformed order of world government or no government at all. There may be powerful reasons apart from patriarchal indoctrination why women who pursue greater equality also often align themselves with the state in times of heightened threat. The alternatives don't work. To meet a threatening world without some kind of organized security state to organize around is more dangerous, not less. An in-principle repudiation of conflict may seem virtuous, but for embattled people, it is not a practical possibility. If not take up arms under an authority, when expansionist Islamists who would enslave them turn up, what are Kurdish female fighters supposed to do instead?

So we should still expect even a postpatriarchal world—a matriarchal world or a purely egalitarian one—to be a realist world. That is not a judgement on the merits of feminism. It is rather an argument that realism and feminism need not be adversaries. The movement for gender equality has notched up impressive gains and may yet lead to greater emancipation. Only, no movement can emancipate humans from anarchy and its pressures.

Realism, as we have seen, is not inherently exclusionary. As a set of assumptions about power and security, if not always as a body of worked-out theory, realism has traveled widely. When we look, we see small and large polities tend to work from realist assumptions, from Cape Town to Beijing, from Haiti to the Solomon Islands. Realism has traveled beyond the Euro-Atlantic or took root there independently. Nor is it necessarily part of a system of overdog oppression. It has proven to be resonant for minor actors as well as the strong, from the smallest microstates to insurgents and rebels. In skilled hands, it is a weapon of the weak. And while it is harder to test and evaluate, history suggests that a feminist world would remain a realist world. Even in a postpatriarchal world, fully emancipated from gender hierarchy, competitive power politics would likely persist. This is not to say that realism is a uniform code. Its form tends to adapt to its particular environment. Only, its fundamentals persist. Realism's core propositions correspond with the experience of our world's harshness. That is precisely why realist instincts, practices, and literature resonate in most places under the sun.

Epilogue

IN THIS BOOK, I've offered three simple points. Realism has a moral basis as the duty of the ruler to the ruled in a hostile world. It is a morality but one of a different kind than most people are accustomed to. This means that governments ought to behave more ruthlessly when caring for their flock than they would in private life. And it means doing things, from time to time, that shock the liberal conscience, as when Churchill sank the Vichy fleet. Yet that must never be an alibi for unchecked morally indifferent barbarism, the exhilarated pursuit and exercise of power for its own sake. Because realism calls for respect for power, realists must remain on their guard against falling in love with it.

As well as being moral in its foundation, realism is realistic. While there are anomalies and puzzles that deserve more attention, realism gets the fundamentals right about how organized groups of people tend to behave and what happens to them if they neglect the need for watchful, prudent self-help. Realism doesn't tell us all we need to know. But it helps explain the return of war and militarized crises, the fair-weatheredness of governments toward rules and institutions, the impossibility of moving into a postnuclear age, the importance of focusing on self-help rather than expecting larger powers to always be providing security, and the value of a pragmatic, incremental, and mitigationist response to climate crisis over an attempt at coordinated global overhaul.

And realism is for all. Claims that it is just an ethos for the West or for white patriarchs or only for post-Westphalian nation-states are oblivious to the appeal and resurgence of realist thought and behavior in space beyond the West and through time, even in antiquity. Indeed, the hard logic of power politics is valuable especially for the weak, such as microstates playing off superpower rivals against one another or insurgents fighting against large occupiers. Realism, if anything, is an antidote against an overemphasis on difference. It is a check against assumptions that cultural fidelities and civilizational ties make the world go around and a guard against focusing on others' skin color or language rather than material strength.

So what should rulers do now? you ask. It would be wrong for this book to offer up a specific, exact blueprint. For one thing, as I've argued, realism as a general paradigm is not a cookbook. Here, I've simply argued that realism is the best, or least bad, intellectual framework from which to grapple with problems. Also, this emphatically isn't just a book for major powers. Different polities face different circumstances and have different capabilities. To outline a set of detailed prescriptive steps would render the book irrelevant to some countries given it would not take into account variations in conditions. Even for those to whom it applied, exact recipes would quickly build in obsolescence since circumstances change.

If there is general practical advice to offer any state today, here are some starting positions: First, assume that in making decisions, *resources are scarce* and that policy is constrained by *trade-offs*. Contrary to the advice of some optimists, deficits do still matter, bills have to be paid, and time and effort devoted to one thing is therefore withheld from something else. Of course, we have not yet mastered economics as a species, and it may be the case that, for the first time, some states can borrow with abandon and get away with it. Yet it would not be prudent to run the national treasury on that experiment. In a similar spirit, military power—people, equipment, platforms, weapons, and logistical stocks—committed in one theater or location are therefore denied to another. It still takes weeks at least and much effort to transport large quantities of materiel and forces even by sea, which is often the fastest way, and that's assuming access can be achieved. Sure, different theaters—like the Indo-Pacific or the Euro-Atlantic—can be connected. But to show connection is not to relieve oneself of the discipline of prioritization.

As well as being mindful of physical constraints, rulers should be wary of allies and partners and *prioritize self-help* as much as they feasibly can. This does not mean forgetting cooperation or alliance building, for these can be valuable. But it does mean building into policy a healthy skepticism about others and not mistaking or revering external cooperation as permanent and natural. An exhortation to greater self-reliance will mean different things to different peoples given they are not all capable of the same level of strength. Small states will not always be able to stand alone against larger states. What they can do, though, is develop the ability to inflict pain and deter. If smaller states cannot defeat a giant, sometimes they can at least develop the ability to rip a giant's limb off.

Self-reliance matters because others are not reliably comembers of a security community, as history suggests. In the final analysis, others are separate states with distinct interests, some of which don't overlap. Don't count on large and powerful friends or, indeed, smaller and useful friends to come and bail you out when they, too, feel pressure. Georgia took part in the war in Iraq from August 2003 in the hope that its commitment would showcase its alliance credentials and that tighter ties with the US superpower would be reciprocated with protection. Yet in the summer of 2008, when Russia invaded, Washington sent stern words and sanctions and officials and humanitarian supplies and helped ship back Georgian forces just as the fighting was ending, but it did not send troops or take risks. For its part, Serbia has long heard Russian leaders invoke the ideal of pan-Slavic and pan-Orthodox solidarity. But beginning in March 1999, when Belgrade was at war with NATO, apart from a brief and dangerous confrontation at Pristina International Airport, Russia did little for its historic partner. Other countries will not necessarily ride to your rescue out of a shared political ethos, culture, or language or because of similar institutions or blood ties. Beware of beguiling sentimental ideas like "friendship" between countries. My ancestors learned that at the capture of Singapore in February 1942. Australia discovered that its interests came second, and its parent country, the United Kingdom, as well as its empire, first—ties of affection and blood be damned. No complaining here: it is the way of things. But Australia thereafter put its interests first, bringing its troops back from North Africa and aligning with another ally whose presence was growing in the region. Remember Singapore. Remember Melos.

And when crafting policy, remember this is a *fallen world*. Don't imagine there to be a morally governed "international community" driven by a humanitarian conscience that will isolate the wicked or reward generosity with allegiance. Resist this assumption no matter how much modern-day prophets herald the rise of civil society or the coming of global norms or the need to hold rogue states to account or the soft power that development aid generates. Much policy these days is accompanied by the false hope that the world will treat offending powers as pariahs or that helping other countries will result in creating leverage and influence. To the contrary, the record of human behavior suggests that as soon as pressure rises or global norms clash with other interests, other countries, like Western states, will behave in a hard-nosed, self-serving, and, at times, hypocritical manner. We've already seen that large swathes of the world have happily done business with Vladimir Putin's Russia even as Ukraine has bled, even including recipients of Western aid. And recall that even in the case of Saddam Hussein's Iraq—under the stranglehold of international sanctions and inspections—UN officials and businesses took what they could by exploiting the Oil-for-Food Programme. Neighbors from Syria to Jordan covertly did business with Baghdad in defiance of sanctions. And French state-owned oil companies secretly negotiated contracts and lobbied for future business. It is hard to turn even the most reviled adversaries into pariahs. You may care morally about the importance of example setting and justice seeking. Others will not or will care less. They have their own citizens to look after. The world does not revolve around your grievances.

Realism can help guide general policy. It can also inspire prudent crisis management. You and I are alive today partly because in October 1962, two leaders of superpowers, John F. Kennedy and Nikita Khrushchev, handled a dangerous confrontation with cool heads.[1] This is no time for hagiography, of course; whole libraries of criticism exist on both leaders. But both navigated the Cuban missile question as adroit realists. Both listened to advice without being prisoners of it. Kennedy in particular resisted the urgings of many of his ExComm (Executive Committee of the National Security Council) counselors to go beyond an intermediate measure of naval blockade and bomb the missile sites in Cuba. He feared that launching direct attacks would force Moscow's hand and trigger a general war. He was more right than he knew. We now know that Red Army commanders, stationed in Cuba, were authorized to use nuclear cruise missiles to destroy the US naval base at Guantanamo. Khrushchev, too, resisted advice to take an unbending position, seeking to extract concessions while limiting his challenge to the US blockade and judging, wisely, that failure to remove the missiles would precipitate invasion. He had survived Stalin's purges, so he knew a thing or two about survival. Both leaders sensed instinctively that in the face of grave danger, they must strike a balance between reckless escalation and passive deficiency. Both looked beyond their country's grievances and complaints to imagine what the scenario looked like for the adversary and to think multiple moves ahead. Both looked to show strength while discretely making concessions their countries could live with to craft an imperfect but workable compromise settlement. Both accepted the need for risk and coercive force while remaining rightly scared of losing control.

If you've made it this far, I hope that you think realism is serious. I hope you are still curious, for a book like this can only be a beginning. With luck, you feel prompted or provoked to read further the great works of realist theory and the practitioners of realpolitik, from Thucydides to Toussaint Louverture, from Kautilya to Anwar Sadat. I hope this book demonstrates what many deny—that a realist understanding of power politics is also for you, whoever or wherever you are. If you are resisting an invasion or agitating to change foreign policy or just trying to understand why countries say one thing and do another, a realist appreciation of power politics is a sound point to begin with. It won't supply all the answers. But it can reveal the nature of the predicament and the constraints you face, out of which you can judge what is achievable and what is wise. Thucydides wanted his history of the Peloponnesian War, with its insights into conflict and the human condition, to be a "possession for all time."[2] He didn't just intend this for the ancient Greeks. It was to be a possession for all, for all time.

Notes

Introduction

1. John F. Kennedy, "Remarks of Senator John F. Kennedy Announcing His Candidacy for the Presidency of the United States—Senate Caucus Room, Washington, DC," January 2, 1960, The American Presidency Project, accessed March 13, 2025, https://www.presidency.ucsb.edu/node/274074.

2. Robert G. Gilpin, "The Richness of the Tradition of Political Realism," *International Organization* 38, no. 2 (1984): 287–304, http://www.jstor.org/stable/2706441; Gilpin, "No One Loves a Political Realist," *Security Studies* 5, no. 3 (1996): 3–26, https://doi.org/10.1080/09636419608429275.

3. For Charles L. Glaser's prescient argument, see Glaser, "Structural Realism in a More Complex World," *Review of International Studies* 29, no. 3 (2003): 403–14, http://www.jstor.org/stable/20097862.

Chapter 1

1. Ken Booth, *A Theory of World Security* (Cambridge University Press, 2007), 35–36.

2. On realist morality, see Jonathan Haslam, *No Virtue like Necessity: Realist Thought in International Relations since Machiavelli* (Yale University Press, 2002), 17–89; Richard K. Betts, "The Realist Persuasion," *National Interest* 139 (2015): 46–55.

3. I use "morality" to refer to sets of values and guiding principles held collectively. Some insist that this really is about "ethics," but for our purposes here, the two are interchangeable.

4. Richard K. Ashley, "The Poverty of Neorealism," *International Organization* 38, no. 2 (1984): 225–286, at 281, http://www.jstor.org/stable/2706440.

5. Helen Milner, "The Assumption of Anarchy in International Relations Theory: A Critique," *Review of International Studies* 17, no. 1 (1991): 67–85, https://doi.org/10.1017/S026021050011232X.

6. E. H. Carr, *The Twenty Years' Crisis: 1919–1939; An Introduction to the Study of International Relations* (Macmillan, 1962), 220. See also Sean Molloy, "Spinoza, Carr,

and the Ethics of *The Twenty Years' Crisis*," *Review of International Studies* 39, no. 2 (2013): 251–71, at 267, http://www.jstor.org/stable/24564658.

7. Gilpin, "Richness of the Tradition," 290.

8. Victor Davis Hanson, *The End of Everything: How Wars Descend into Annihilation* (Basic Books, 2024), 270–79.

9. Chris Mullin, "The Terror Was Absolute," review of *Vietnam: An Epic Tragedy*, by Max Hastings, *London Review of Books* 41, no. 14 (2019), https://www.lrb.co.uk/the-paper/v41/n14/chris-mullin/terror-was-absolute.

10. For an anatomy of different traditions, see Stephen M. Walt, "International Relations: One World, Many Theories," *Foreign Policy*, no. 110 (1998): 29–32, 34–46, https://doi.org/10.2307/1149275.

11. For an entrée to liberal internationalism, see Duncan S. Bell, "What Is Liberalism?," *Political Theory* 42, no. 6 (2014): 682–715, https://doi.org/10.1177/0090591714535103; Andrew Moravcsik, "Taking Preferences Seriously: A Liberal Theory of International Politics," *International Organization* 51, no. 4 (1997): 513–53, https://doi.org/10.1162/002081897550447; John Gerard Ruggie, "International Regimes, Transactions, and Change: Embedded Liberalism in the Post-war Economic Order," *International Organization* 36, no. 2 (1982): 379–415, http://www.jstor.org/stable/2706527.

12. For a sharp diagnosis of the clash within liberalism between egalitarianism and empire, see Jeanne Morefield, *Covenants without Swords: Idealist Liberalism and the Spirit of Empire* (Princeton University Press, 2004).

13. Dillon Stone Tatum, "Toward a Radical IR: Transformation, Praxis, and Critique in a (Neo)Liberal World Order," *International Studies Review* 23, no. 4 (2021): 1751–70, https://doi.org/10.1093/isr/viab043.

14. Colin S. Gray, *Weapons Don't Make War: Policy, Strategy and Military Technology* (University of Kansas, 2005).

15. I am grateful to Arthur M. Eckstein for conversations on this point.

16. Lawrence H. Keeley, *War before Civilization: The Myth of the Peaceful Savage* (Oxford University Press, 1996).

17. Dominic P. Johnson and Bradley Thayer, "The Evolution of Offensive Realism: Survival under Anarchy from the Pleistocene to the Present," *Politics and the Life Sciences* 35, no. 1 (2016): 1–20, https://www.jstor.org/stable/26372766.

18. Raymond C. Kelly, *Warless Societies and the Origin of War* (University of Michigan Press, 2000); Douglas P. Fry, ed., *War, Peace and Human Nature: The Convergence of Evolutionary and Cultural Views* (Oxford University Press, 2015); Dean Folk and Charles Hildebolt, "Annual War Deaths in Small-Scale versus State Societies Scale with Population Size Rather Than Violence," *Current Anthropology* 58, no. 6 (2017): 805–13, https://doi.org/10.1086/694568.

19. Stefanos Geroulanos, *The Invention of Prehistory: Empire, Violence, and Our Obsession with Human Origins* (Liveright, 2025).

20. Azar Gat, "Proving Communal Warfare among Hunter-Gatherers: The Quasi-Rousseauan Error," *Evolutionary Anthropology* 24, no. 3 (2015): 111–26, at 115, https://doi.org/10.1002/evan.21446.

21. Richard K. Betts, *Surprise Attack: Lessons for Defense Planning* (Brookings Institution Press, 1981).

22. Mark Galeotti, "Even Putin Knows Invading Ukraine Won't Pay Off," *Foreign Policy*, February 22, 2022, https://foreignpolicy.com/2022/02/22/invasion-russia-ukraine-pay-off/; Harun Yilmaz, "No, Russia Will Not Invade Ukraine," Al Jazeera, February 9, 2022, https://www.aljazeera.com/opinions/2022/2/9/no-russia-will-not-invade-ukraine; Eugene Chausovsky, "Why Russia Probably Won't Attack Ukraine," *Foreign Policy*, December 27, 2022, https://foreignpolicy.com/2021/12/27/how-russia-decides-when-to-invade/; Harald Malmgren, "What the West Gets Wrong about Putin," UnHerd, January 13, 2022, https://unherd.com/2022/01/what-the-west-gets-wrong-about-putin/. See also Jonas J. Driedger and Mikhail Polianskii, "Utility-Based Predictions of Military Escalation: Why Experts Forecasted Russia Would Not Invade Ukraine," *Contemporary Security Policy* 44, no. 4 (2023): 544–60, https://doi.org/10.1080/13523260.2023.2259153.

23. Patrick Porter, "Out of the Shadows: Ukraine and the Shock of Non-hybrid War," *Journal of Global Security Studies* 8, no. 3 (2023): 1–15, https://doi.org/10.1093/jogss/ogad014.

24. Carr, *Twenty Years' Crisis*, 229.

25. Tricia Ruiz, "Feminist Theory and International Relations: The Feminist Challenge to Realism and Liberalism," *Soundings Journal* 88, no. 1 (2005): 1–7, https://giwps.georgetown.edu/dei-resources/feminist-theory-and-international-relations-the-feminist-challenge-to-realism-and-liberalism/.

26. Hugh White, "The Idea of National Security: What Use Is It to Policymakers?" (working paper, National Security College, Australian National University, Canberra, 2012), 8, https://openresearch-repository.anu.edu.au/items/c47b7b4b-b5d4-43a0-ab1c-3dcfcdd30a56.

27. Reinhold Niebuhr, *Moral Man and Immoral Society* (Westminster John Knox Press, 1932), 108.

28. William Bain, *Political Theology of International Order* (Oxford University Press, 2020).

29. Augustine, *The City of God against the Pagans*, trans. Robert Dyson (Cambridge University Press, 1998), 929.

30. Haslam, *No Virtue*, 29.

31. Steven Spielberg, dir., *Lincoln* (Walt Disney Studios, 2014).

32. Hans J. Morgenthau, *Politics among Nations: The Struggle for Power and Peace*, rev. ed. (Alfred A. Knopf, 1956), 9.

33. See C. A. J. Coady, "The Moral Reality in Realism," *Journal of Applied Philosophy* 22, no. 2 (2005): 121–36, www.jstor.org/stable/24354875.

34. Martin Thomas, "After Mers-el-Kébir: The Armed Neutrality of the Vichy French Navy, 1940–43," *English Historical Review* 112, no. 447 (1997): 643–70, http://www.jstor.org/stable/576348.

35. Winston S. Churchill, *The Second World War*, vol. 2, *Their Finest Hour* (Cassell, 1949), 206.

36. Paul R. Viotti, *Kenneth Waltz: An Intellectual Biography* (Columbia University Press, 2023), 47; Jennifer W. See, "A Prophet without Honor: Hans Morgenthau and the War in Vietnam, 1955–1965," *Pacific Historical Review* 70, no. 3 (2001): 419–48, https://doi.org/10.1525/phr.2001.70.3.419; Paul Starobin, "The Realists," *National Journal* 39, no. 37 (2006): 24–31.

37. Bill Barrow and Tom Raum, "CIA Declassifies Camp David Accords Intelligence," Associated Press, November 14, 2013, https://apnews.com/general-news-889eea23a43a4831808e1bdfd439ba4e.

38. Fouad Ajami, "The End of Pan-Arabism," *Foreign Affairs* 57, no. 2 (1978): 355–73.

39. For reports of Stalin's pet piece of sarcasm, see William D. Leahy, *I Was There* (Victor Gollancz, 1950), 408; Valentin Berezhkov, *At Stalin's Side: His Interpreter's Memoirs from the October Revolution to the Fall of the Dictator's Empire* (Carol, 1994), 310.

40. Alexander Wendt, "Anarchy Is What States Make of It: The Social Construction of Power Politics," *International Organization*, 46, no. 2 (1992): 391–425, http://www.jstor.org/stable/2706858.

41. Michael C. Desch, "It Is Kind to Be Cruel: The Humanity of American Realism," *Review of International Studies* 29, no. 3 (2003): 415–26, at 419–21, http://www.jstor.org/stable/20097863.

42. Van Jackson, *Grand Strategies of the Left: The Foreign Policy of Progressive World Making* (Cambridge University Press, 2023).

43. Gabriel Gorodetsky, "When Soviet Ideals Met International Reality," *Le Monde Diplomatique*, October 7, 2017, https://mondediplo.com/2017/10/05SovietIdeal.

44. For a recent rearticulation of this position, see Marc Mulholland, "Distrust Your Government," *Weekly Worker*, March 14, 2024, https://weeklyworker.co.uk/worker/1482/distrust-your-government/.

45. Leon D. Trotsky, "Uneven and Combined Development and the Role of American Imperialism: Minutes of a Discussion," in *Writings of Leon Trotsky [1932–1933]*, ed. George Breitman and Sarah Lovell (Pathfinder, 1972), 116–20.

46. David Blagden, "Uneven and Combined Development: Convergence Realism in Communist Regalia?," *Cambridge Review of International Affairs* 34, no. 2 (2021): 250–66, https://doi.org/10.1080/09557571.2020.1843002; Justin Rosenberg, "Uneven and Combined Development and International Relations—a Special Affinity?" *Millennium* 50, no. 2 (2022): 291–327, at 294–97, https://doi.org/10.1177/03058298211064346.

47. Stephen Pinker, *The Better Angels of Our Nature: A History of Violence and Humanity* (Penguin, 2012); Nils Petter Gleditsch, "Toward a Social-Democratic Peace?," *Ethics and International Affairs* 34, no. 1 (2020): 67–75, at 67, https://doi.org/10.1017/S0892679420000076.

48. Hedley Bull, *The Anarchical Society: A Study of Order in World Politics* (Macmillan, 1977); Barry Buzan, "The English School: An Underexploited Resource in IR," *Review of International Studies* 27, no. 3 (2001): 471–88, https://www.jstor.org/stable/20097749.

49. Adam Gopnik, "The Big One: Historians Rethink the War to End All Wars," *New Yorker*, August 23, 2004.

50. Daryl Press and Eugene Gholz, "The Effects of Wars on Neutral Countries: Why It Doesn't Pay to Preserve the Peace," *Security Studies* 10, no. 4 (2001): 1–57, https://doi.org/10.1080/09636410108429444.

51. Joshua R. Itzkowitz Shifrinson and Patrick Porter, "Why We Can't Be Friends with Our Allies," *Politico*, October 22, 2020, https://www.politico.com/news/magazine/2020/10/22/why-we-cant-be-friends-with-our-allies-431015.

52. Erica Chenoweth and Maria J. Stephan, "Why Civil Resistance Works: The Strategic Logic of Nonviolent Conflict," *International Security* 33, no. 1 (2008): 7–44, https://doi.org/10.1162/isec.2008.33.1.7.

53. On all three cases, see Lorenzo Raymond, "Why Nonviolent Civil Resistance Doesn't Work (Unless You Have Lots of Bombs)," *CounterPunch*, May 27, 2016, https://www.counterpunch.org/2016/05/27/why-nonviolent-civil-resistance-doesnt-work-unless-you-have-lots-of-bombs/.

54. Michael Mandelbaum, "Is Major War Obsolete?," *Survival* 40, no. 4 (1998): 20–38, https://doi.org/10.1093/survival/40.4.20.

55. See Campbell Craig, *Glimmer of a New Leviathan: Total War in the Realism of Niebuhr, Morgenthau and Waltz* (Columbia University Press, 2003).

56. Keir A. Lieber and Daryl G. Press, *The Myth of the Nuclear Revolution: Power Politics in the Atomic Age* (Cornell University Press, 2020); Kenneth N. Waltz and Scott D. Sagan, *The Spread of Nuclear Weapons: A Debate Renewed* (Stanford University Press, 2002).

57. For a strong articulation of the disarmament case, see Ward Hayes Wilson, *It Is Possible: A Future without Nuclear Weapons* (World School Press, 2023).

58. David Blagden, "Reactive Rearmament: The Instability of a Post-nuclear World" (paper presented at the 47th Annual British International Studies Association Conference, Glasgow, Scotland, June 2023).

59. Francis J. Gavin, "Strategies of Inhibition: U.S. Grand Strategy, the Nuclear Revolution, and Nonproliferation," *International Security* 40, no. 1 (2015): 9–46, https://doi.org/10.1162/ISEC_a_00205.

60. Joseph Joffe and James W. Davis, "Less Than Zero: Bursting the New Disarmament Bubble," *Foreign Affairs* 90, no. 1 (2011): 7–13, at 12.

61. Thomas C. Schelling, "The Future of Arms Control," *Operations Research* 9, no. 5 (1961): 722–31, at 723, http://www.jstor.org/stable/166817.

62. Malcolm Browne, "Nuclear Winter Theorists Pull Back," *New York Times*, January 23, 1990, C1; Andrew Revkin, "Hard Facts about Nuclear Winter," *Science Digest* 93 (1985): 62–68, 77–83; Alexandra Witze, "How a Small Nuclear War Would Transform the Entire Planet," *Nature* 579, no. 7800 (2020): 485–87.

63. Mattias Eken, "The Understandable Fear of Nuclear Weapons Doesn't Match Reality," The Conversation, March 14, 2017, https://theconversation.com/the-understandable-fear-of-nuclear-weapons-doesnt-match-reality-73563.

64. Matthew Rendall, "Nuclear Weapons and Intergenerational Exploitation," *Security Studies* 16, no. 4 (2007): 525–54, at 533, https://doi.org/10.1080/09636410701741070.

65. Craig, *Glimmer*, 172.

66. On this point, see Michael Quinlan, *Thinking about Nuclear Weapons: Principles, Problems, Prospects* (Oxford University Press, 2009), 67–71.

67. Keir A. Lieber and Daryl G. Press, "The Return of Nuclear Escalation: How America's Adversaries Have Hijacked Its Old Deterrence Strategy," *Foreign Affairs* 102, no. 6 (2023): 45–55.

68. E.g., see Elbridge Colby, "Restoring Deterrence," *Orbis* 51, no. 3 (2007): 413–28, https://doi.org/10.1016/j.orbis.2007.04.004; Richard Betts, "The Lost Logic of Deterrence: What the Strategy That Won the Cold War Can—and Can't—Do Now," *Foreign Affairs* 92, no. 2 (2013): 87–99.

69. Hugh White, *How to Defend Australia* (La Trobe University Press, 2019); Patrick Porter, "Why Australia Needs a Bomb in the Basement," *Australian Financial Review*, April 9, 2021, https://www.afr.com/policy/foreign-affairs/australia-needs-a-bomb-in-the-basement-20210329-p57eya.

70. Marina Yue Zhang, "Lithium, Lightest Metal on Earth, Carries Heavy Geopolitical Weight," Lowy Institute, December 28, 2023, https://www.lowyinstitute.org/the-interpreter/lithium-lightest-metal-earth-carries-heavy-geopolitical-weight.

71. See also Stephen M. Walt, "The Realist Guide to Solving Climate Change," *Foreign Policy*, August 13, 2021, https://foreignpolicy.com/2021/08/13/realist-guide-to-solving-climate-change/.

72. Chelsea Harvey, "The World Will Likely Miss 1.5 Degrees C—Why Isn't Anyone Saying So?," *Scientific American*, November 11, 2022, https://www.scientificamerican.com/article/the-world-will-likely-miss-1-5-degrees-c-why-isnt-anyone-saying-so/.

73. Nick Robins, *The Road to Net-Zero Finance* (Advisory Group on Finance, UK Climate Change Committee, December 2020), 3, https://www.theccc.org.uk/wp-content/uploads/2020/12/Finance-Advisory-Group-Report-The-Road-to-Net-Zero-Finance.pdf.

74. See also Tom Switzer, "Political Realism and the Environment: Why the United Nations Cannot Slash Global Emissions," in *The Edinburgh Companion to Political Realism*, ed. Robert Schuett and Miles Hollingworth (Edinburgh University Press, 2018), 517–27.

75. John Constantelos, Polly J. Diven, and H. Whitt Kilburn, "Can't Buy Me Love (with Foreign Aid)," *Foreign Policy Analysis* 19, no. 4 (2023): 1–24, https://doi.org/10.1093/fpa/orad024.

76. G. John Ikenberry et al., *The Crisis of American Foreign Policy: Wilsonianism in the Twenty-First Century* (Princeton University Press, 2008), 10.

77. George W. Bush, "President Sworn-In to Second Term," second inaugural address, transcript, White House, January 20, 2005, https://georgewbush-whitehouse.archives.gov/news/releases/2005/01/20050120-1.html.

78. Dale C. Copeland, *The Origins of Major War* (Cornell University Press, 2000).

79. The first two decades after 1989 of the unipolar Pax Americana, which made up less than 10 percent of America's history, generated 25 percent of the nation's total time at war. That period is more bellicose by an order of magnitude than the preceding eras of bipolarity and multipolarity in terms of frequency, if not intensity. See Nuno Mon-

teiro, "Unrest Assured: Why Unipolarity Is Not Peaceful," *International Security* 36, no. 3 (Winter 2011–2012): 9–40, http://www.jstor.org/stable/41428108; Bruce Porter, "The Warfare State," *American Heritage* 45, no. 4 (1994): 56–69.

80. David M. Edelstein, *Occupational Hazards: Success and Failure in Military Occupation* (Cornell University Press, 2008).

81. For a powerful counterargument, though one that affirms the picture of half measures, see Alex J. Bellamy, *Syria Betrayed: Atrocities, War and the Failure of Diplomacy* (Columbia University Press, 2022).

82. Robert D. Kaplan, *The Tragic Mind: Fear, Fate and the Burden of Power* (Yale University Press, 2023), 9.

83. For realist critiques of Kissinger, see Michael C. Desch, "Henry Kissinger: An Occasional Realist," *American Conservative*, September 15, 2020, https://www.theamericanconservative.com/henry-kissinger-an-occasional-realist/; Patrick Porter, "The Man Who Loved Power," *The Critic*, November 30, 2023, https://thecritic.co.uk/the-man-who-loved-power/.

84. On the Chennault affair—that is, the deliberate sabotage of the Paris peace talks and Kissinger's part in it—see Ken Hughes, *Chasing Shadows: The Nixon Tapes, the Chennault Affair and the Origins of Watergate* (University of Virginia Press, 2014). Hughes draws on the Federal Bureau of Investigation's transcripts; the notes of Richard Nixon's campaign chief of staff, H. R. Halderman; memoirs of officials from the Lyndon B. Johnson administration; Nixon's campaign foreign policy advisor, Richard V. Allen; and Kissinger's own recorded words to Nixon.

85. Mark Danner, "Words in a Time of War," *Los Angeles Times*, June 1, 2007, https://www.latimes.com/la-oe-danner1jun01-story.html; Bob Woodward, *State of Denial* (Simon and Schuster, 2006), 408.

86. Hans J. Morgenthau, *Politics among Nations: The Struggle for Power and Peace*, 5th rev. ed. (Knopf, 1978), 240. See also Sean Molloy, "Aristotle, Epicurus, Morgenthau and the Political Ethics of the Lesser Evil," *Journal of International Political Theory* 5, no. 1 (2009): 94–112, at 106.

87. Douglas L. Kriner and Francis X. Shen, "Battlefield Casualties and Ballot-Box Defeat: Did the Bush-Obama Wars Cost Clinton the White House?," *Political Science and Politics* 53, no. 2 (2020): 248–52, https://doi.org/10.1017/S104909651900204X; David Blagden and Patrick Porter, "Desert Shield of the Republic? A Realist Case for Abandoning the Middle East," *Security Studies* 30, no. 1 (2021): 5–48, at 38, https://doi.org/10.1080/09636412.2021.1885727.

88. Fouad Ajami, "The Summoning," *Foreign Affairs* 72, no. 4 (1993): 2–9, at 9.

89. Steven Forde, "Varieties of Realism: Thucydides and Machiavelli," *Journal of Politics* 54, no. 2 (1992): 372–93, at 384, https://www.jstor.org/stable/2132031.

90. Daniel Edward Grissom, "Thucydides' Dangerous World: Dual Forms of Danger in Classical Greek Interstate Relations" (PhD diss., University of Maryland, 2012), https://drum.lib.umd.edu/items/30acfa4d-b172-4543-8ebf-d9daeeb830f7.

91. Thucydides, *The Peloponnesian War*, trans. Rex Warner (Penguin, 1974), 2.65, 1.18, 7.29.

92. Erich S. Gruen, "Thucydides, His Critics and Interpreters," *Journal of Interdisciplinary History* 1, no. 2 (1971): 327–37, at 336, https://doi.org/10.2307/202647.

Chapter 2

1. Duncan S. Bell, e.g., claims realism is primarily an ideology built around negations. Bell, "Anarchy, Power and Death: Contemporary Political Realism as Ideology," *Journal of Political Ideologies* 7, no. 2 (2002): 221–39, https://doi.org/10.1080/1356931022 0137557.

2. Emma Ashford, "In Praise of Lesser Evils: Can Realism Repair Foreign Policy?," *Foreign Affairs* 101, no. 5 (2002): 211–18, at 218.

3. Jack Donnelly, "The Discourse of Anarchy in IR," *International Theory* 7, no. 3 (2015): 393–425, https://doi.org/10.1017/S1752971915000111; Laura Sjoberg, "Gender, Structure and War: What Waltz Couldn't See," *International Theory* 4, no. 1 (2012): 1–38, https://doi.org/10.1017/S175297191100025X.

4. Robert Axelrod and Robert O. Keohane, "Achieving Cooperation under Anarchy: Strategies and Institutions," *World Politics* 38, no. 1 (1985): 226–54, https://doi.org/10.2307/2010357.

5. Samuel J. Barkin, "Realist Constructivism," *International Studies Review* 5, no. 3 (2003): 325–42, at 328, https://doi.org/10.1046/j.1079-1760.2003.00503002.x; John J. Mearsheimer, *The Tragedy of Great Power Politics* (W. W. Norton, 2001), 407–9.

6. Hans J. Morgenthau, *Scientific Man versus Power Politics* (University of Chicago Press, 1946); Kenneth N. Waltz, *Theory of International Politics* (McGraw-Hill Education, 1979).

7. Jonathan Kirshner, *An Unwritten Future: Realism and Uncertainty in World Politics* (Princeton University Press, 2022); Richard Ned Lebow, "The Ancient Greeks and Modern Realism: Ethics, Persuasion, and Power," in *Political Thought and International Relations: Variations on a Realist Theme*, ed. Duncan Bell (Oxford University Press, 2009), 26–40.

8. Chris Brown, "Structural Realism, Classical Realism and Human Nature," *International Relations* 23, no. 2 (2009): 257–70, https://doi.org/10.1177/0047117809104638; Joseph Parent and J. M. Baron, "Elder Abuse: How the Moderns Mistreat Classical Realism," *International Studies Review* 13, no. 2 (2011): 193–213, https://doi.org/10.1111/j.1468-2486.2011.01021.x.

9. On the offensive-defensive realism debate, see Jeffrey W. Taliaferro, "Security-Seeking under Anarchy: Defensive Realism Revisited," *International Security* 25, no. 3 (2000–2001): 128–61, http://www.jstor.org/stable/2626708.

10. Mearsheimer, *Great Power Politics*.

11. Charles L. Glaser, *Rational Theory of International Politics: The Logic of Competition and Cooperation* (Princeton University Press, 2010).

12. Copeland, *Origins of Major War*.

13. In the next chapter, I will discuss Chinese realism and Beijing's shift from a "hide-and-bide" strategy to a pursuit of primacy in Asia on the back of a shift in power and wealth.

14. An honourable exception is Charles L. Glaser, who allows more for security-dilemma dynamics—that is, inadvertent escalation—as a source of the US-China rivalry. See Glaser, "Fear Factor: How to Know When You're in a Security Dilemma," *Foreign Affairs* 103, no. 4 (2024): 122–28.

15. On the debate about how best to check China's bid for primacy in Asia and how much to ideologize the competition, see Jeremy Friedman, "The Case for Inclusive Alliances: American Must Rediscover the Ideological Flexibility That Helped It Win the Cold War," *Foreign Affairs*, July 17, 2024, https://www.foreignaffairs.com/united-states/case-inclusive-alliances-cold-war; Matt Pottinger and Mike Gallagher, "No Substitute for Victory: America's Competition with China Must Be Won, Not Managed," *Foreign Affairs* 103, no. 3 (2024): 25–39; Elbridge Colby and Robert D. Kaplan, "The Ideology Delusion: America's Competition with China Is Not about Doctrine," *Foreign Affairs*, September 4, 2020, https://www.foreignaffairs.com/articles/united-states/2020-09-04/ideology-delusion.

16. Elbridge A. Colby, *The Strategy of Denial: American Defence in an Age of Great Power Conflict* (Yale University Press, 2021).

17. Dale C. Copeland, *A World Safe for Commerce: American Foreign Policy from the Revolution to the Rise of China* (Princeton University Press, 2024), 389.

18. On the criteria for judging realism's theoretical performance, see Stephen M. Walt, "The Enduring Relevance of the Realist Tradition," in *Political Science: The State of the Discipline*, ed. Ira Katznelson and Helen V. Milner (W. W. Norton, 2002), 197–235.

19. David A. Lake, "Escape from the State of Nature: Authority and Hierarchy in World Politics," *International Security* 32, no. 1 (2007): 47–79, https://doi.org/10.1162/isec.2007.32.1.47.

20. John Vasquez, "The Realist Paradigm and Degenerative versus Progressive Research Programs," *American Political Science Review* 91, no. 4 (1997): 899–912, https://doi.org/10.2307/2952172; Daniel H. Nexon, "The Balance of Power in the Balance," *World Politics* 61, no. 2 (2009): 330–59, at 353, https://doi.org/10.1017/S0043887109000124.

21. Paul W. Schroeder, "Historical Reality vs. Neo-realist Theory," *International Security* 19, no. 1 (1994): 108–48, https://doi.org/10.2307/2539150; Schroeder, *The Transformation of European Politics: 1763–1848* (Clarendon Press, 1994).

22. Schroeder, "Historical Reality," 129.

23. Bull, *Anarchical Society*; Buzan, "English School."

24. See the collected essays in Stuart J. Kaufman, Richard Little, and William C. Wohlforth, eds., *The Balance of Power in World History* (Palgrave Macmillan, 2007).

25. Randall L. Schweller, *Unanswered Threats: Political Constraints on the Balance of Power* (Princeton University Press, 2006).

26. Susan B. Martin, "From Balance of Power to Balancing Behavior: The Long and Winding Road," in *Perspectives on Structural Realism*, ed. Andrew K. Hanami (Palgrave Macmillan, 2003), 61–74.

27. Brian C. Rathbun, "The Rarity of Realpolitik: What Bismarck's Rationality

Tells Us about International Politics," *International Security* 43, no. 1 (2018): 7–55, https://doi.org/10.1162/isec_a_00323.

28. Imre Lakatos, *Philosophical Papers*, vol. 1, *The Methodology of Scientific Research Programmes* (1978; repr., Cambridge University Press, 2012). See also Jeffrey W. Legro and Andrew Moravcsik, "Is Anybody Still a Realist?," *International Security* 24, no. 2 (1999): 5–55, https://muse.jhu.edu/article/447679.

29. Keir A. Lieber and Gerard Alexander, "Waiting for Balancing: Why the World Is Not Pushing Back," *International Security* 30, no. 1 (2005): 109–39, http://www.jstor.org/stable/4137460; Stephen G. Brooks and William C. Wohlforth, *World out of Balance: International Politics and the Challenge of American Primacy* (Princeton University Press, 2008); Carla Norrlof, *America's Global Advantage: U.S. Hegemony and International Cooperation* (Cambridge University Press, 2010).

30. Stacey E. Goddard, "The Rhetoric of Appeasement: Hitler's Legitimation and British Foreign Policy, 1938–39," *Security Studies* 24, no. 1 (2015): 95–130, https://doi.org/10.1080/09636412.2015.1001216; Martha Finnemore, "Legitimacy, Hypocrisy, and the Social Structure of Unipolarity: Why Being a Unipole Isn't All That It's Cracked Up to Be," *World Politics* 61, no. 1 (2009): 58–85, https://doi.org/10.1017/S0043887109000082.

31. Geoffrey Parker, *Imprudent King: A New Life of Philip II* (Yale University Press, 2014).

32. Warren Kimball, ed., *Churchill and Roosevelt: The Complete Correspondence* (HarperCollins, 1988); Abraham M. Roof, "A Separate Peace? The Soviet Union and the Making of British Strategy in the Wake of 'Barbarossa,' June–September 1941," *Journal of Slavic Military Studies* 22, no. 2 (2009): 236–52, https://doi.org/10.1080/13518040902918121.

33. Alex Ilari Aissaoui, "Was There a Balance of Power System in the Ancient Near East?," *Diplomacy and Statecraft* 30, no. 3 (2019): 421–42, at 424–29, https://doi.org/10.1080/09592296.2019.1641916.

34. Joseph M. Parent and Sebastian Rosato, "Balancing in Neorealism," *International Security* 40, no. 2 (2015): 51–86, http://www.jstor.org/stable/43828295.

35. Steven E. Lobell, "A Granular Theory of Balancing," *International Studies Quarterly* 62, no. 3 (2018): 593–605, https://doi.org/10.1093/isq/sqy011.

36. Stephen Schlesinger, *Act of Creation: The Founding of the United Nations* (Westview Press, 2003), 331.

37. Michael Martinez, "Allies Spy on Allies Because a Friend Today May Not Be One Tomorrow," CNN, October 31, 2013, https://edition.cnn.com/2013/10/30/us/spying-on-allies-everybody-does-it/index.html.

38. William V. Harris, *War and Imperialism in Republican Rome: 327–70 BC* (Oxford University Press, 1985).

39. Arthur M. Eckstein, *Mediterranean Anarchy, Interstate War and the Rise of Rome* (University of California Press, 2006).

40. Marcus Fischer, "Feudal Europe, 800–1300: Communal Discourse and Conflictual Practices," *International Organization* 46, no. 2 (1992): 427–65, at 428, http://www.jstor.org/stable/2706859.

41. Richard N. Rosecrance, "A Concert of Powers," *Foreign Affairs* 71, no. 2 (1992): 64–68; Jennifer Mitzen, *Power in Concert: The Nineteenth-Century Origins of Global Governance* (University of Chicago Press, 2013), 22–23; Richard B. Elrod, "The Concert of Europe: A Fresh Look at the International System," *World Politics* 28, no. 2 (1976): 159–74, at 161–62.

42. Korina Kagan, "The Myth of the European Concert: The Realist-Institutionalist Debate and Great Power Behavior in the Eastern Question, 1821–41," *Security Studies* 7, no. 2 (1997): 1–57, at 54, https://doi.org/10.1080/09636419708429341.

43. Victoria Tin-Bor Hui, *War and State Formation in Ancient China and Early Modern Europe* (Cambridge University Press, 2003).

44. Colin Elman and Miriam Fendius Elman, "History versus Neo-realism: A Second Look," *International Security* 20, no. 1 (1995): 182–95, at 188–90, https://doi.org/10.2307/2539222.

45. Rush Doshi, *The Long Game: China's Grand Strategy to Displace American Order* (Oxford University Press, 2021), 159–83.

46. For a circumspect treatment of whether this constitutes an axis, see Eugene Rumer, "The United States and the 'Axis' of its Enemies," Carnegie Endowment for International Peace, November 25, 2024, https://carnegieendowment.org/research/2024/11/the-united-states-and-the-axis-of-its-enemies-myths-vs-reality?lang=en.

47. Christopher Layne, "The Unipolar Illusion: Why New Great Powers Will Rise," *International Security* 17, no. 4 (1993): 5–51, https://doi.org/10.2307/2539020.

48. Kevin Narizny, "On Systemic Paradigms and Domestic Politics: A Critique of the Newest Realism," *International Security* 42, no. 2 (2017): 155–90, https://doi.org/10.1162/ISEC_a_00296.

49. Jonathan Monten, "Thucydides and Modern Realism," *International Studies Quarterly* 50, no. 1 (2006): 3–25, https://doi.org/10.1111/j.1468-2478.2006.00390.x.

50. Robert Jervis, "Explaining the War in Iraq," in *Why Did the United States Invade Iraq?*, ed. Jane A. Kramer and A. Trevor Thrall (Routledge, 2012), 25–49, at 27.

51. For one study of predation, see Joshua R. Itzkowitz Shifrinson, *Rising Titans, Falling Giants: How Great Powers Exploit Power Shifts* (Cornell University Press, 2018).

52. Richard Ned Lebow offers this version of classical realist morality, linking downfall to moral misbehavior. See Lebow, *The Tragic Vision of Politics: Ethics, Interests and Orders* (Cambridge University Press, 2009).

53. Robert Jervis, "Realism, Neoliberalism, and Cooperation: Understanding the Debate," *International Security* 24, no. 1 (1999): 42–63, at 53, http://www.jstor.org/stable/2539347.

54. Andrew Kydd, "Sheep in Sheep's Clothing: Why Security Seekers Do Not Fight Each Other," *Security Studies* 7, no. 1 (1997): 114–55, https://doi.org/10.1080/09636419708429336.

55. Bull, *Anarchical Society*.

56. Joseph Grieco, "Anarchy and the Limits of Cooperation: A Realist Critique of the Newest Liberal Institutionalism," *International Organization* 42, no. 3 (1988): 485–507, https://doi.org/10.1017/S0020818300027715.

57. Robert O. Keohane and Lisa L. Martin, "The Promise of Institutionalist Theory," *International Security* 20, no. 1 (1995): 40, https://doi.org/10.2307/2539214.

58. Lloyd Gruber, *Ruling the World: Power Politics and the Rise of Supranational Institutions* (Princeton University Press, 2000).

59. Andrew J. Cole and Jane Vaynman, "Why Arms Control Is So Rare," *American Political Science Review* 114, no. 2 (2020): 324–55, https://doi.org/10.1017/S0003055420000167.

60. Jane Vaynman and Vipin Narang, "There Are Signs North Korea Is Working on Its Nuclear Program: Here's Why 'Denuclearization' Is So Problematic," *Washington Post*, June 30, 2018, https://www.washingtonpost.com/news/monkey-cage/wp/2018/06/30/there-are-signs-north-korea-is-still-working-on-its-nuclear-program-heres-why-denuclearization-is-so-problematic/.

61. Barton Gellman, "U.S. Spied on Iraq Via U.N.," *Washington Post*, March 2, 1999, https://www.washingtonpost.com/wp-srv/inatl/daily/march99/unscom2.htm.

62. Caitlin Talmadge, Lisa Michelini, and Vipin Narang, "When Actions Speak Louder Than Words: Adversary Perceptions of Nuclear No-First-Use Pledges," *International Security* 48, no. 4 (2024): 7–46, https://doi.org/10.1162/isec_a_00482.

63. Jack L. Goldsmith and Erica A. Posner, *The Limits of International Law* (Oxford University Press, 2007), 9.

64. Pratik Jakhar, "Whatever Happened to the South China Sea Ruling?," *The Interpreter*, July 12, 2021, https://www.lowyinstitute.org/the-interpreter/whatever-happened-south-china-sea-ruling.

65. Tanisha M. Fazal, "Dead Wrong? Battle Deaths, Military Medicine, and Exaggerated Reports of War's Demise," *International Security* 39, no. 1 (2014): 95–125, www.jstor.org/stable/24480546.

66. E.g., see Brian R. Urlacher, "Introducing Native American Conflict History (NACH) Data," *Journal of Peace Research* 58, no. 5 (2021): 1117–25, https://doi.org/10.1177/0022343320987274.

67. Bear F. Braumoeller, *Only the Dead: The Persistence of War in the Modern Age* (Oxford University Press, 2019).

68. Oona A. Hathaway and Scott J. Shapiro, *The Internationalists: How a Radical Plan to Outlaw War Remade the World* (Simon and Schuster, 2017), 13.

69. Dan Altman, "The Evolution of Territorial Conquest after 1945 and the Limits of the Territorial Conquest Norm," *International Organization* 74, no. 3 (2020): 490–522, https://doi.org/10.1017/S0020818320000119.

70. Michael Doyle, "Liberalism and World Politics," *American Political Science Review* 80, no. 4 (1986): 1151–69, https://doi.org/10.2307/1960861; Spencer Weart, *Never at War: Why Democracies Will Not Fight One Another* (Yale University Press, 1998).

71. Bruce Russet and William Antholis, "Do Democracies Fight Each Other? Evidence from the Peloponnesian War," *Journal of Peace Research* 29, no. 4 (1992): 415–34, https://doi.org/10.1177/0022343392029004005.

72. From the critique in Eric Robinson, "Reading and Misreading the Ancient Evidence for Democratic Peace," *Journal of Peace Research* 38, no. 5 (2001): 593–608, at 595–99, https://doi.org/10.1177/0022343301038005003.

73. Patrick J. McDonald, "Great Powers, Hierarchy, and Endogenous Regimes: Rethinking the Domestic Causes of Peace," *International Organization* 69, no. 3 (2015): 557–88, https://doi.org/10.1017/S0020818315000120.

74. Michael Doyle, "Why They Don't Fight: The Surprising Endurance of the Democratic Peace," *Foreign Affairs* 103, no. 4 (2024): 135–41.

75. Thomas C. Schelling, *Arms and Influence* (Yale University Press, 1966), 19.

76. This is as Bruno Tertrais reminds us. See Tertrais, *In Defense of Deterrence: The Relevance, Morality and Cost-Effectiveness of Nuclear Weapons* (Institut français des relations internationales, Fall 2011), 10, https://www.nonproliferation.eu/wp-content/uploads/2018/09/brunotertrais4ebbda42d7115.pdf.

77. Tertrais, *In Defense of Deterrence*, 9.

78. Victor Gobarev, "Soviet Military Plans and Actions during the First Berlin Crisis, 1948–1949," *Journal of Slavic Military Studies* 10, no. 3 (1997): 1–24, at 5, https://doi.org/10.1080/13518049708430303.

79. "Pak's N-Bomb Prevented Indian Retaliation after 26/11," *Indian Express*, March 9, 2009, https://indianexpress.com/article/india/india-others/paks-nbomb-prevented-indian-retaliation-after-26-11/, cited in Keith Payne, "Realism, Idealism, Deterrence and Disarmament," *Strategic Studies Quarterly* 13, no. 3 (2019): 7–37, at 35n53.

80. Edward Kaplan, *The End of Victory: Prevailing in the Thermonuclear Age* (Cornell University Press, 2022).

81. Keir A. Lieber and Daryl G. Press, "Why States Won't Give Nuclear Weapons to Terrorists," *International Security* 38, no. 1 (2013): 80–104, https://doi.org/10.1162/ISEC_a_00127.

82. Dan Sagir, *Weapons of Mass Deterrence: The Secret behind Israel's Nuclear Power* (Carmel Publishing House, 2024), 87; Sagir, "The Story of Restraint: The Yom Kippur War and Israel's Nuclear Capability," *Times of Israel*, August 11, 2023, https://blogs.timesofisrael.com/a-story-of-restraint-the-yom-kippur-war-and-israels-nuclear-capability/.

83. Wilson, *It Is Possible*.

84. George F. Kennan, *American Diplomacy: 1900–1950* (University of Chicago Press, 1951), 95–96.

85. Nina Tannenwald (@NinaTannenwald), "I'm sure Patrick will do a good job. However, let's help him out with the scope conditions by identifying some things realism doesn't expain [*sic*]. I'll start," X, March 28, 2024, 8:34 a.m., https://x.com/NinaTannenwald/status/1773342844159140246.

86. Roderick Bailey, "COVID Vaccines: Countries Have a History of Acting Selfishly—and When They Do, Everyone Loses Out," The Conversation, February 1, 2021, https://www.history.ox.ac.uk/article/covid-vaccines-countries-have-a-history-of-acting-selfishly-and-when-they-do-everyone-loses.

87. Seth A. Johnson, "The Pandemic and the Limits of Realism," *Foreign Policy*, June 24, 2020, https://foreignpolicy.com/2020/06/24/coronavirus-pandemic-realism-limited-international-relations-theory/.

88. William C. Wohlforth, "Realism and the End of the Cold War," *International Security* 19, no. 3 (1995): 91–129, https://doi.org/10.2307/2539233.

89. This information is derived from ICC's own list. See International Criminal Court, "Defendants," accessed March 1, 2025, https://www.icc-cpi.int/defendants.

90. Linda Hunt, "U.S. Coverup of Nazi Scientists," *Bulletin of the Atomic Scientists* 41, no. 4 (1985): 16–24.

91. Herbert P. Bix, *Hirohito and the Making of Modern Japan* (Perennial, 2000), 533–81.

92. Oumar Ba, "A Truly International Criminal Court: Why the New Prosecutor Should Look beyond Africa," *Foreign Affairs*, June 16, 2021, https://www.foreignaffairs.com/articles/africa/2021-06-18/truly-international-criminal-court.

93. Tim Sahay, "A New Non-alignment," *The Polycrisis*, November 9, 2022, https://www.phenomenalworld.org/analysis/non-alignment-brics/.

94. Human Rights Watch, "War Crimes, Crimes against Humanity, Ethnic Cleansing in West Darfur," May 9, 2024, https://www.hrw.org/news/2024/05/09/qa-war-crimes-crimes-against-humanity-ethnic-cleansing-west-darfur.

95. Sebastian Rosato, *Europe United: Power Politics and the Making of the European Community* (Cornell University Press, 2010). See also the critique in Andrew Moravcsik, "Did Power Politics Cause European Integration? Realist Theory Meets Qualitative Methods," *Security Studies* 22, no. 4 (2013): 773–90, https://doi.org/10.1080/09636412.2013.844511.

96. Marc Tran, "France and Germany Evade Deficit Fines," *The Guardian*, November 25, 2003, https://www.theguardian.com/business/2003/nov/25/theeuro.politics.

97. Guy Chazan, "How the Far Right Is Winning Over Young Europeans," *Financial Times*, May 29, 2024, https://www.ft.com/content/e77e1863-5a78-4d16-933c-6a665a66f261.

98. "Who Is in Charge of Europe?," *The Economist*, January 8, 2024, https://www.economist.com/europe/2024/01/08/who-is-in-charge-of-europe.

99. Nina Tannenwald, *The Nuclear Taboo: The United States and the Non-use of Nuclear Weapons since 1945* (Cambridge University Press, 2009).

100. Lieber and Press, "Return of Nuclear Escalation."

101. Daryl G. Press, Scott D. Sagan, and Benjamin A. Valentino, "Atomic Aversion: Experimental Evidence on Taboos, Traditions, and the Non-use of Nuclear Weapons," *American Political Science Review* 107, no. 1 (2013): 188–206, http://www.jstor.org/stable/23357763; Scott D. Sagan and Benjamin A. Valentino, "Revisiting Hiroshima in Iran: What Americans Really Think about Using Nuclear Weapons and Killing Noncombatants," *International Security* 42, no. 1 (2017): 41–79, https://doi.org/10.1162/ISEC_a_00284.

102. Matthew Sparkes, "Could Nuclear Weapons Testing Resume as Global Tensions Rise?," *New Scientist*, October 17, 2023, https://www.newscientist.com/article/2397254-could-nuclear-weapons-testing-resume-as-global-tensions-rise/.

103. Chaim D. Kaufmann and Robert A. Pape, "Explaining Costly International Moral Action: Britain's Sixty-Year Campaign against the Atlantic Slave Trade," *International Organization* 53, no. 4 (1989): 631–68, https://doi.org/10.1162/002081899551020.

104. John J. Mearsheimer and Stephen M. Walt, *The Israel Lobby and U.S. Foreign Policy* (Farrar, Straus and Giroux, 2007).

Chapter 3

1. Karen Smith and Arlene B. Tickner, "Introduction: International Relations from the Global South," in *International Relations from the Global South: Worlds of Difference*, ed. Tickner and Smith (Routledge, 2020), 1–14, at 1.

2. On non-Western realism, see Michiel Foulon and Gustav Meibauer, "Realist Avenues to Global International Relations," *European Journal of International Relations* 26, no. 4 (2020): 1203–29.

3. For a recent restatement of this position, see John M. Hobson, "Unmasking the Racism of Orthodox International Relations/International Political Economy Theory," *Security Dialogue* 53, no. 1 (2022): 3–20, https://doi.org/10.1177/09670106211061084.

4. Kelebogile Zvobgo and Meredith Loken, "Why Race Matters in International Relations," *Foreign Policy*, June 19, 2020, https://foreignpolicy.com/2020/06/19/why-race-matters-international-relations-ir/.

5. Edward W. Said, *Orientalism*, 25th anniversary ed. (Penguin, 2003), xix.

6. Sanjay Seth, *Beyond Reason: Postcolonial Theory and the Social Sciences* (Oxford University Press, 2021).

7. John M. Hobson, *The Eurocentric Conception of World Politics* (Cambridge University Press, 2012), 188.

8. Amitav Acharya and Barry Buzan, eds., *Non-Western International Relations Theory: Perspectives on and beyond Asia* (Routledge, 2009).

9. Arlene Tickner, "Seeing IR Differently: Notes from the Third World," *Millennium* 32, no. 2 (2003): 295–324, https://doi.org/10.1177/03058298030320020301.

10. Amitav Acharya, "Global International Relations (IR) and Regional Worlds: A New Agenda for International Studies," *International Studies Quarterly* 58, no. 4 (2014): 647–59, https://www.jstor.org/stable/43868815; Antonia Witt et al., "How to Problematize the Global?," *Millennium* 51, no. 1 (2022): 34–80, https://doi.org/10.1177/03058298221139330.

11. Robert W. Cox, "Social Forces, States and World Orders: Beyond International Relations Theory," *Millennium* 10, no. 2 (1981): 126–55, at 128, https://doi.org/10.1177/03058298810100020501.

12. Tickner, "Seeing IR Differently," 302–3.

13. Samuel P. Huntington, *The Clash of Civilizations and the Remaking of World Order* (Simon and Schuster, 1996).

14. Tickner, "Seeing IR Differently," 305n42.

15. Ted Hopf, "The Promise of Constructivism in International Relations Theory," *International Security* 23, no. 1 (1998): 171–200, https://doi.org/10.2307/2539267.

16. Lawrence Sondhaus, *Strategic Culture and Ways of War* (Routledge, 2006), 122.

17. Colin S. Gray, "National Style in Strategy: The American Example," *International Security*, 6, no. 2 (1981): 21–47, https://www.jstor.org/stable/2538645. On realism specifically, see Gray, "Out of the Wilderness: Prime Time for Strategic Culture," *Comparative Strategy* 26, no. 1 (2007): 1–20, at 6, https://doi.org/10.1080/01495930701271478; Richard Pipes, "Why the Soviet Union Thinks It Could Fight and Win a Nuclear War," *Commentary* 64, no. 1 (1977): 21–23.

18. Robert Lieber, "The Folly of Containment," *Commentary* 115, no. 4 (2003): 15–21;

Robert Kaufman, *In Defense of the Bush Doctrine* (Kentucky University Press, 2007); H. R. McMaster, *Battlegrounds: The Fight to Defend the Free World* (HarperCollins, 2020); Alexander Vindman, *The Folly of Realism: How the West Deceived Itself about Russia and Betrayed Ukraine* (Public Affairs, 2025).

19. David Adesnik, "War and Responsibility," *Free Beacon*, June 23, 2014, https://freebeacon.com/national-security/war-and-responsibility/.

20. Hal Brands and Peter Feaver, "Saving Realism from the So-Called Realists," *Commentary* 144, no. 2 (2017): 15–22.

21. Peter J. Katzenstein and Nobuo Okawara, "Japan's National Security: Structures, Norms, and Policies," *International Security* 17, no. 4 (1993): 84–118, https://doi.org/10.2307/2539023.

22. See Kevin C. Dunn and Timothy M. Shaw, eds., *Africa's Challenge to International Relations Theory* (Palgrave, 2000); Scarlett Cornelissen, Fantu Cheru, and Timothy M. Shaw, eds., *Africa and International Relations in the 21st Century* (Springer, 2012); Stephanie Neuman, *International Relations Theory and the Third World* (Macmillan, 1998); Siba N. Grovogui, "Regimes of Sovereignty: International Morality and the African Condition," *European Journal of International Relations* 8, no. 3 (2002): 315–38, https://doi.org/10.1177/1354066102008003001; Tandeka C. Nkiwane, "Africa and International Relations: Regional Lessons for a Global Discourse," *International Political Science Review* 22, no. 3 (2001): 279–90, https://doi.org/10.1177/0192512101221223005.

23. Ahmed Rashid, *The Resurgence of Central Asia: Islam or Nationalism* (Zed, 1994); Jennifer Knepper, "Nuclear Weapons and Iranian Strategic Culture," *Comparative Strategy* 27, no. 5 (2008): 451–68, https://doi.org/10.1080/01495930802430080. For a more qualified argument, see Ali Parchami, "An Iranian World View: The Strategic Culture of the Islamic Republic," *Journal of Advanced Military Studies* 13, no. 1 (2022): 9–23, https://doi.org/10.21140/mcuj.2022SIstratcul001.

24. Kate Sullivan, "Exceptionalism in Indian Diplomacy: The Origins of India's Moral Leadership Aspirations," *South Asia: Journal of South Asian Studies* 37, no. 4 (2014): 640–55, at 651, https://doi.org/10.1080/00856401.2014.939738; Baldev Raj Nayar and T. V. Paul, *India in the World Order: Searching for Major-Power Status* (Cambridge University Press, 2003), 140; Ian Hall, "The Persistence of Nehruvianism in India's Strategic Culture," in *Strategic Asia 2016–17: Understanding Strategic Cultures in the Asia-Pacific*, ed. Michael Wills, Ashley J. Tellis, and Alison Szalwinski (National Bureau of Asia Research, 2016), 141–67.

25. George Tanham, "India's Strategic Culture," *Washington Quarterly* 15, no. 1 (1992): 129–42, https://doi.org/10.1080/01636609209550082; R. M. Basrur, "Nuclear Weapons and Indian Strategic Culture," *Journal of Peace Research* 38, no. 2 (2001): 181–98, http://www.jstor.org/stable/425494; Rodney W. Jones, "India's Strategic Culture and the Origins of Omniscient Paternalism," in *Strategic Culture and Weapons of Mass Destruction: Culturally Based Insights into Comparative National Security Policymaking*, ed. Jeannie L. Johnson, Kerry M. Kartchner, and Jeffrey A. Larsen (Palgrave Macmillan, 2009), 117–36.

26. Huiyun Feng, *Chinese Strategic Culture and Foreign Policy Decision-Making: Confucianism, Leadership and War* (Routledge, 2007), 27. The literature on this varies on the extent to which the authors judge the culture determinative or how far culturally rooted preferences are changeable under pressure. See Jonathan Adelman and Chih-yu Shih, *Symbolic War: The Chinese Use of Force, 1840–1980* (Institute of International Relations, 1993); Barry Gills, "The Hegemonic Transition in East Asia: A Historical Perspective," in *Gramsci, Historical Materialism and International Relations*, ed. Stephen Gill (Cambridge University Press, 1993), 186–213, at 195; Derek M. C. Yuen, *Deciphering Sun Tzu: How to Read "The Art of War"* (Hurst, 2014); John K. Fairbank, "Varieties of the Chinese Military Experience," in *Chinese Ways in Warfare*, ed. Frank A. Kierman, Fairbank, and Edward L. Dreyer (Harvard University Press, 1974), 1–26.

27. I am grateful to John Sullivan for his remarks on this point. See also Nicola Di Cosmo, "The Origins of the Great Wall," *Silk Road* 4, no. 1 (2006): 14–19, at 18.

28. Jeffrey Lewis, *The Minimum Means of Reprisal: China's Search for Security in a Nuclear Age* (MIT Press, 2007).

29. Steve Chan, *Thucydides' Trap? Historical Interpretation, Logic of Inquiry and the Future of Sino-American Relations* (University of Michigan Press, 2020).

30. Alastair Iain Johnston, *Cultural Realism: Strategic Culture and Grand Strategy in Chinese History* (Princeton University Press, 1997).

31. On the "Chinese cult of defense," see Andrew Scobell, *China's Use of Military Force: Beyond the Great Wall and the Long March* (Cambridge University Press, 2003), 15–39.

32. David C. Kang, "Power Transitions: Thucydides Didn't Live in Asia," *Washington Quarterly* 41, no. 1 (2018): 137–54, https://doi.org/10.1080/0163660X.2018.1445905. This draws on his earlier work: see Kang, *China Rising: Power, Peace and Order in East Asia* (Columbia University Press, 2007); Kang, "Getting Asia Wrong: The Need for New Analytical Frameworks," *International Security* 27, no. 4 (2003): 57–85, http://www.jstor.org/stable/4137604.

33. See Nicola Nymalm and Johannes Plagemann, "Comparative Exceptionalism: Universality and Particularity in Foreign Policy Discourses," *International Studies Review* 21, no. 1 (2019): 12–37, https://doi.org/10.1093/isr/viy008.

34. Madeleine K. Albright, interview by Matt Lauer, *The Today Show*, NBC, February 19, 1998, transcript, US Department of State Archive, https://1997-2001.state.gov/statements/1998/980219a.html.

35. Said, preface, xxi.

36. Aaron Beers Sampson, "Tropical Anarchy: Waltz, Wendt, and the Way We Imagine International Politics," *Alternatives* 27, no. 4 (2002): 429–57, https://doi.org/10.1177/030437540202700402.

37. Matthew Specter, *The Atlantic Realists: Empire and International Political Thought between Germany and the United States* (Stanford University Press, 2022).

38. Adam Tooze, "John Mearsheimer and the Dark Origins of Realism," *New Statesman*, March 8, 2022, https://www.newstatesman.com/ideas/2022/03/john-mearsheimer-dark-origins-realism-russia.

39. I am grateful to Michael Lind for our exchange on this point.

40. Waltz, *Theory of International Politics*, 25.

41. Robert Gilpin, *War and Change in World Politics* (Cambridge University Press, 1986), 23.

42. Gilpin, "Richness of the Tradition," 290.

43. Errol Henderson, *African Realism: International Relations Theory and Africa's Wars in the Postcolonial Era* (Rowman and Littlefield, 2015).

44. William Brown, "Africa and International Relations: A Comment on IR Theory, Anarchy and Statehood," *Review of International Studies* 32, no. 1 (2006): 119–43, at 129, https://doi.org/10.1017/S0260210506006954.

45. Paul Kennedy, *The Rise and Fall of the Great Powers* (Random House, 1987), 14–16, 458–71.

46. Hans J. Morgenthau, *Politics among Nations: The Struggle for Power and Peace*, 3rd rev. ed. (Knopf, 1960), 359–61 (originally published in 1948). See also Francis P. Sempa, "Hans Morgenthau and the Balance of Power in Asia," *The Diplomat*, May 25, 2015, https://thediplomat.com/2015/05/hans-morgenthau-and-the-balance-of-power-in-asia/.

47. Thomas J. Christensen, "Chinese Realpolitik," *Foreign Affairs* 75, no. 5 (1996): 37–52, at 37.

48. Henrik Stalhane Hiim, "Hardening Chinese Realpolitik in the 21st Century: The Evolution of Beijing's Thinking about Arms Control," *Journal of Contemporary China* 31, no. 133 (2022): 86–100, https://www.tandfonline.com/doi/full/10.1080/10670564.2021.1926095.

49. I am grateful to Will Liley for suggesting some of these lines of criticism.

50. Alvaro Morcillo Laiz, "The Cold War Origins of Global IR: The Rockefeller Foundation and Realism in Latin America," *International Studies Review* 24, no. 1 (2022): 1–26, https://doi.org/10.1093/isr/viab061.

51. Huang Yang, "Thucydides in China," *KNOW: A Journal on the Formation of Knowledge* 6, no. 2 (2022): 351–71, at 365–66, https://doi.org/10.1086/721421.

52. Jun Mai, "'China's Military Must Spend More' to Meet US War Threat," *South China Morning Post*, March 8, 2021, https://www.scmp.com/news/china/politics/article/3124591/chinas-military-must-spend-more-meet-us-war-threat.

53. Yaping Qin, "Development of International Relations Theory in China: Progress through Debates," *International Relations of the Asia Pacific* 11, no. 2 (2011): 231–57, at 238, https://doi.org/10.1093/irap/lcr003.

54. Kenneth N. Waltz, *Man, the State, and War: A Theoretical Analysis* (Columbia University Press, 1954).

55. Parent and Baron, "Elder Abuse."

56. Waltz, *Man, the State, and War*.

57. Carr, *Twenty Years' Crisis*.

58. "The international community is without government, without a central authority to preserve law and order, and it does not guarantee the member states either their territorial integrity, their political independence, or their rights under interna-

tional law. States exist, therefore, primarily in terms of their own strength or that of their protector states and, if they wish to maintain their independence, they must make the preservation or improvement of their power position the principal objective of foreign policy." Nicholas J. Spykman, *America's Strategy in World Politics* (Harcourt, Brace, 1942), 446.

59. "For national policy, we must never forget, controls at the most only national action: thus the pacifist nation can disarm itself but it does not disarm its enemies . . . until all the nation's rivals and potential enemies are irrevocably committed to the pacifist ideal, it is a form of criminal negligence to act as if they were already committed to it." Walter Lippmann, *U.S. Foreign Policy: Shield of the Republic* (Little, Brown, 1943), 52.

60. Hans J. Morgenthau, "The Primacy of the National Interest," *American Scholar* 18, no. 2 (1949): 207–12, at 211, http://www.jstor.org/stable/41205156.

61. "War with Iraq Is Not in America's National Interest," *New York Times*, September 26, 2002. See also John J. Mearsheimer and Stephen M. Walt, "An Unnecessary War," *Foreign Policy*, November 3, 2009, https://foreignpolicy.com/2009/11/03/an-un necessary-war-2/.

62. Haro Karkour and Felix Rösch, "Towards IR's 'Fifth Debate': Racial Justice and the National Interest in Classical Realism," *International Studies Review* 26, no. 2 (2024): viae030, https://doi.org/10.1093/isr/viae030.

63. This is also acknowledged by commentators sympathetic with the idea that India has a restraining strategic culture. See Nabarun Roy, "India's Use of Military Power and the Sovereignty Principle: Insights from the Neighborhood," *India Review* 23, no. 2 (2024): 95–114, https://doi.org/10.1080/14736489.2024.2324637.

64. C. Raja Mohan, "Explained: How Balakot Changed the Familiar Script of India-Pakistan Military Crises," *Indian Express*, March 4, 2019, https://carnegieendow ment.org/posts/2019/03/explained-how-balakot-changed-the-familiar-script-of-india -pakistan-military-crises?lang=en.

65. Office of the Director of National Intelligence, *Annual Threat Assessment of the U.S. Intelligence Community* (DNI, February 2023), 34, https://www.dni.gov/files/ ODNI/documents/assessments/ATA-2023-Unclassified-Report.pdf.

66. According to US intelligence, India's foreign-intelligence agency, the Research and Analysis Wing (RAW), oversees this assassination program. Hannah Ellis-Petersen, Aakash Hassan, and Shah Meer Baloch, "Indian Government Ordered Killings in Pakistan, Intelligence Officials Claim," *The Guardian*, April 4, 2024, https:// www.theguardian.com/world/2024/apr/04/indian-government-assassination-allega tions-pakistan-intelligence-officials.

67. Arpan Banerjee, "Indian Surgical Strikes: Accelerating the Emergence of Nascent Norms of Use of Force Against Non-state Actors," *Cambridge International Law Journal*, September 6, 2017, https://cilj.co.uk/2017/09/06/indian-surgical-strikes-accel erating-the-emergence-of-nascent-norms-of-use-of-force-against-non-state-actors/.

68. "Narendra Modi Is Remaking India's 1.4m Strong Military," *The Economist*, November 29, 2023, https://www.economist.com/asia/2023/11/29/narendra-modi-is -remaking-indias-14m-strong-military.

69. M. Misra, "The Indian Machiavelli: Pragmatism versus Morality, and the Reception of *Arthasastra* in India, 1905–2014," *Modern Asian Studies* 50, no. 1 (2016): 310–44, https://doi.org/10.1017/S0026749X14000638.

70. Deepshikha Shahi, *Kautilya and Non-Western IR Theory* (Palgrave, 2019), 3; Harsh V. Pant, "Is India Developing a Strategy for Power?," *Washington Quarterly* 38, no. 4 (2015): 99–113, at 104–5, https://doi.org/10.1080/0163660X.2015.1125831.

71. Arshid Iqbal Dar, "Beyond Eurocentrism: Kautilya's Realism and India's Regional Diplomacy," *Humanities and Social Sciences Education* 8 (2021): 1–7, https://doi.org/10.1057/s41599-021-00888-6.

72. Yuan-Kang Wang, *Harmony and War: Confucian Culture and Chinese Power* (Columbia University Press, 2011), 111. On the Ordu debate, see ibid., 130–35.

73. Wang, *Harmony and War*, 132.

74. Michael C. Desch, "Culture Clash: Assessing the Importance of Ideas in Security Studies," *International Security* 23, no. 1 (1998): 141–70, https://doi.org/10.2307/2539266.

75. John F. Sullivan, "Sun Tzu's Fighting Words," *Strategy Bridge*, June 15, 2020, https://thestrategybridge.org/the-bridge/2020/6/15/sun-tzus-fighting-words.

76. Peter Jorge, *Sun Tzu in the West: The Anglo-American Art of War* (Cambridge University Press, 2022).

77. Fiona S. Cunningham and M. Taylor Fravel, "Assuring Assured Retaliation: China's Nuclear Posture and U.S.-China Strategic Stability," *International Security* 40, no. 2 (2015): 7–50, at 10, http://www.jstor.org/stable/43828294. The leaked document, "Lowering the Threshold of Nuclear Threats," lowers the threshold to a greater degree: "Targets that could draw such a response include any of China's leading urban centers or its atomic or hydroelectric power facilities." Agence France-Presse, "China Shifting Nuclear Rules of Engagement: Report," Defense Talk, January 6, 2011, https://www.defencetalk.com/china-shifting-nuclear-rules-of-engagement-report-31090/.

78. See in particular the skeptical accounts collected in Brenda Shaffer, ed., *The Limits of Culture: Islam and Foreign Policy* (MIT Press, 2006), especially the essays by Shaffer and Svante E. Cornell: Shaffer, "The Islamic Republic of Iran: Is It Really?," in Shaffer, *Limits of Culture*, 219–41; Cornell, "Pakistan's Foreign Policy: Islamic or Pragmatic?," in Shaffer, *Limits of Culture*, 291–325.

79. An alternative argument suggests that Iran's outward religious rhetoric, posing as the leader of pan-Islamic resistance to America's corrupt order, is still consequential because it has helped generate enmity in Washington. This is true, but common interests have led even these adversaries to also collaborate in the shadows from the Reagan-era Contra affair to tacit cooperation in containing the expansion of the Islamic State.

80. Lynn E. Davis et al., *Iran's Nuclear Future: Critical U.S. Policy Choices* (RAND, 2011), 12n10, https://www.rand.org/content/dam/rand/pubs/monographs/2011/RAND_MG1087.pdf.

81. Andrew Small, *The China-Pakistan Axis: Asia's New Geopolitics* (Hurst, 2015).

82. Ivan Arreguin-Toft, "How the Weak Win Wars: A Theory of Asymmetric Con-

flict," *International Security* 26, no. 1 (2001): 93–128, at 96, http://www.jstor.org/stable/3092079. Arreguín-Toft uses the rough-and-ready measure of population and armed forces size, which doesn't tell us everything, but it is a good start.

83. Waltz, *Theory of International Politics*, 72.

84. Christian Burger and Anders Wivel, "Sneaky Foreign Policy? A Realist-Pragmatist Framework of Agency and the Case of the Solomon Islands" (unpublished manuscript, paper presented at the 65th Annual Conference of the International Studies Association, San Francisco, CA, April 2024); Anders Wivel and Kajsa Ji Noe Oest, "Security, Profit or Shadow of the Past? Explaining the Security Strategies of Microstates," *Cambridge Review of International Affairs* 23, no. 3 (2010): 429–53, https://doi.org/10.1080/09557571.2010.484047; Revecca Pedi and Anders Wivel, "The Power (Politics) of the Weak Revisited: Realism and the Study of Small-State Foreign Policy," in *Agency, Security and Governance of Small States: A Global Perspective*, ed. I. T. Kolnberger and H. Koff (Routledge, 2023), 13–28.

85. Zongyuan Zoe Liu, "What the China-Solomon Islands Pact Means for the U.S. and the South Pacific," Council on Foreign Relations, May 4, 2022, https://www.cfr.org/in-brief/china-solomon-islands-security-pact-us-south-pacific.

86. Nick Sas and Chrisnrita Aumanu-Leong, "Solomon Islands Receives Visits from United States, China and Japan as 'Friends to All, Enemy to None' Policy Proves Popular," ABC News, March 21, 2023, https://www.abc.net.au/news/2023-03-22/solomon-islands-china-us-japan-visits/102123368.

87. Burger and Wivel, "Sneaky Foreign Policy," 8.

88. Arnold Wolfers, *Discord and Collaboration: Essays on International Politics* (Johns Hopkins University Press, 1962), 112.

89. Hans Mouritzen, "Tension between the Strong, and the Strategies of the Weak," *Journal of Peace Research* 28, no. 2 (1991): 217–30, https://doi.org/10.1177/0022343391028002007.

90. Thucydides, *Peloponnesian War*, 5.103.1.

91. For a strong call for a return to hybridity partly via the case of Toussaint Louverture, see Marco Viera, "The Decolonial Subject and the Problem of Non-Western Authenticity," *Postcolonial Studies* 22, no. 2 (2019): 150–67, https://doi.org/10.1080/13688790.2019.1608795.

92. Tarak Barkawi, "Empire and Order in International Relations and Security Studies," in *Oxford Research Encyclopedia of International Studies*, 16, last modified November 30, 2017, https://doi.org/10.1093/acrefore/9780190846626.013.164.

93. David Martin, "Five Years Later: An Axiom of War," CBS News, March 18, 2008, https://www.cbsnews.com/news/five-years-later-an-axiom-of-war/; David Petraeus, "Learning Counterinsurgency: Observations from Soldiering in Iraq," *Military Review* 86, no. 1 (January–February 2006): 2–12.

94. Stephen Biddle, "Afghanistan's Legacy: Emerging Lessons of an Ongoing War," *Washington Quarterly* 37, no. 2 (2014): 73–86, at 80, https://doi.org/10.1080/0163660X.2014.926210.

95. Fernando Coimbra, dir., *Sand Castle* (Treehouse Pictures, 2017).

96. Jacqueline Hazelton, *Bullets Not Ballots: Success in Counterinsurgency Warfare* (Cornell University Press, 2021).

97. Charles S. Meier, *Among Empires: American Ascendancy and Its Predecessors* (Harvard University Press, 2006), 131.

98. This logic also helps explain why the US-led multinational force successfully suppressed resistance and reduced the level of conflict for a period. With more troops and trillions of dollars, Petraeus was able to help the new regime in Baghdad realign Sunni communities that had once revolted and to defeat al-Qaeda in Iraq. The Sons of Iraq, former insurgents, already loathed al-Qaeda in Iraq's predatory behavior, but the "surge" strengthened US forces and bolstered the state in Baghdad, making both look strong enough to align with.

99. Christine Sylvester, *Feminist International Relations: An Unfinished Journey* (Cambridge University Press, 2009); J. Ann Tickner, *Gender in International Relations: Feminist Perspectives on Achieving Global Security* (Columbia University Press, 1992); Anne Sisson Runyan and V. Spike Peterson, "The Radical Future of Realism: Feminist Subversions of IR Theory," *Alternatives* 16, no. 1 (1991): 67–106, https://www.jstor.org/stable/40644702; Sandra Whitworth, "Gender in the Inter-paradigm Debate," *Millennium* 18, no. 2 (1989): 265–72, https://doi.org/10.1177/03058298890180020201.

100. Adam Durbin, "Johnson Says If Putin Were a Woman He Would Not Have Invaded," BBC News, June 29, 2022, https://www.bbc.co.uk/news/uk-61976526.

101. Joan Michelson, "'The Biggest Challenge Is Men Starting Wars'—Hillary Clinton to Women Peace Activists," *Forbes*, October 8, 2023, https://www.forbes.com/sites/joanmichelson2/2023/10/08/the-biggest-challenge-is-men-starting-wars--hillary-clinton-to-women-peace-activists/.

102. Pinker, *Better Angels*, 684.

103. Daniel P. Barr, *Unconquered: The Iroquois League at War in Colonial America* (Bloomsbury, 2006), 12.

104. Madison Schramm and Alexandra Stark, "Peacemakers or Iron Ladies? A Cross-National Study of Gender and International Conflict," *Security Studies* 29, no. 3 (2020): 515–48, https://doi.org/10.1080/09636412.2020.1763450.

105. Oeindrila Dube and S. P. Harish, "Queens," *Journal of Political Economy* 128, no. 7 (2020): 2579–652, https://doi.org/10.1086/707011.

Epilogue

1. On what we now know about the Cuban missile crisis, see Sheldon M. Stern, *The Cuban Missile Crisis in American Memory: Myth versus Reality* (Stanford University Press, 2012).

2. Thucydides, *Peloponnesian War*, 1.22.18.

Bibliography

Acharya, Amitav. "Global International Relations (IR) and Regional Worlds: A New Agenda for International Studies." *International Studies Quarterly* 58, no. 4 (2014): 647–59. https://www.jstor.org/stable/43868815.

Acharya, Amitav, and Barry Buzan, eds. *Non-Western International Relations Theory: Perspectives on and beyond Asia*. Routledge, 2009.

Adelman, Jonathan, and Chih-yu Shih. *Symbolic War: The Chinese Use of Force, 1840–1980*. Institute of International Relations, 1993.

Adesnik, David. "War and Responsibility." *Free Beacon*, June 23, 2014. https://freebeacon.com/national-security/war-and-responsibility/.

Aissaoui, Alex Ilari. "Was There a Balance of Power System in the Ancient Near East?" *Diplomacy and Statecraft* 30, no. 3 (2019): 421–42. https://doi.org/10.1080/09592296.2019.1641916.

Ajami, Fouad. "The End of Pan-Arabism." *Foreign Affairs* 57, no. 2 (1978): 355–73.

Ajami, Fouad. "The Summoning." *Foreign Affairs* 72, no. 4 (1993): 2–9.

Albright, Madeleine K. Interview by Matt Lauer. *The Today Show*, NBC, February 19, 1998. Transcript. US Department of State Archive. https://1997-2001.state.gov/statements/1998/980219a.html.

Altman, Dan. "The Evolution of Territorial Conquest after 1945 and the Limits of the Territorial Conquest Norm." *International Organization* 74, no. 3 (2020): 490–522. https://doi.org/10.1017/S0020818320000119.

Arreguin-Toft, Ivan. "How the Weak Win Wars: A Theory of Asymmetric Conflict." *International Security* 26, no. 1 (2001): 93–128. http://www.jstor.org/stable/3092079.

Ashford, Emma. "In Praise of Lesser Evils: Can Realism Repair Foreign Policy?" *Foreign Affairs* 101, no. 5 (2002): 211–18.

Ashley, Richard K. "The Poverty of Neorealism." *International Organization* 38, no. 2 (1984): 225–86. http://www.jstor.org/stable/2706440.

Axelrod, Robert, and Robert O. Keohane. "Achieving Cooperation under Anarchy: Strategies and Institutions." *World Politics* 38, no. 1 (1985): 226–54. https://doi.org/10.2307/2010357.

Augustine. *The City of God against the Pagans*. Translated by Robert Dyson. Cambridge University Press, 1998.

Ba, Oumar. "A Truly International Criminal Court: Why the New Prosecutor Should Look Beyond Africa." *Foreign Affairs*, June 16, 2021. https://www.foreignaffairs.com/articles/africa/2021-06-18/truly-international-criminal-court.

Bailey, Roderick. "COVID Vaccines: Countries Have a History of Acting Selfishly—and When They Do, Everyone Loses Out." The Conversation, February 1, 2021. https://www.history.ox.ac.uk/article/covid-vaccines-countries-have-a-history-of-acting-selfishly-and-when-they-do-everyone-loses.

Bain, William. *Political Theology of International Order*. Oxford University Press, 2020.

Banerjee, Arpan. "Indian Surgical Strikes: Accelerating the Emergence of Nascent Norms of Use of Force against Non-state Actors." *Cambridge International Law Journal*, September 6, 2017. https://cilj.co.uk/2017/09/06/indian-surgical-strikes-accelerating-the-emergence-of-nascent-norms-of-use-of-force-against-non-state-actors/.

Barkawi, Tarak. "Empire and Order in International Relations and Security Studies." In *Oxford Research Encyclopedia of International Studies*. Last modified November 30, 2017. https://doi.org/10.1093/acrefore/9780190846626.013.164.

Barkin, Samuel J. "Realist Constructivism." *International Studies Review* 5, no. 3 (2003): 325–42. https://doi.org/10.1046/j.1079-1760.2003.00503002.x.

Barr, Daniel P. *Unconquered: The Iroquois League at War in Colonial America*. Bloomsbury, 2006.

Barrow, Bill, and Tom Raum. "CIA Declassifies Camp David Accords Intelligence." Associated Press, November 14, 2013. https://apnews.com/general-news-889eea23a43a4831808e1bdfd439ba4e.

Basrur, R. M. "Nuclear Weapons and Indian Strategic Culture." *Journal of Peace Research* 38, no. 2 (2001): 181–98. http://www.jstor.org/stable/425494.

Bell, Duncan S. "Anarchy, Power and Death: Contemporary Political Realism as Ideology." *Journal of Political Ideologies* 7, no. 2 (2002): 221–39. https://doi.org/10.1080/13569310220137557.

Bell, Duncan S. "What Is Liberalism?" *Political Theory* 42, no. 6 (2014): 682–715. https://doi.org/10.1177/0090591714535103.

Bellamy, Alex J. *Syria Betrayed: Atrocities, War and the Failure of Diplomacy*. Columbia University Press, 2022.

Berezhkov, Valentin. *At Stalin's Side: His Interpreter's Memoirs from the October Revolution to the Fall of the Dictator's Empire*. Carol, 1994.

Betts, Richard K. "The Lost Logic of Deterrence: What the Strategy That Won the Cold War Can—and Can't—Do Now." *Foreign Affairs* 92, no. 2 (2013): 87–99.

Betts, Richard K. "The Realist Persuasion." *National Interest* 139 (2015): 46–55.

Betts, Richard K. *Surprise Attack: Lessons for Defense Planning*. Brookings Institution Press, 1981.

Biddle, Stephen. "Afghanistan's Legacy: Emerging Lessons of an Ongoing War."

Washington Quarterly 37, no. 2 (2014): 73–86. https://doi.org/10.1080/0163660X.2014.926210.

Bix, Herbert P. *Hirohito and the Making of Modern Japan*. Perennial, 2000.

Blagden, David. "Reactive Rearmament: The Instability of a Post-nuclear World." Paper presented at the 47th Annual British International Studies Association Conference, Glasgow, Scotland, June 2023.

Blagden, David. "Uneven and Combined Development: Convergence Realism in Communist Regalia?" *Cambridge Review of International Affairs* 34, no. 2 (2021): 250–66. https://doi.org/10.1080/09557571.2020.1843002.

Blagden, David, and Patrick Porter. "Desert Shield of the Republic? A Realist Case for Abandoning the Middle East." *Security Studies* 30, no. 1 (2021): 5–48. https://doi.org/10.1080/09636412.2021.1885727.

Booth, Ken. *A Theory of World Security*. Cambridge University Press, 2007.

Brands, Hal, and Peter Feaver. "Saving Realism from the So-Called Realists." *Commentary* 144, no. 2 (2017): 15–22.

Braumoeller, Bear F. *Only the Dead: The Persistence of War in the Modern Age*. Oxford University Press, 2019.

Brooks, Stephen G., and William C. Wohlforth. *World out of Balance: International Politics and the Challenge of American Primacy*. Princeton University Press, 2008.

Brown, Chris. "Structural Realism, Classical Realism and Human Nature." *International Relations* 23, no. 2 (2009): 257–70. https://doi.org/10.1177/0047117809104638.

Brown, William. "Africa and International Relations: A Comment on IR Theory, Anarchy and Statehood." *Review of International Studies* 32, no. 1 (2006): 119–43. https://doi.org/10.1017/S0260210506006954.

Browne, Malcolm. "Nuclear Winter Theorists Pull Back." *New York Times*, January 23, 1990, C1.

Bull, Hedley. *The Anarchical Society: A Study of Order in World Politics*. Macmillan, 1977.

Burger, Christian, and Anders Wivel. "Sneaky Foreign Policy? A Realist-Pragmatist Framework of Agency and the Case of the Solomon Islands." Paper presented at the 65th Annual Conference of the International Studies Association, San Francisco, CA, April 2024.

Bush, George W. "President Sworn-In to Second Term." Second inaugural address. White House, January 20, 2005. https://georgewbush-whitehouse.archives.gov/news/releases/2005/01/20050120-1.html.

Buzan, Barry. "The English School: An Underexploited Resource in IR." *Review of International Studies* 27, no. 3 (2001): 471–88. https://www.jstor.org/stable/20097749.

Carr, E. H. *The Twenty Years' Crisis: 1919–1939; An Introduction to the Study of International Relations*. Macmillan, 1962.

Chan, Steve. *Thucydides' Trap? Historical Interpretation, Logic of Inquiry and the Future of Sino-American Relations*. University of Michigan Press, 2020.

Chausovsky, Eugene. "Why Russia Probably Won't Attack Ukraine." *Foreign Policy*,

December 27, 2022. https://foreignpolicy.com/2021/12/27/how-russia-decides-when-to-invade.

Chazan, Guy. "How the Far Right Is Winning Over Young Europeans." *Financial Times*, May 29, 2024. https://www.ft.com/content/e77e1863-5a78-4d16-933c-6a665a66f261.

Chenoweth, Erica, and Maria J. Stephan. "Why Civil Resistance Works: The Strategic Logic of Nonviolent Conflict." *International Security* 33, no. 1 (2008): 7–44. https://doi.org/10.1162/isec.2008.33.1.7.

Christensen, Thomas J. "Chinese Realpolitik." *Foreign Affairs* 75, no. 5 (1996): 37–52.

Churchill, Winston S. *The Second World War*. Vol. 2, *Their Finest Hour*. Cassell, 1949.

Coady, C. A. J. "The Moral Reality in Realism." *Journal of Applied Philosophy* 22, no. 2 (2005): 121–36. www.jstor.org/stable/24354875.

Coimbra, Fernando, dir. *Sand Castle*. Treehouse Pictures, 2017.

Colby, Elbridge A. "Restoring Deterrence." *Orbis* 51, no. 3 (2007): 413–28. https://doi.org/10.1016/j.orbis.2007.04.004.

Colby, Elbridge A. *The Strategy of Denial: American Defence in an Age of Great Power Conflict*. Yale University Press, 2021.

Colby, Elbridge A., and Robert D. Kaplan. "The Ideology Delusion: America's Competition with China Is Not about Doctrine." *Foreign Affairs*, September 4, 2020. https://www.foreignaffairs.com/articles/united-states/2020-09-04/ideology-delusion.

Cole, Andrew J., and Jane Vaynman. "Why Arms Control Is So Rare." *American Political Science Review* 114, no. 2 (2020): 324–55. https://doi.org/10.1017/S0003055420000167.

Constantelos, John, Polly J. Diven, and H. Whitt Kilburn. "Can't Buy Me Love (with Foreign Aid)." *Foreign Policy Analysis* 19, no. 4 (2023): 1–24. https://doi.org/10.1093/fpa/orad024.

Copeland, Dale C. *The Origins of Major War*. Cornell University Press, 2000.

Copeland, Dale C. *A World Safe for Commerce: American Foreign Policy from the Revolution to the Rise of China*. Princeton University Press, 2024.

Cornelissen, Scarlett, Fantu Cheru, and Timothy M. Shaw, eds. *Africa and International Relations in the 21st Century*. Springer, 2012.

Cornell, Svante E. "Pakistan's Foreign Policy: Islamic or Pragmatic?" In *The Limits of Culture: Islam and Foreign Policy*, edited by Brenda Shaffer, 291–325. MIT Press, 2006.

Cox, R. W. "Social Forces, States and World Orders: Beyond International Relations Theory." *Millennium* 10, no. 2 (1981): 126–55. https://doi.org/10.1177/03058298810100020501.

Craig, Campbell. *Glimmer of a New Leviathan: Total War in the Realism of Niebuhr, Morgenthau and Waltz*. Columbia University Press, 2003.

Cunningham, Fiona S., and M. Taylor Fravel. "Assuring Assured Retaliation: China's Nuclear Posture and U.S.-China Strategic Stability." *International Security* 40, no. 2 (2015): 7–50. http://www.jstor.org/stable/43828294.

Danner, Mark. "Words in a Time of War." *Los Angeles Times*, June 1, 2007. https://www.latimes.com/la-oe-danner1jun01-story.html.

Dar, Arshid Iqbal. "Beyond Eurocentrism: Kautilya's Realism and India's Regional Diplomacy." *Humanities and Social Sciences Education* 8 (2021): 1–7. https://doi.org/10.1057/s41599-021-00888-6.

Davis, Lynn E., Jeffrey Martini, Alireza Nader, Dalia Dassa Kaye, James T. Quinlivan, and Paul Steinberg. *Iran's Nuclear Future: Critical U.S. Policy Choices*. RAND, 2011. https://www.rand.org/content/dam/rand/pubs/monographs/2011/RAND_MG1087.pdf.

Desch, Michael C. "Culture Clash: Assessing the Importance of Ideas in Security Studies." *International Security* 23, no. 1 (1998): 141–70. https://doi.org/10.2307/2539266.

Desch, Michael C. "Henry Kissinger: An Occasional Realist." *American Conservative*, September 15, 2020. https://www.theamericanconservative.com/henry-kissinger-an-occasional-realist/.

Desch, Michael C. "It Is Kind to Be Cruel: The Humanity of American Realism." *Review of International Studies* 29, no. 3 (2003): 415–26. http://www.jstor.org/stable/20097863.

Di Cosmo, Nicola. "The Origins of the Great Wall." *Silk Road* 4, no. 1 (2006): 14–19.

Donnelly, Jack. "The Discourse of Anarchy in IR." *International Theory* 7, no. 3 (2015): 393–425. https://doi.org/10.1017/S1752971915000111.

Doshi, Rush. *The Long Game: China's Grand Strategy to Displace American Order*. Oxford University Press, 2021.

Doyle, Michael. "Liberalism and World Politics." *American Political Science Review* 80, no. 4 (1986): 1151–69. https://doi.org/10.2307/1960861.

Doyle, Michael. "Why They Don't Fight: The Surprising Endurance of the Democratic Peace." *Foreign Affairs* 103, no. 4 (2024): 135–41.

Driedger, Jonas J., and Mikhail Polianskii. "Utility-Based Predictions of Military Escalation: Why Experts Forecasted Russia Would Not Invade Ukraine." *Contemporary Security Policy* 44, no. 4 (2023): 544–60. https://doi.org/10.1080/13523260.2023.2259153.

Dube, Oeindrila, and S. P. Harish. "Queens." *Journal of Political Economy* 128, no. 7 (2020): 2579–652. https://doi.org/10.1086/707011.

Dunn, Kevin C., and Timothy M. Shaw, eds. *Africa's Challenge to International Relations Theory*. Palgrave, 2000.

Durbin, Adam. "Johnson Says If Putin Were a Woman He Would Not Have Invaded." BBC News, June 29, 2022. https://www.bbc.co.uk/news/uk-61976526.

Eckstein, Arthur M. *Mediterranean Anarchy, Interstate War and the Rise of Rome*. University of California Press, 2006.

Edelstein, David M. *Occupational Hazards: Success and Failure in Military Occupation*. Cornell University Press, 2008.

Eken, Mattias. "The Understandable Fear of Nuclear Weapons Doesn't Match Reality." The Conversation, March 14, 2017. https://theconversation.com/the-understandable-fear-of-nuclear-weapons-doesnt-match-reality-73563.

Ellis-Petersen, Hannah, Aakash Hassan, and Shah Meer Baloch. "Indian Government Ordered Killings in Pakistan, Intelligence Officials Claim." *The Guardian*, April 4, 2024. https://www.theguardian.com/world/2024/apr/04/indian-government-assassination-allegations-pakistan-intelligence-officials.

Elman, Colin, and Mirium Fendius Elman. "History versus Neo-realism: A Second Look." *International Security* 20, no. 1 (1995): 182–95. https://doi.org/10.2307/2539222.

Elrod, Richard B. "The Concert of Europe: A Fresh Look at the International System." *World Politics* 28, no. 2 (1976): 159–74.

Fairbank, John K. "Varieties of the Chinese Military Experience." In *Chinese Ways in Warfare*, edited by Frank A. Kierman, Fairbank, and Edward L. Dreyer, 1–26. Harvard University Press, 1974.

Fazal, Tanisha M. "Dead Wrong? Battle Deaths, Military Medicine, and Exaggerated Reports of War's Demise." *International Security* 39, no. 1 (2014): 95–125. www.jstor.org/stable/24480546.

Feng, Huiyun. *Chinese Strategic Culture and Foreign Policy Decision-Making: Confucianism, Leadership and War*. Routledge, 2007.

Finnemore, Martha. "Legitimacy, Hypocrisy, and the Social Structure of Unipolarity: Why Being a Unipole Isn't All That It's Cracked Up to Be." *World Politics* 61, no. 1 (2009): 58–85. https://doi.org/10.1017/S0043887109000082.

Fischer, Marcus. "Feudal Europe, 800–1300: Communal Discourse and Conflictual Practices." *International Organization* 46, no. 2 (1992): 427–65. http://www.jstor.org/stable/2706859.

Folk, Dean, and Charles Hildebolt. "Annual War Deaths in Small-Scale versus State Societies Scale with Population Size Rather Than Violence." *Current Anthropology* 58, no. 6 (2017): 805–13. https://doi.org/10.1086/694568.

Forde, Steven. "Varieties of Realism: Thucydides and Machiavelli." *Journal of Politics* 54, no. 2 (1992): 372–93. https://www.jstor.org/stable/2132031.

Foulon, Michiel, and Gustav Meibauer. "Realist Avenues to Global International Relations." *European Journal of International Relations* 26, no. 4 (2020): 1203–29.

France-Presse, Agence. "China Shifting Nuclear Rules of Engagement: Report." *Defense Talk*, January 6, 2011. https://www.defencetalk.com/china-shifting-nuclear-rules-of-engagement-report-31090/.

Friedman, Jeremy. "The Case for Inclusive Alliances: American Must Rediscover the Ideological Flexibility That Helped It Win the Cold War." *Foreign Affairs*, July 17, 2024. https://www.foreignaffairs.com/united-states/case-inclusive-alliances-cold-war.

Fry, Douglas P., ed. *War, Peace and Human Nature: The Convergence of Evolutionary and Cultural Views*. Oxford University Press, 2015.

Galeotti, Mark. "Even Putin Knows Invading Ukraine Won't Pay Off." *Foreign Policy*, February 22, 2022. https://foreignpolicy.com/2022/02/22/invasion-russia-ukraine-pay-off/.

Gat, Azar. "Proving Communal Warfare among Hunter-Gatherers: The Quasi-Rousseauan Error." *Evolutionary Anthropology* 24, no. 3 (2015): 111–26. https://doi.org/10.1002/evan.21446.

Gavin, Francis J. "Strategies of Inhibition: U.S. Grand Strategy, the Nuclear Revolution, and Nonproliferation." *International Security* 40, no. 1 (2015): 9–46. https://doi.org/10.1162/ISEC_a_00205.

Gellman, Barton. "U.S. Spied on Iraq Via U.N." *Washington Post*, March 2, 1999. https://www.washingtonpost.com/wp-srv/inatl/daily/march99/unscom2.htm.

Geroulanos, Stefanos. *The Invention of Prehistory: Empire, Violence, and Our Obsession with Human Origins*. Liveright, 2025.

Gills, Barry. "The Hegemonic Transition in East Asia: A Historical Perspective." In *Gramsci, Historical Materialism and International Relations*, edited by Stephen Gill, 186–213. Cambridge University Press, 1993.

Gilpin, Robert G. "No One Loves a Political Realist." *Security Studies* 5, no. 3 (1996): 3–26. https://doi.org/10.1080/09636419608429275.

Gilpin, Robert G. "The Richness of the Tradition of Political Realism." *International Organization* 38, no. 2 (1984): 287–304. http://www.jstor.org/stable/2706441.

Gilpin, Robert G. *War and Change in World Politics*. Cambridge University Press, 1986.

Glaser, Charles L. "Fear Factor: How to Know When You're in a Security Dilemma." *Foreign Affairs* 103, no. 4 (2024): 122–28.

Glaser, Charles L. *Rational Theory of International Politics: The Logic of Competition and Cooperation*. Princeton University Press, 2010.

Glaser, Charles L. "Structural Realism in a More Complex World." *Review of International Studies* 29, no. 3 (2003): 403–14. http://www.jstor.org/stable/20097862.

Gleditsch, Nils Petter. "Toward a Social-Democratic Peace?" *Ethics and International Affairs* 34, no. 1 (2020): 67–75. https://doi.org/10.1017/S0892679420000076.

Gobarev, Victor. "Soviet Military Plans and Actions during the First Berlin Crisis, 1948–1949." *Journal of Slavic Military Studies* 10, no. 3 (1997): 1–24. https://doi.org/10.1080/13518049708430303.

Goddard, Stacey E. "The Rhetoric of Appeasement: Hitler's Legitimation and British Foreign Policy, 1938–39." *Security Studies* 24, no. 1 (2015): 95–130. https://doi.org/10.1080/09636412.2015.1001216.

Goldsmith, Jack L., and Erica A. Posner. *The Limits of International Law*. Oxford University Press, 2007.

Gopnik, Adam. "The Big One: Historians Rethink the War to End All Wars." *New Yorker*, August 23, 2004, 78–84.

Gorodetsky, Gabriel. "When Soviet Ideals Met International Reality." *Le Monde Diplomatique*, October 7, 2017. https://mondediplo.com/2017/10/05SovietIdeal.

Gray, Colin S. "National Style in Strategy: The American Example." *International Security* 6, no. 2 (1981): 21–47. https://www.jstor.org/stable/2538645.

Gray, Colin S. "Out of the Wilderness: Prime Time for Strategic Culture." *Comparative Strategy* 26, no. 1 (2007): 1–20. https://doi.org/10.1080/01495930701271478.

Gray, Colin S. *Weapons Don't Make War: Policy, Strategy and Military Technology*. University of Kansas, 2005.

Grieco, Joseph. "Anarchy and the Limits of Cooperation: A Realist Critique of the

Newest Liberal Institutionalism." *International Organization* 42, no. 3 (1988): 485–507. https://doi.org/10.1017/S0020818300027715.

Grissom, Daniel Edward. "Thucydides' Dangerous World: Dual Forms of Danger in Classical Greek Interstate Relations." PhD diss., University of Maryland, 2012. https://drum.lib.umd.edu/items/30acfa4d-b172-4543-8ebf-d9daeeb830f7.

Grovogui, Siba N. "Regimes of Sovereignty: International Morality and the African Condition." *European Journal of International Relations* 8, no. 3 (2002): 315–38. https://doi.org/10.1177/1354066102008003001

Gruber, Lloyd. *Ruling the World: Power Politics and the Rise of Supranational Institutions*. Princeton University Press, 2000.

Gruen, Erich S. "Thucydides, His Critics and Interpreters." *Journal of Interdisciplinary History* 1, no. 2 (1971): 327–37. https://doi.org/10.2307/202647.

Hall, Ian. "The Persistence of Nehruvianism in India's Strategic Culture." In *Strategic Asia 2016–17: Understanding Strategic Cultures in the Asia-Pacific*, edited by Michael Wills, Ashley J. Tellis, and Alison Szalwinski, 141–67. National Bureau of Asia Research, 2017.

Hanson, Victor Davis. *The End of Everything: How Wars Descend into Annihilation*. Basic Books, 2024.

Harris, William V. *War and Imperialism in Republican Rome: 327–70 BC* (Oxford University Press, 1985).

Harvey, Chelsea. "The World Will Likely Miss 1.5 Degrees C—Why Isn't Anyone Saying So?" *Scientific American*, November 11, 2022. https://www.scientificamerican.com/article/the-world-will-likely-miss-1-5-degrees-c-why-isnt-anyone-saying-so/.

Haslam, Jonathan. *No Virtue like Necessity: Realist Thought in International Relations since Machiavelli*. Yale University Press, 2002.

Hathaway, Oona A., and Scott J. Shapiro. *The Internationalists: How a Radical Plan to Outlaw War Remade the World*. Simon and Schuster, 2017.

Hazelton, Jacqueline. *Bullets Not Ballots: Success in Counterinsurgency Warfare*. Cornell University Press, 2021.

Henderson, Errol. *African Realism: International Relations Theory and Africa's Wars in the Postcolonial Era*. Rowman and Littlefield, 2015.

Hiim, Henrik Stalhane. "Hardening Chinese Realpolitik in the 21st Century: The Evolution of Beijing's Thinking about Arms Control." *Journal of Contemporary China* 31, no. 133 (2022): 86–100. https://www.tandfonline.com/doi/full/10.1080/10670564.2021.1926095.

Hobson, John M. *The Eurocentric Conception of World Politics*. Cambridge University Press, 2012.

Hobson, John M. "Unmasking the Racism of Orthodox International Relations/International Political Economy Theory." *Security Dialogue* 53, no. 1 (2022): 3–20. https://doi.org/10.1177/09670106211061084.

Hopf, Ted. "The Promise of Constructivism in International Relations Theory." *International Security* 23, no. 1 (1998): 171–200. https://doi.org/10.2307/2539267.

Hughes, Ken. *Chasing Shadows: The Nixon Tapes, the Chennault Affair and the Origins of Watergate*. University of Virginia Press, 2014.
Hui, Victoria Tin-Bor. *War and State Formation in Ancient China and Early Modern Europe*. Cambridge University Press, 2003.
Human Rights Watch. "War Crimes, Crimes against Humanity, Ethnic Cleansing in West Darfur." May 9, 2024. https://www.hrw.org/news/2024/05/09/qa-war-crimes-crimes-against-humanity-ethnic-cleansing-west-darfur.
Hunt, Linda. "U.S. Coverup of Nazi Scientists." *Bulletin of the Atomic Scientists* 41, no. 4 (1985): 16–24.
Huntington, Samuel P. *The Clash of Civilizations and the Remaking of World Order* (Simon and Schuster, 1996).
Ikenberry, G. John, Thomas J. Knock, Anne-Marie Slaughter, and Tony Smith. *The Crisis of American Foreign Policy: Wilsonianism in the Twenty-First Century*. Princeton University Press, 2008.
International Criminal Court. "Defendants." Accessed March 1, 2025. https://www.icc-cpi.int/defendants.
Jackson, Van. *Grand Strategies of the Left: The Foreign Policy of Progressive World Making*. Cambridge University Press, 2023.
Jakhar, Pratik. "Whatever Happened to the South China Sea Ruling?" *The Interpreter*, July 12, 2021. https://www.lowyinstitute.org/the-interpreter/whatever-happened-south-china-sea-ruling.
Jervis, Robert. "Explaining the War in Iraq." In *Why Did the United States Invade Iraq?*, edited by Jane A. Kramer and A. Trevor Thrall, 25–49. Routledge, 2012.
Jervis, Robert. "Realism, Neoliberalism, and Cooperation: Understanding the Debate." *International Security* 24, no. 1 (1999): 42–63. http://www.jstor.org/stable/2539347.
Joffe, Joseph, and James W. Davis. "Less Than Zero: Bursting the New Disarmament Bubble." *Foreign Affairs* 90, no. 1 (2011): 7–13.
Johnson, Dominic P., and Bradley Thayer. "The Evolution of Offensive Realism: Survival under Anarchy from the Pleistocene to the Present." *Politics and the Life Sciences* 35, no. 1 (2016): 1–20. https://www.jstor.org/stable/26372766.
Johnson, Seth A. "The Pandemic and the Limits of Realism." *Foreign Policy*, June 24, 2020. https://foreignpolicy.com/2020/06/24/coronavirus-pandemic-realism-limited-international-relations-theory/.
Johnston, Alastair Iain. *Cultural Realism: Strategic Culture and Grand Strategy in Chinese History*. Princeton University Press, 1997.
Jones, Rodney W. "India's Strategic Culture and the Origins of Omniscient Paternalism." In *Strategic Culture and Weapons of Mass Destruction: Culturally Based Insights into Comparative National Security Policymaking*, edited by Jeannie L. Johnson, Kerry M. Kartchner, and Jeffrey A. Larsen, 117–36. Palgrave Macmillan, 2009.
Jorge, Peter. *Sun Tzu in the West: The Anglo-American Art of War*. Cambridge University Press, 2022.

Bibliography

Kagan, Korina. "The Myth of the European Concert: The Realist-Institutionalist Debate and Great Power Behavior in the Eastern Question, 1821–41." *Security Studies* 7, no. 2 (1997): 1–57. https://doi.org/10.1080/09636419708429341.

Kang, David C. *China Rising: Power, Peace and Order in East Asia.* Columbia University Press, 2007.

Kang, David C. "Getting Asia Wrong: The Need for New Analytical Frameworks." *International Security* 27, no. 4 (2003): 57–85. http://www.jstor.org/stable/4137604.

Kang, David C. "Power Transitions: Thucydides Didn't Live in Asia." *Washington Quarterly* 41, no. 1 (2018): 137–54. https://doi.org/10.1080/0163660X.2018.1445905.

Kaplan, Edward. *The End of Victory: Prevailing in the Thermonuclear Age.* Cornell University Press, 2022.

Kaplan, Robert D. *The Tragic Mind: Fear, Fate and the Burden of Power.* Yale University Press, 2023.

Karkour, Haro, and Felix Rösch. "Towards IR's 'Fifth Debate': Racial Justice and the National Interest in Classical Realism." *International Studies Review* 26, no. 2 (2024): viae030. https://doi.org/10.1093/isr/viae030.

Katzenstein, Peter J., and Nobuo Okawara. "Japan's National Security: Structures, Norms, and Policies." *International Security* 17, no. 4 (1993): 84–118. https://doi.org/10.2307/2539023.

Kaufman, Robert. *In Defense of the Bush Doctrine.* Kentucky University Press, 2007.

Kaufman, Stuart J., Richard Little, and William C. Wohlforth, eds. *The Balance of Power in World History.* Palgrave Macmillan, 2007.

Kaufmann, Chaim D., and Robert A. Pape. "Explaining Costly International Moral Action: Britain's Sixty Year Campaign against the Slave Trade." *International Organization* 53, no .4 (1989): 631–68. https://doi.org/10.1162/002081899551020.

Keeley, Lawrence H. *War before Civilization: The Myth of the Peaceful Savage.* Oxford University Press, 1996.

Kelly, Raymond C. *Warless Societies and the Origin of War.* University of Michigan Press, 2000.

Kennan, George F. *American Diplomacy: 1900–1950.* University of Chicago Press, 1951.

Kennedy, John F. "Remarks of Senator John F. Kennedy Announcing His Candidacy for the Presidency of the United States—Senate Caucus Room, Washington, DC." January 2, 1960. The American Presidency Project. Accessed March 13, 2025. https://www.presidency.ucsb.edu/node/274074.

Kennedy, Paul. *The Rise and Fall of the Great Powers.* Random House, 1987.

Keohane, Robert O., and Lisa L. Martin. "The Promise of Institutionalist Theory." *International Security* 20, no. 1 (1995): 39–51. https://doi.org/10.2307/2539214.

Kimball, Warren, ed. *Churchill and Roosevelt: The Complete Correspondence.* HarperCollins, 1988.

Kirshner, Jonathan. *An Unwritten Future: Realism and Uncertainty in World Politics.* Princeton University Press, 2022.

Knepper, Jennifer. "Nuclear Weapons and Iranian Strategic Culture." *Comparative Strategy* 27, no. 5 (2008): 451–68. https://doi.org/10.1080/01495930802430080.

Kriner, Douglas L., and Francis X. Shen. "Battlefield Casualties and Ballot-Box Defeat:

Did the Bush-Obama Wars Cost Clinton the White House?" *Political Science and Politics* 53, no. 2 (2020): 248–52. https://doi.org/10.1017/S104909651900204X.
Kydd, Andrew. "Sheep in Sheep's Clothing: Why Security Seekers Do Not Fight Each Other." *Security Studies* 7, no. 1 (1997): 114–55. https://doi.org/10.1080/09636419708429336.
Laiz, Alvaro Morcillo. "The Cold War Origins of Global IR: The Rockefeller Foundation and Realism in Latin America." *International Studies Review* 24, no. 1 (2022): 1–26. https://doi.org/10.1093/isr/viab061.
Lakatos, Imre. *Philosophical Papers*. Vol. 1, *The Methodology of Scientific Research Programmes*. 1978; repr., Cambridge University Press, 2012.
Lake, David A. "Escape from the State of Nature: Authority and Hierarchy in World Politics." *International Security* 32, no. 1 (2007): 47–79. https://doi.org/10.1162/isec.2007.32.1.47.
Layne, Christopher. "The Unipolar Illusion: Why New Great Powers Will Rise." *International Security* 17, no. 4 (1993): 5–51. https://doi.org/10.2307/2539020.
Leahy, William D. *I Was There*. Victor Gollancz, 1950.
Lebow, Richard Ned. "The Ancient Greeks and Modern Realism: Ethics, Persuasion, and Power." In *Political Thought and International Relations: Variations on a Realist Theme*, edited by Duncan Bell, 26–40. Oxford University Press, 2009.
Lebow, Richard Ned. *The Tragic Vision of Politics: Ethics, Interests and Orders*. Cambridge University Press, 2009.
Legro, Jeffrey W., and Andrew Moravcsik. "Is Anybody Still a Realist?" *International Security* 24, no. 2 (1999): 5–55. https://muse.jhu.edu/article/447679.
Lewis, Jeffrey. *The Minimum Means of Reprisal: China's Search for Security in a Nuclear Age*. MIT Press, 2007.
Lieber, Keir A., and Gerard Alexander. "Waiting for Balancing: Why the World Is Not Pushing Back." *International Security* 30, no. 1 (2005): 109–39. http://www.jstor.org/stable/4137460.
Lieber, Keir A., and Daryl G. Press. *The Myth of the Nuclear Revolution: Power Politics in the Atomic Age*. Cornell University Press, 2020.
Lieber, Keir A., and Daryl G. Press. "The Return of Nuclear Escalation: How America's Adversaries Have Hijacked Its Old Deterrence Strategy." *Foreign Affairs* 102, no. 6 (2023): 45–55.
Lieber, Keir A., and Daryl G. Press. "Why States Won't Give Nuclear Weapons to Terrorists." *International Security* 38, no. 1 (2013): 80–104. https://doi.org/10.1162/ISEC_a_00127.
Lieber, Robert. "The Folly of Containment." *Commentary* 115, no. 4 (2003): 15–21.
Lippmann, Walter. *U.S. Foreign Policy: Shield of the Republic*. Little, Brown, 1943.
Liu, Zongyuan Zoe. "What the China-Solomon Islands Pact Means for the U.S. and the South Pacific." Council on Foreign Relations, May 4, 2022. https://www.cfr.org/in-brief/china-solomon-islands-security-pact-us-south-pacific.
Lobell, Steven E. "A Granular Theory of Balancing." *International Studies Quarterly* 62, no. 3 (2018): 593–605. https://doi.org/10.1093/isq/sqy011.
Mai, Jun. "'China's Military Must Spend More' to Meet US War Threat." *South China

Morning Post, March 8, 2021. https://www.scmp.com/news/china/politics/article/3124591/chinas-military-must-spend-more-meet-us-war-threat.

Malmgren, Harald. "What the West Gets Wrong about Putin." UnHerd, January 13, 2022. https://unherd.com/2022/01/what-the-west-gets-wrong-about-putin/.

Mandelbaum, Michael. "Is Major War Obsolete?" *Survival* 40, no. 4 (1998): 20–38. https://doi.org/10.1093/survival/40.4.20.

Martin, David. "Five Years Later: An Axiom of War." CBS News, March 18, 2008. https://www.cbsnews.com/news/five-years-later-an-axiom-of-war/.

Martin, Susan B. "From Balance of Power to Balancing Behavior: The Long and Winding Road." In *Perspectives on Structural Realism*, edited by Andrew K. Hanami, 61–74. Palgrave Macmillan, 2003.

Martinez, Michael. "Allies Spy on Allies Because a Friend Today May Not Be One Tomorrow." CNN, October 31, 2013. https://edition.cnn.com/2013/10/30/us/spying-on-allies-everybody-does-it/index.html.

McDonald, Patrick J. "Great Powers, Hierarchy, and Endogenous Regimes: Rethinking the Domestic Causes of Peace." *International Organization* 69, no. 3 (2015): 557–88. https://doi.org/10.1017/S0020818315000120.

McMaster, H. R. *Battlegrounds: The Fight to Defend the Free World*. HarperCollins, 2020.

Mearsheimer, John J. *The Tragedy of Great Power Politics*. W. W. Norton, 2001.

Mearsheimer, John J., and Stephen M. Walt. *The Israel Lobby and U.S. Foreign Policy*. Farrar, Straus and Giroux, 2007.

Mearsheimer, John J., and Stephen M. Walt. "An Unnecessary War." *Foreign Policy*, November 3, 2009. https://foreignpolicy.com/2009/11/03/an-unnecessary-war-2/.

Meier, Charles S. *Among Empires: American Ascendancy and Its Predecessors*. Harvard University Press, 2006.

Michelson, Joan. "'The Biggest Challenge Is Men Starting Wars'—Hillary Clinton to Women Peace Activists." *Forbes*, October 8, 2023. https://www.forbes.com/sites/joanmichelson2/2023/10/08/the-biggest-challenge-is-men-starting-wars--hillary-clinton-to-women-peace-activists/.

Milner, Helen. "The Assumption of Anarchy in International Relations Theory: A Critique." *Review of International Studies* 17, no. 1 (1991): 67–85. https://doi.org/10.1017/S026021050011232X.

Misra, M. "The Indian Machiavelli: Pragmatism versus Morality, and the Reception of *Arthasastra* in India, 1905–2014." *Modern Asian Studies* 50, no. 1 (2016): 310–44. https://doi.org/10.1017/S0026749X14000638.

Mitzen, Jennifer. *Power in Concert: The Nineteenth-Century Origins of Global Governance*. University of Chicago Press, 2013.

Mohan, C. Raja. "Explained: How Balakot Changed the Familiar Script of India-Pakistan Military Crises." *Indian Express*, March 4, 2019. https://carnegieendowment.org/posts/2019/03/explained-how-balakot-changed-the-familiar-script-of-india-pakistan-military-crises?lang=en.

Molloy, Sean. "Aristotle, Epicurus, Morgenthau and the Political Ethics of the Lesser

Evil." *Journal of International Political Theory* 5, no. 1 (2009): 94–112. https://doi.org/10.3366/E1755088209000034.

Molloy, Sean. "Spinoza, Carr, and the Ethics of *The Twenty Years' Crisis*." *Review of International Studies* 39, no. 2 (2013): 251–71. http://www.jstor.org/stable/24564658.

Monteiro, Nuno. "Unrest Assured: Why Unipolarity Is Not Peaceful." *International Security* 36, no. 3 (Winter 2011–2012): 9–40. http://www.jstor.org/stable/41428108.

Monten, Jonathan. "Thucydides and Modern Realism." *International Studies Quarterly* 50, no. 1 (2006): 3–25. https://doi.org/10.1111/j.1468-2478.2006.00390.x.

Moravcsik, Andrew. "Did Power Politics Cause European Integration? Realist Theory Meets Qualitative Methods." *Security Studies* 22, no. 4 (2013): 773–90. https://doi.org/10.1080/09636412.2013.844511.

Moravcsik, Andrew. "Taking Preferences Seriously: A Liberal Theory of International Politics." *International Organization* 51, no. 4 (1997): 513–53. https://doi.org/10.1162/002081897550447.

Morefield, Jeanne. *Covenants without Swords: Idealist Liberalism and the Spirit of Empire*. Princeton University Press, 2004.

Morgenthau, Hans J. *Politics among Nations: The Struggle for Power and Peace*. Rev. ed. Alfred A. Knopf, 1956.

Morgenthau, Hans J. *Politics among Nations: The Struggle for Power and Peace*. 3rd rev. ed. Knopf, 1960.

Morgenthau, Hans J. *Politics among Nations: The Struggle for Power and Peace*. 5th rev. ed. Knopf, 1978.

Morgenthau, Hans J. "The Primacy of the National Interest." *American Scholar* 18, no. 2 (1949): 207–12. http://www.jstor.org/stable/41205156.

Morgenthau, Hans J. *Scientific Man versus Power Politics*. University of Chicago Press, 1946.

Mouritzen, Hans. "Tension between the Strong, and the Strategies of the Weak." *Journal of Peace Research* 28, no. 2 (1991): 217–30. https://doi.org/10.1177/0022343391028002007.

Mulholland, Marc. "Distrust Your Government." *Weekly Worker*, March 14, 2024. https://weeklyworker.co.uk/worker/1482/distrust-your-government/.

Mullin, Chris. "The Terror Was Absolute." Review of *Vietnam: An Epic Tragedy*, by Max Hastings. *London Review of Books* 41, no. 14 (2019). https://www.lrb.co.uk/the-paper/v41/n14/chris-mullin/terror-was-absolute.

"Narendra Modi Is Remaking India's 1.4m Strong Military." *The Economist*, November 29, 2023. https://www.economist.com/asia/2023/11/29/narendra-modi-is-remaking-indias-14m-strong-military.

Narizny, Kevin. "On Systemic Paradigms and Domestic Politics: A Critique of the Newest Realism." *International Security* 42, no. 2 (2017): 155–90. https://doi.org/10.1162/ISEC_a_00296.

Nayar, Baldev Raj, and T. V. Paul. *India in the World Order: Searching for Major-Power Status*. Cambridge University Press, 2003.

Neuman, Stephanie. *International Relations Theory and the Third World*. Macmillan, 1998.

Nexon, Daniel H. "The Balance of Power in the Balance." *World Politics* 61, no. 2 (2009): 330–59. https://doi.org/10.1017/S0043887109000124.

Niebuhr, Reinhold. *Moral Man and Immoral Society*. Westminster John Knox Press, 1932.

Nkiwane, Tandeka C. "Africa and International Relations: Regional Lessons for a Global Discourse." *International Political Science Review* 22, no. 3 (2001): 279–90. https://doi.org/10.1177/0192512101223005.

Norrlof, Carla. *America's Global Advantage: U.S. Hegemony and International Cooperation*. Cambridge University Press, 2010.

Nymalm, Nicola, and Johannes Plagemann. "Comparative Exceptionalism: Universality and Particularity in Foreign Policy Discourses." *International Studies Review* 21, no. 1 (2019): 12–37. https://doi.org/10.1093/isr/viy008.

Office of the Director of National Intelligence. *Annual Threat Assessment of the U.S. Intelligence Community*. DNI, February 2023.

Pant, Harsh V. "Is India Developing a Strategy for Power?" *Washington Quarterly* 38, no. 4 (2015): 99–113. https://doi.org/10.1080/0163660X.2015.1125831.

Parchami, Ali. "An Iranian World View: The Strategic Culture of the Islamic Republic." *Journal of Advanced Military Studies* 13, no. 1 (2022): 9–23. https://doi.org/10.21140/mcuj.2022SIstratcul001.

Parent, Joseph, and J. M. Baron. "Elder Abuse: How the Moderns Mistreat Classical Realism." *International Studies Review* 13, no. 2 (2011): 193–213. https://doi.org/10.1111/j.1468-2486.2011.01021.x.

Parent, Joseph, and Sebastian Rosato. "Balancing in Neorealism." *International Security* 40, no. 2 (2015): 51–86. http://www.jstor.org/stable/43828295.

Parker, Geoffrey. *Imprudent King: A New Life of Philip II*. Yale University Press, 2014.

Petraeus, David. "Learning Counterinsurgency: Observations from Soldiering in Iraq." *Military Review* 86, no. 1 (January–February 2006): 2–12.

Payne, Keith. "Realism, Idealism, Deterrence and Disarmament." *Strategic Studies Quarterly* 13, no. 3 (2019): 7–37.

Pedi, Revecca, and Anders Wivel. "The Power (Politics) of the Weak Revisited: Realism and the Study of Small-State Foreign Policy." In *Agency, Security and Governance of Small States: A Global Perspective*, edited by I. T. Kolnberger and H. Koff, 13–28. Routledge, 2023.

Pinker, Stephen. *The Better Angels of Our Nature: A History of Violence and Humanity*. Penguin, 2012.

Pipes, Richard. "Why the Soviet Union Thinks It Could Fight and Win a Nuclear War." *Commentary* 64, no. 1 (1977): 21–23.

Porter, Bruce. "The Warfare State." *American Heritage* 45, no. 4 (1994): 56–69.

Porter, Patrick. "The Man Who Loved Power." *The Critic*, November 30, 2023. https://thecritic.co.uk/the-man-who-loved-power/.

Porter, Patrick. "Out of the Shadows: Ukraine and the Shock of Non-hybrid War." *Journal of Global Security Studies* 8, no. 3 (2023): 1–15. https://doi.org/10.1093/jogss/ogad014.

Porter, Patrick. "Why Australia Needs a Bomb in the Basement." *Australian Financial Review*, April 9, 2021. https://www.afr.com/policy/foreign-affairs/australia-needs-a-bomb-in-the-basement-20210329-p57eya.

Pottinger, Matt, and Mike Gallagher. "No Substitute for Victory: America's Competition with China Must Be Won, Not Managed." *Foreign Affairs* 103, no. 3 (2024): 25–39.

Press, Daryl, and Eugene Gholz. "The Effects of Wars on Neutral Countries: Why It Doesn't Pay to Preserve the Peace." *Security Studies* 10, no. 4 (2001): 1–57. https://doi.org/10.1080/09636410108429444.

Press, Daryl, Scott D. Sagan, and Benjamin A. Valentino. "Atomic Aversion: Experimental Evidence on Taboos, Traditions, and the Non-use of Nuclear Weapons." *American Political Science Review* 107, no. 1 (2013): 188–206. http://www.jstor.org/stable/23357763.

Press, Daryl G., Scott D. Sagan, and Benjamin A. Valentino. "Revisiting Hiroshima in Iran: What Americans Really Think about Using Nuclear Weapons and Killing Noncombatants." *International Security* 42, no. 1 (2017): 41–79. https://doi.org/10.1162/ISEC_a_00284.

Qin, Yaping. "Development of International Relations Theory in China: Progress through Debates." *International Relations of the Asia Pacific* 11, no. 2 (2011): 231–57. https://doi.org/10.1093/irap/lcr003.

Quinlan, Michael. *Thinking about Nuclear Weapons: Principles, Problems, Prospects*. Oxford University Press, 2009.

Rashid, Ahmed. *The Resurgence of Central Asia: Islam or Nationalism*. Zed, 1994.

Rathbun, Brian C. "The Rarity of Realpolitik: What Bismarck's Rationality Tells Us about International Politics." *International Security* 43, no. 1 (2018): 7–55. https://doi.org/10.1162/isec_a_00323.

Raymond, Lorenzo. "Why Nonviolent Civil Resistance Doesn't Work (Unless You Have Lots of Bombs)." *CounterPunch*, May 27, 2016. https://www.counterpunch.org/2016/05/27/why-nonviolent-civil-resistance-doesnt-work-unless-you-have-lots-of-bombs/.

Rendall, Matthew. "Nuclear Weapons and Intergenerational Exploitation." *Security Studies* 16, no. 4 (2007): 525–54. https://doi.org/10.1080/09636410701741070.

Revkin, Andrew. "Hard Facts about Nuclear Winter." *Science Digest* 93 (1985): 62–68, 77–83.

Robins, Nick. *The Road to Net-Zero Finance*. Advisory Group on Finance, UK Climate Change Committee, December 2020. https://www.theccc.org.uk/wp-content/uploads/2020/12/Finance-Advisory-Group-Report-The-Road-to-Net-Zero-Finance.pdf.

Robinson, Eric. "Reading and Misreading the Ancient Evidence for Democratic Peace." *Journal of Peace Research* 38, no. 5 (2001): 593–608. https://doi.org/10.1177/0022343301038005003.

Roof, Abraham M. "A Separate Peace? The Soviet Union and the Making of British Strategy in the Wake of 'Barbarossa,' June–September 1941." *Journal of Slavic Military Studies* 22, no. 2 (2009): 236–52. https://doi.org/10.1080/13518040902918121.

Rosato, Sebastian. *Europe United: Power Politics and the Making of the European Community*. Cornell University Press, 2010.

Rosecrance, Richard N. "A Concert of Powers." *Foreign Affairs* 71, no. 2 (1992): 64–68.

Rosenberg, Justin. "Uneven and Combined Development and International Relations—a Special Affinity?" *Millennium* 50, no. 2 (2022): 294–97. https://doi.org/10.1177/03058298211064346.

Roy, Nabarun. "India's Use of Military Power and the Sovereignty Principle: Insights from the Neighborhood." *India Review* 23, no. 2 (2024): 95–114. https://doi.org/10.1080/14736489.2024.2324637.

Ruggie, John Gerard. "International Regimes, Transactions, and Change: Embedded Liberalism in the Post-war Economic Order." *International Organization* 36, no. 2 (1982): 379–415. http://www.jstor.org/stable/2706527.

Ruiz, Tricia. "Feminist Theory and International Relations: The Feminist Challenge to Realism and Liberalism." *Soundings Journal* 88, no. 1 (2005): 1–7. https://giwps.georgetown.edu/dei-resources/feminist-theory-and-international-relations-the-feminist-challenge-to-realism-and-liberalism/.

Rumer, Eugene. "The United States and the 'Axis' of Its Enemies." Carnegie Endowment for International Peace, November 25, 2024. https://carnegieendowment.org/research/2024/11/the-united-states-and-the-axis-of-its-enemies-myths-vs-reality?lang=en.

Runyan, Anne Sisson, and V. Spike Peterson. "The Radical Future of Realism: Feminist Subversions of IR Theory." *Alternatives* 16, no. 1 (1991): 67–106. https://www.jstor.org/stable/40644702.

Russet, Bruce, and William Antholis. "Do Democracies Fight Each Other? Evidence from the Peloponnesian War." *Journal of Peace Research* 29, no. 4 (1992): 415–34. https://doi.org/10.1177/0022343392029004005.

Sagir, Dan. "The Story of Restraint: The Yom Kippur War and Israel's Nuclear Capability." *Times of Israel*, August 11, 2023. https://blogs.timesofisrael.com/a-story-of-restraint-the-yom-kippur-war-and-israels-nuclear-capability/.

Sagir, Dan. *Weapons of Mass Deterrence: The Secret behind Israel's Nuclear Power*. Carmel, 2024.

Sahay, Tim. "A New Non-alignment." The Polycrisis, November 9, 2022. https://www.phenomenalworld.org/analysis/non-alignment-brics/.

Said, Edward W. *Orientalism*. 25th anniversary ed. Penguin, 2003.

Sampson, Aaron Beers. "Tropical Anarchy: Waltz, Wendt, and the Way We Imagine International Politics." *Alternatives* 27, no. 4 (2002): 429–57. https://doi.org/10.1177/030437540202700402.

Sas, Nick, and Chrisnrita Aumanu-Leong. "Solomon Islands Receives Visits from United States, China and Japan as 'Friends to All, Enemy to None' Policy Proves Popular." ABC News, March 21, 2023. https://www.abc.net.au/news/2023-03-22/solomon-islands-china-us-japan-visits/102123368.

Schelling, Thomas C. *Arms and Influence*. Yale University Press, 1966.

Schelling, Thomas C. "The Future of Arms Control." *Operations Research* 9, no. 5 (1961): 722–31. http://www.jstor.org/stable/166817.

Schlesinger, Stephen. *Act of Creation: The Founding of the United Nations.* Westview Press, 2003.

Schramm, Madison, and Alexandra Stark. "Peacemakers or Iron Ladies? A Cross-National Study of Gender and International Conflict." *Security Studies* 29, no. 3 (2020): 515–48. https://doi.org/10.1080/09636412.2020.1763450.

Schroeder, Paul W. "Historical Reality vs. Neo-realist Theory." *International Security* 19, no. 1 (1994): 108–48. https://doi.org/10.2307/2539150.

Schroeder, Paul W. *The Transformation of European Politics: 1763–1848.* Clarendon Press, 1994.

Schweller, Randall L. *Unanswered Threats: Political Constraints on the Balance of Power.* Princeton University Press, 2006.

Scobell, Andrew. *China's Use of Military Force: Beyond the Great Wall and the Long March.* Cambridge University Press, 2003.

See, Jennifer W. "A Prophet without Honor: Hans Morgenthau and the War in Vietnam, 1955–1965." *Pacific Historical Review* 70, no. 3 (2001): 419–48. https://doi.org/10.1525/phr.2001.70.3.419.

Sempa, Francis P. "Hans Morgenthau and the Balance of Power in Asia." *The Diplomat,* May 25, 2015. https://thediplomat.com/2015/05/hans-morgenthau-and-the-balance-of-power-in-asia/.

Seth, Sanjay. *Beyond Reason: Postcolonial Theory and the Social Sciences.* Oxford University Press, 2021.

Shaffer, Brenda. "The Islamic Republic of Iran: Is It Really?" In *The Limits of Culture: Islam and Foreign Policy,* edited by Shaffer, 219–41. MIT Press, 2006.

Shaffer, Brenda. ed. *The Limits of Culture: Islam and Foreign Policy.* MIT Press, 2006.

Shahi, Deepshikha. *Kautilya and Non-Western IR Theory.* Palgrave, 2019.

Shifrinson, Joshua R. Itzkowitz. *Rising Titans, Falling Giants: How Great Powers Exploit Power Shifts.* Cornell University Press, 2018.

Shifrinson, Joshua R. Itzkowitz, and Patrick Porter. "Why We Can't Be Friends with Our Allies." *Politico,* October 22, 2020. https://www.politico.com/news/magazine/2020/10/22/why-we-cant-be-friends-with-our-allies-431015.

Sjoberg, Laura. "Gender, Structure and War: What Waltz Couldn't See." *International Theory* 4, no. 1 (2012): 1–38. https://doi.org/10.1017/S175297191100025X.

Small, Andrew. *The China-Pakistan Axis: Asia's New Geopolitics.* Hurst, 2015.

Smith, Karen, and Arlene B. Tickner. "Introduction: International Relations from the Global South." In *International Relations from the Global South: Worlds of Difference,* edited by Tickner and Smith, 1–14. Routledge, 2020.

Sondhaus, Lawrence. *Strategic Culture and Ways of War.* Routledge, 2006.

Sparkes, Matthew. "Could Nuclear Weapons Testing Resume as Global Tensions Rise?" *New Scientist,* October 17, 2023. https://www.newscientist.com/article/2397254-could-nuclear-weapons-testing-resume-as-global-tensions-rise/.

Specter, Matthew. *The Atlantic Realists: Empire and International Political Thought between Germany and the United States.* Stanford University Press, 2022.

Spielberg, Steven, dir. *Lincoln.* Walt Disney Studios, 2014.

Spykman, Nicholas J. *America's Strategy in World Politics.* Harcourt, Brace, 1942.

Starobin, Paul. "The Realists." *National Journal* 39, no. 37 (2006): 24–31.

Stern, Sheldon M. *The Cuban Missile Crisis in American Memory: Myth versus Reality.* Stanford University Press, 2012.

Sullivan, John F. "Sun Tzu's Fighting Words." *Strategy Bridge*, June 15, 2020. https://thestrategybridge.org/the-bridge/2020/6/15/sun-tzus-fighting-words.

Sullivan, Kate. "Exceptionalism in Indian Diplomacy: The Origins of India's Moral Leadership Aspirations." *South Asia: Journal of South Asian Studies* 37, no. 4 (2014): 640–55. https://doi.org/10.1080/00856401.2014.939738.

Switzer, Tom. "Political Realism and the Environment: Why the United Nations Cannot Slash Global Emissions." In *The Edinburgh Companion to Political Realism*, edited by Robert Schuett and Miles Hollingworth, 517–27. Edinburgh University Press, 2018.

Sylvester, Christine. *Feminist International Relations: An Unfinished Journey.* Cambridge University Press, 2009.

Taliaferro, Jeffrey W. "Security-Seeking under Anarchy: Defensive Realism Revisited." *International Security* 25, no. 3 (2000–2001): 128–61. http://www.jstor.org/stable/2626708.

Talmadge, Caitlin, Lisa Michelini, and Vipin Narang. "When Actions Speak Louder Than Words: Adversary Perceptions of Nuclear No-First-Use Pledges." *International Security* 48, no. 4 (2024): 7–46. https://doi.org/10.1162/isec_a_00482.

Tanham, George. "India's Strategic Culture." *Washington Quarterly* 15, no. 1 (1992): 129–42. https://doi.org/10.1080/01636609209550082.

Tannenwald, Nina (@NinaTannenwald). "I'm sure Patrick will do a good job. However, let's help him out with the scope conditions by identifying some things realism doesn't expain [sic]. I'll start." X, March 28, 2024, 8:34 a.m. https://x.com/NinaTannenwald/status/1773342844159140246.

Tannenwald, Nina. *The Nuclear Taboo: The United States and the Non-use of Nuclear Weapons Since 1945.* Cambridge University Press, 2009.

Tatum, Dillon Stone. "Toward a Radical IR: Transformation, Praxis, and Critique in a (Neo)Liberal World Order." *International Studies Review* 23, no. 4 (2021): 1751–70. https://doi.org/10.1093/isr/viab043.

Tertrais, Bruno. *In Defense of Deterrence: The Relevance, Morality and Cost-Effectiveness of Nuclear Weapons.* Institut français des relations internationales, Fall 2011. https://www.nonproliferation.eu/wp-content/uploads/2018/09/brunotertrais4ebbda42d7115.pdf.

Thomas, Martin. "After Mers-el-Kébir: The Armed Neutrality of the Vichy French Navy, 1940–43." *English Historical Review* 112, no. 447 (1997): 643–70. http://www.jstor.org/stable/576348.

Thucydides. *The Peloponnesian War.* Translated by Rex Warner. Penguin, 1974.

Tickner, Arlene. "Seeing IR Differently: Notes from the Third World." *Millennium* 32, no. 2 (2003): 295–324. https://doi.org/10.1177/03058298030320020301.

Tickner, J. Ann. *Gender in International Relations: Feminist Perspectives on Achieving Global Security.* Columbia University Press, 1992.

Tooze, Adam. "John Mearsheimer and the Dark Origins of Realism." *New Statesman*, March 8, 2022. https://www.newstatesman.com/ideas/2022/03/john-mearsheimer-dark-origins-realism-russia.

Tran, Marc. "France and Germany Evade Deficit Fines." *The Guardian*, November 25, 2003. https://www.theguardian.com/business/2003/nov/25/theeuro.politics.

Trotsky, Leon D. "Uneven and Combined Development and the Role of American Imperialism: Minutes of a Discussion." In *Writings of Leon Trotsky [1932–1933]*, edited by George Breitman and Sarah Lovell, 116–20. Pathfinder, 1972.

Urlacher, Brian R. "Introducing Native American Conflict History (NACH) Data." *Journal of Peace Research* 58, no. 5 (2021): 1117–25. https://doi.org/10.1177/0022343320987274.

Vasquez, John. "The Realist Paradigm and Degenerative versus Progressive Research Programs." *American Political Science Review* 91, no. 4 (1997): 899–912. https://doi.org/10.2307/2952172.

Vaynman, Jane, and Vipin Narang. "There Are Signs North Korea Is Working on Its Nuclear Program: Here's Why 'Denuclearization' Is So Problematic." *Washington Post*, June 30, 2018. https://www.washingtonpost.com/news/monkey-cage/wp/2018/06/30/there-are-signs-north-korea-is-still-working-on-its-nuclear-program-heres-why-denuclearization-is-so-problematic/.

Viera, Marco. "The Decolonial Subject and the Problem of Non-Western Authenticity." *Postcolonial Studies* 22, no. 2 (2019): 150–67. https://doi.org/10.1080/13688790.2019.1608795.

Vindman, Alexander. *The Folly of Realism: How the West Deceived Itself about Russia and Betrayed Ukraine*. Public Affairs, 2025.

Viotti, Paul R. *Kenneth Waltz: An Intellectual Biography*. Columbia University Press, 2023.

Walt, Stephen M. "The Enduring Relevance of the Realist Tradition." In *Political Science: The State of the Discipline*, edited by Ira Katznelson and Helen V. Milner, 197–235. W. W. Norton, 2002.

Walt, Stephen M. "International Relations: One World, Many Theories." *Foreign Policy*, no. 110 (1998): 29–32, 34–46. https://doi.org/10.2307/1149275.

Walt, Stephen M. "The Realist Guide to Solving Climate Change." *Foreign Policy*, August 13, 2021. https://foreignpolicy.com/2021/08/13/realist-guide-to-solving-climate-change/.

Waltz, Kenneth N. *Man, the State, and War: A Theoretical Analysis*. Columbia University Press, 1954.

Waltz, Kenneth N. *Theory of International Politics*. McGraw-Hill Education, 1979.

Waltz, Kenneth N., and Scott D. Sagan. *The Spread of Nuclear Weapons: A Debate Renewed*. Stanford University Press, 2002.

Wang, Yuan-Kang. *Harmony and War: Confucian Culture and Chinese Power*. Columbia University Press, 2011.

"War with Iraq Is Not in America's National Interest." *New York Times*, September 26, 2002.

Weart, Spencer. *Never at War: Why Democracies Will Not Fight One Another.* Yale University Press, 1998.
Wendt, Alexander. "Anarchy Is What States Make of It: The Social Construction of Power Politics." *International Organization* 46, no. 2 (1992): 391–425. http://www.jstor.org/stable/2706858.
White, Hugh. *How to Defend Australia.* La Trobe University Press, 2019.
White, Hugh. "The Idea of National Security: What Use Is It to Policymakers?" Working paper, National Security College, Australian National University, Canberra, 2012. https://openresearch-repository.anu.edu.au/items/c47b7b4b-b5d4-43a0-ab1c-3dcfcdd30a56.
Whitworth, Sandra. "Gender in the Inter-paradigm Debate." *Millennium* 18, no. 2 (1989): 265–72. https://doi.org/10.1177/03058298890180020201.
"Who Is in Charge of Europe?" *The Economist*, January 8, 2024. https://www.economist.com/europe/2024/01/08/who-is-in-charge-of-europe.
Wilson, Ward Hayes. *It Is Possible: A Future without Nuclear Weapons.* World School Press, 2023.
Witt, Antonia, Felix Anderl, Amitav Acharya, Deepshikha Shahi, Isaac Kamola, and Scarlett Cornelissen. "How to Problematize the Global?" *Millennium* 51, no. 1 (2022): 34–80. https://doi.org/10.1177/03058298221139330.
Witze, Alexandra. "How a Small Nuclear War Would Transform the Entire Planet." *Nature* 579, no. 7800 (2020): 485–87.
Wivel, Anders, and Kajsa Ji Noe Oest. "Security, Profit or Shadow of the Past? Explaining the Security Strategies of Microstates." *Cambridge Review of International Affairs* 23, no. 3 (2010): 429–53. https://doi.org/10.1080/09557571.2010.484047.
Wohlforth, William C. "Realism and the End of the Cold War." *International Security* 19, no. 3 (1995): 91–129. https://doi.org/10.2307/2539233.
Wolfers, Arnold. *Discord and Collaboration: Essays on International Politics.* Johns Hopkins University Press, 1962.
Woodward, Bob. *State of Denial.* Simon and Schuster, 2006.
Yang, Huang. "Thucydides in China." *KNOW: A Journal on the Formation of Knowledge* 6, no. 2 (2022): 351–71. https://doi.org/10.1086/721421.
Yilmaz, Harun. "No, Russia Will Not Invade Ukraine." Al Jazeera, February 9, 2022. https://www.aljazeera.com/opinions/2022/2/9/no-russia-will-not-invade-ukraine.
Yuen, Derek M. C. *Deciphering Sun Tzu: How to Read "The Art of War."* Hurst, 2014.
Zhang, Marina Yue. "Lithium, Lightest Metal on Earth, Carries Heavy Geopolitical Weight." Lowy Institute, December 28, 2023. https://www.lowyinstitute.org/the-interpreter/lithium-lightest-metal-earth-carries-heavy-geopolitical-weight.
Zvobgo, Kelebogile, and Meredith Loken. "Why Race Matters in International Relations." *Foreign Policy*, June 19, 2020. https://foreignpolicy.com/2020/06/19/why-race-matters-international-relations-ir/.

Index

Able Archer incident, 33
accidents, nuclear weapons and, 36
Adesnik, David, 107
African National Congress, 31
Ajami, Fouad, 52–53
al-Assad, Bashar, 44–45
Albright, Madeleine, 110–11
Alexander of Macedon, 69
Ali, Muhammad, 128
alternative worldviews, 23–32
altruism, 98
anarchy, 8, 25, 29–30, 57–58, 59, 79, 117–18, 138
ancient democracies, 83
Aristotle, 83
arms control, 79
Arthashastra (Kautilya), 122
The Art of War (Sun Tzu), 125
Ashford, Emma, 57
Athens, 83
Auden, W. H., 94
Augustine of Hippo, 18

Ba'ath rule, 46
bad-genealogy version, 111
balance-of-power dynamic, 64, 122
Balkans wars, 70, 81
Barkawi, Tarak, 132
Behind Closed Doors (documentary), 96
Beijing, 126, 129

Belfast Agreement, 21
Berlin airlift crisis, 87
bin Laden, Osama, 44
Bismarck, Otto von, 64
Bolton, John, 50, 51
Booth, Ken, 5–6
Braumoeller, Bear F., 81
Brexit, 96
Brok, Elmar, 96
Brzezinski, Zbigniew, 119
Bullets Not Ballots (Hazelton), 134
Bush, George H. W., 106
Bush, George W., 45

Campbell, Kurt, 129
Carr, E. H., 7, 16, 104, 117
Catherine the Great, 135–36
central powers, formation and hardening of, 72
Cesaire, Aime, 103
Chamberlain, Neville, 67
Charles V, King, 65
China, 43, 109–10, 120–21, 122–23, 124–25, 129; Belt and Road Initiative, 129; bid for primacy, 153n15; culture, 161n26; growth in power and ambition of, 73; main cause of current competition between America and, 60–61; moral legitimacy of Beijing, 80
Christendom, 69

187

Churchill, Winston, 20–21, 65–66
classical realism, 58–59
climate change, 39–44
Climate Change Committee, 41
Clinton, Bill, 99, 135
Clinton, Hillary, 135–36
complexification, 14
Comprehensive Nuclear Test Ban Treaty (CTBT) of 1996, 97–100
Concert of Europe, 82, 85
Confucius, 109, 123, 124
cookbook model, of realism, 57
cooperation, problem of, 77–90
Copeland, Dale C., 59
counterbalancing, 65
Cox, Robert W., 104
crisis stability, 106
Cuban missile crisis, 33, 50, 143
culture, Chinese, 161n26

Dagalo, Mohamed Hamdan, 94
defensive realists, 62
democracies, 47–49, 82–83
democracy-war debate, 84
democratic peace, 82
deterrence, 87, 89, 106
dictators, dealing with, 44–49
disarmament, 33–34, 38
donor-recipient behavior, 44
Doshi, Rush, 71–72
Doyle, Michael, 84
dynamic realists, 62

Eckstein, Arthur M., 68
economic growth, variations of, 27
Egypt, 22–23, 66
Eisenhower, Dwight, 87, 128–29
Elman, Colin, 71
Elman, Miriam Fendius, 71
emancipatory policies, 25–26
English school, 64
ethnocentricity, of realism, 105
Eurocentrism, 101–2

European Coal and Steel Community, 95
European Parliament Committee on Foreign Affairs, 96
European Union (EU), 94–96
external balancing, 70–71, 121

Falklands War (1982), 87
fallen world, 142–43
Fanon, Franz, 103
fatal casualties, 81
Fazal, Tanisha M., 81
fearlessness, state of, 54
feminism, 11–12
Finland, 21
Fischer, Marcus, 69
Five Nations, 137
Floyd, George, 103
Foreign Affairs, 102
foreign policy, 48–49
Foreign Policy, 103
Foreman, George, 128

Gandhi, Mahatma, 31
Gaza, invasion of, 93–94, 103
gender, realism and, 134–39
general policy, realism and, 143
George, Lloyd, 30
"Germany-first" war strategy, 115
Gilpin, Robert, 3, 9; *War and Change in World Politics*, 113
Glaser, Charles L., 59
Gleditsch, Nils Petter, 29–30
global pandemics, 90–91
"Global South," 93
Great East Asian War, 31–32
Great Turkish War, 31–32
Great Wall, 109
Great War, 81
Greco-Turkish conflict, 70
groups, primacy of, 16
Gruber, Lloyd, 78
guerilla forces, 131–32

Habsburgs, 65
The Hague, 80
The Hague Conventions, 82
The Hague Invasion Act, 80
Haiti, 131
hardheadedness, 71
Harmony and War (Wang), 123
Hathaway, Oona A., 82
Haushofer, Karl, 111–12
Hazelton, Jacqueline, *Bullets Not Ballots*, 134
hearts-and-minds worldview, 133–34
Henderson, Errol, 114
"hide-and-abide" strategy, 71, 126
hierarchy, problem of, 63–77
Hirohito, Emperor, 92
Hiroshima, 35
Hitler, Adolf, 20–21, 65, 66
Hobson, John M., 104, 114
human rights, rise of, 90–91
Human Rights Watch, 94
human security, 17
Huntington, Samuel P., 105, 109
Hussein, Saddam, 38, 44–45, 46, 50, 79, 87, 106

Ikenberry, G. John, 45
India, 108, 120–22, 163n66
India-Pakistan wars, 86
"inside-out" views, 84
institutions: about, 77–78; limits of, 78–81
internal balancing, 67–68, 121
international community, 69
International Court of Justice, 93
International Criminal Court (ICC), 80, 90, 91–94
international institutions, 77
international politics, 4, 9
International Relations (IR) theory, 2, 63, 66, 68, 101–2, 104, 114, 116, 122, 135
Iran, 108, 127, 164n79
Iraq, invasion of, 21, 50

Iroquois Confederacy, 136–37
Islamic Renaissance Party of Tajikistan, 127
Islamic State, 46–47
Islamic State of Iraq and the Levant (ISIL), 76
Israel, invasion of Gaza by, 93–94
Israel Lobby, 99

Jackson, Van, 25
Japan, 51, 105–6
Jervis, Robert, 75
Johnson, Boris, 135
Joint Comprehensive Plan of Action with Iran, 99

Kagan, Korina, 70
Kang, David, 110
Kautilya, 144; *Arthashastra*, 122
Kazakhstan, 127
Kellogg-Briand Peace Pact of 1928, 82
Kennan, George F., 89, 91, 119
Kennedy, John F., 50, 143
Kennedy, Paul, *The Rise and Fall of Great Powers*, 114
Khamenei, Ali, 127
Khan, Herman, 50
Khrushchev, Nikita, 143
Kissinger, Henry, 50
Korean War, 21
Kyoto, 115

Lakatos, Imre, 65
Layne, Christopher, 73
League of Nations, 29, 82, 85, 117
Lenin, Vladimir, 25, 26
Leninism, 113
liberal internationalism, 11, 12, 71
Libyan Civil War, 21
Liebknecht, Wilhelm, 26
Lincoln (film), 19
Lindisfarne community, 51
Line of Control, 120

Lippmann, Walter, 117
lithium, 40
Lobell, Steven, 67
Loken, Meredith, 102–3, 114
Louis XIV, King of France, 65
Louverture, Toussaint, 131, 144

Machiavelli, Niccolò, 17, 18; *The Prince*, 118–19
major wars: about, 86–87; absence of, 31–32
Man, the State, and War (Waltz), 117
Mandela, Nelson, 50
Manilla, military coup in, 31
Mao Zedong, 21
Martin, Susan B., 64
Marxism, 11–12
Maurya, Chandragupta, 122
McDonald, Patrick J., 84
Mearsheimer, John J., 59, 99, 111–12
Meier, Charles S., 134
Meinecke, Friedrich, 111–12
Meir, Golda, 50
Merkel, Angela, 30
microstates, 128, 130–31
Middle Kingdom, 124
military power, centrality of, 31
Milosevic, Slobodan, 31
Ming era, 123
Mitanni, 66
mitigationist strategy, 42–43
Mongols, 123
morality: about, 145n3; of realism, 3, 140; of realists, 6–23
moral legitimacy, of Beijing, 80
Moralpolitik, 93–94
Morgenthau, Hans J., 19, 51, 58, 104, 111–12, 114–15, 116, 117, 119
Mullin, Chris, 10

Napoleon, 65, 128
Napoleonic Wars, 31–32
national policy, 163n59

nation-state, 16
near misses, nuclear weapons and, 36
Nehru, Jawaharlal, 108, 120
neighborhood-first diplomacy, 122
neoclassical realism, 74
neopatrimonial model, 114
neo-realism, 58
Netanyahu, Benjamin, 99
net-zero goals, 41–43
Niebuhr, Reinhold, 18, 117
Nijaar, Hardeep Singh, 121
Nixon-Kissinger realignment, 106
Nixon-Mao rapprochment, 21
No First Use doctrine, 109
nondemocracy, World War One as, 82
nonfatal casualties, 81
Non-Proliferation Treaty of 1968, 121
non-Western International Relations theory, 104
North American Free Trade Agreement (NAFTA), 78
North Atlantic Treaty Organization (NATO), 31, 73, 74, 77
nuclear deterrence, 37
nuclear peace, 85–90
nuclear weapons, moral case for, 32–39
nuclear winter, 33, 35
Nuremberg trials, 92

Obama, Barak, 106
offensive-defensive realism, 60, 120
offensive realists, 62
offshore balancers, 61
Oil-for-Food Programme, 143
one-China principle, 129
Operation Iraqi Freedom, 94
oppression, realists and, 6
Osirak dilemma, 38–39
Ottoman powers, 70
"outside-in" views, 84

Pakistan, 108, 120–21, 122, 127
Palestine, 23

Palmerston, Lord, 48
pandemics, 40, 90–91
Parent, Joseph, 66
patriarchies, 135, 136, 137
Pax Americana, 72, 129, 150–51n79
peace: about, 81–84; nuclear, 85–90
peace chiefs, 136
Pearl Harbor attack, 115
Peloponnesian War, 52, 54, 118, 144
Pericles, 54
Permanent Court of Arbitration, 80
Petraeus, David, 132–33, 166n98
Petrovna, Elizabeth, 135
Philip II, King, 65
Philippines, revolution in, 31
Pinker, Stephen, 135
Pinochet, Augusto, 48
postcolonialism, 11–12
postcolonial literature, 104
postpositivists, 104
power: institutions and, 78; respecting, 49–55
power hierarchy, of the world, 116
power politics, 9, 12
primacy realists, 61
The Prince (Machiavelli), 18, 118–19
prioritizers, 61
Putin, Vladimir, 15–16, 44–45, 73, 76, 92, 106, 112, 135, 143

Qaddafi, Muammar, 47, 87
Quad, 121

radical traditions, 11–12
Ramaphosa, Cyril, 94
Rathbun, Brian, 64
realism: about, 2, 5–12; beyond the West, 113–27; gender and, 134–39; general policy and, 143; morality of, 3, 140; in our time, 32–49; of realism, 3, 140; realism of, 56–100; taxonomy of, 58–63; of the weak, 128–34; who it's for, 3, 140–41

realists, morality of, 6–23
real*politik*, 9
regime change, 44–45, 79
regime expediency, 127
Research and Analysis Wing (RAW), 163n66
resistant behavior, 65
resource scarcity, 141
reverse leverage, 128
The Rise and Fall of Great Powers (Kennedy), 114
rogue states, 106
Roosevelt, Franklin, 65–66
Rosato, Sebastian, 66
Rothschild, Lord, 30

Sadat, Anwar, 22–23, 50, 87, 114, 144
Sahay, Tim, 93
Said, Edward W., 103–4, 111
Sampson, Aaron Beers, 111, 116
Sand Castle (film), 133–34
Schelling, Thomas C., 85
Schmitt, Carl, 111–12, 116
Schroeder, Paul W., 63, 65
Schweller, Randall L., 64
"second strike," 32
security regime, 70
self-help, 70–72, 141–42
self-regard, 70
self-reliance, 142
Serbia, revolution in, 31
Seth, Sanjay, 104
Shanghai Communiqué, 21
Shapiro, Scott J., 82
Solomon Islands, 128–30
South Africa, revolution in, 31
Soviet Union, collapse of, 91
Specter, Matthew, 111, 112
sphere of influence, 129–30
Spykman, Nicholas J., 117
Stability and Growth Pact, 95–96
Stalin, Joseph, 20, 21, 24, 87, 144
"state-of-the-art" judgement, 13–14

states: about, 3-4, 12-23, 162-63n58; coldness of, 6-7; institutions and, 78
strategic-culture literature, 105, 107, 123
structural realism, 58-59
stupid behavior, 75
Sun Tzu, *The Art of War*, 125
Syracuse, 83
Syria, 47
Syrian civil war, 81

Tannenwald, Nina, 90
taxonomy, of realism, 58-63
tensions active measures to defuse, 79
Thach, Nguyen Co, 10
Theory of International Politics (Waltz), 58-59
third world knowledge, 104
Thucydides, 17, 52, 53-54, 83, 116, 118, 144
Tickner, Arlene, 104-5
Tokyo trials, 92
Tooze, Adam, 112
trade-offs, 141
Treaty of Westphalia (1648), 86
Trotsky, Leon, 27
true feminism, 138
Truman, Harry, 68, 115
Trump, Donald, 52
Tsar Bomba, 35
The Twenty Years' Crisis (Waltz), 117

Ukraine, 15-16, 29, 73, 74, 86, 93, 96, 103, 106, 112, 135, 143
underbalancing, 67
unipolar movement, 72, 110-11
United Nations (UN), 24, 29
United Nations Children's Fund, 29
United Nations Security Council, 68
United States, main cause of current competition between China and, 60-61
UN Security Council, 93
US Net Evaluation Subcommittee, 87
Uzbekistan, 127

veto, 68
vibes model, of realism, 57
Vienna Congress (1815), 86
Vietnam, 10, 21
virtù, 20-22
virtue, 20-22
Vulcans, 106

Walt, Stephen M., 90, 99, 114
Waltz, Kenneth N., 38, 104, 111, 113, 116, 117, 128; *Man, the State, and War*, 117; *Theory of International Politics*, 58-59; *The Twenty Years' Crisis*, 117
Wang, Yuan-Kang, *Harmony and War*, 123
war: avoidance of, 12-13; in Gaza, 103; rise of war crime prosecutions, 91-94; on terror, 103
War and Change in World Politics (Gilpin), 113
warmongers, 10
Washington, George, 71
Weart, Spencer, 83
Western International Relations theory, 104
Whiggish thesis, 81
White, Hugh, 17
Wilson, Ward, 87
Wilson, Woodrow, 117
Wohlforth, William C., 91, 112
Wolfers, Arnold, 130
worldviews, alternative, 23-32
World War One, 31-32, 82
World War Two, 31-32

Xi Jinping, 106
Xu Qiliang, 116

Yom Kippur war (1973), 87
Yongle Emperor, 123

Zhang, Marina Yue, 40
Zvobgo, Kelebogile, 102-3, 114

Made in the USA
Middletown, DE
25 November 2025